THE ESSENTIAL
NIETZSCHE

BEYOND GOOD AND EVIL

·

THE GENEALOGY OF MORALS

THE ESSENTIAL
NIETZSCHE

BEYOND GOOD AND EVIL

•

THE GENEALOGY OF MORALS

CHARTWELL
BOOKS

Brimming with creative inspiration, how-to projects, and useful information to enrich your everyday life, Quarto Knows is a favorite destination for those pursing their interests and passions. Visit our site and dig deeper with our books into your area of interest: Quarto Creates, Quarto Cooks, Quarto Homes, Quarto Lives, Quarto Drives, Quarto Explores, Quarto Gifts, or Quarto Kids.

This edition published in 2017 by Chartwell Books,
an imprint of The Quarto Group
142 West 36th Street, 4th Floor
New York, NY 10018 USA
www.QuartoKnows.com

ISBN-13: 978-0-7858-3543-1

Design: Rachael Cronin

10 9 8 7 6 5 4 3 2 1

Printed in China

Beyond Good and Evil

The Genealogy of Morals

BEYOND GOOD AND EVIL

Prelude to a Philosophy of the Future

[1886]

by
Friedrich Nietzsche

Translated by Helen Zimmern

Preface

Supposing that Truth is a woman—what then? Is there not ground for suspecting that all philosophers, in so far as they have been dogmatists, have failed to understand women—that the terrible seriousness and clumsy importunity with which they have usually paid their addresses to Truth, have been unskilled and unseemly methods for winning a woman? Certainly she has never allowed herself to be won; and at present every kind of dogma stands with sad and discouraged mien—*If*, indeed, it stands at all! For there are scoffers who maintain that it has fallen, that all dogma lies on the ground—nay more, that it is at its last gasp.

But to speak seriously, there are good grounds for hoping that all dogmatizing in philosophy, whatever solemn, whatever conclusive and decided airs it has assumed, may have been only a noble puerilism and tyronism; and probably the time is at hand when it will be once and again understood *what* has actually sufficed for the basis of such imposing and absolute philosophical edifices as the dogmatists have hitherto reared: perhaps some popular superstition of immemorial time (such as the soul-superstition, which, in the form of subject- and ego-superstition, has not yet ceased doing mischief): perhaps some play upon words, a deception on the part of grammar, or an audacious generalization of very restricted, very personal, very human—all-too-human facts.

The philosophy of the dogmatists, it is to be hoped, was only a promise for thousands of years afterwards, as was astrology in still earlier times, in the service of which probably more labor, gold, acuteness, and patience have been spent than on any actual science hitherto: we owe to it, and to its "super-terrestrial" pretensions in Asia and Egypt, the grand style of architecture. It seems that in order to inscribe themselves upon the heart of humanity with everlasting claims, all great things have first to wander about the earth as enormous and awe-inspiring caricatures: dogmatic philosophy has been a caricature of this kind—for instance, the Vedanta doctrine in Asia, and Platonism in Europe.

Let us not be ungrateful to it, although it must certainly be confessed that the worst, the most tiresome, and the most dangerous of errors hitherto has been a dogmatist error—namely, Plato's invention of Pure Spirit and the Good in Itself. But now when it has been surmounted, when Europe, rid of this nightmare, can again draw breath freely and at least enjoy a healthier—sleep, we,

9

whose duty is wakefulness itself, are the heirs of all the strength which the struggle against this error has fostered. It amounted to the very inversion of truth, and the denial of the *perspective*—the fundamental condition—of life, to speak of Spirit and the Good as Plato spoke of them; indeed one might ask, as a physician: "How did such a malady attack that finest product of antiquity, Plato? Had the wicked Socrates really corrupted him? Was Socrates after all a corrupter of youths, and deserved his hemlock?"

But the struggle against Plato, or—to speak plainer, and for the "people"— the struggle against the ecclesiastical oppression of millenniums of Christianity (*for Christianity is Platonism for the "people"*), produced in Europe a magnificent tension of soul, such as had not existed anywhere previously; with such a tensely strained bow one can now aim at the furthest goals. As a matter of fact, the European feels this tension as a state of distress, and twice attempts have been made in grand style to unbend the bow: once by means of Jesuitism, and the second time by means of democratic enlightenment—which, with the aid of liberty of the press and newspaper-reading, might, in fact, bring it about that the spirit would not so easily find itself in "distress"! (The Germans invented gunpowder—all credit to them! but they again made things square—they invented printing.) But we, who are neither Jesuits, nor democrats, nor even sufficiently Germans, we *good Europeans*, and free, *very* free spirits—we have it still, all the distress of spirit and all the tension of its bow! And perhaps also the arrow, the duty, and, who knows? *The goal to aim at....*

Sils-Maria, Upper Engadine,
June 1885.

Part One:
Prejudices of Philosophers

1

The Will to Truth, which is to tempt us to many a hazardous enterprise, the famous Truthfulness of which all philosophers have hitherto spoken with respect, what questions has this Will to Truth not laid before us! What strange, perplexing, questionable questions! It is already a long story; yet it seems as if it were hardly commenced. Is it any wonder if we at last grow distrustful, lose patience, and turn impatiently away? That this Sphinx teaches us at last to ask questions ourselves? *who* is it really that puts questions to us here? *what* really is this "Will to Truth" in us?

In fact we made a long halt at the question as to the origin of this Will—until at last we came to an absolute standstill before a yet more fundamental question. We inquired about the *value* of this Will. Granted that we want the truth: *why not rather* untruth? And uncertainty? Even ignorance?

The problem of the value of truth presented itself before us—or was it we who presented ourselves before the problem? Which of us is the Oedipus here? Which the Sphinx? It would seem to be a rendezvous of questions and notes of interrogation.

And could it be believed that it at last seems to us as if the problem had never been propounded before, as if we were the first to discern it, get a sight of it, and *risk raising* it? For there is risk in raising it, perhaps there is no greater risk.

2

"How *could* anything originate out of its opposite? For example, truth out of error? or the Will to Truth out of the will to deception? or the generous deed out of selfishness? or the pure sun-bright vision of the wise man out of covetousness? Such genesis is impossible; whoever dreams of it is a fool, nay, worse than a fool; things of the highest value must have a different origin, an origin of *their* own—in this transitory, seductive, illusory, paltry world, in this turmoil of delusion and cupidity, they cannot have their source. But rather in the lap of Being, in the intransitory, in the concealed God, in the 'Thing-in-itself—*there* must be their source, and nowhere else!"

This mode of reasoning discloses the typical prejudice by which metaphysicians of all times can be recognized, this mode of valuation is at the back of all their logical procedure; through this "belief" of theirs, they exert themselves for their "knowledge," for something that is in the end solemnly christened "the Truth." The fundamental belief of metaphysicians is *the belief in antitheses of values*. It never occurred even to the wariest of them to doubt here on the very threshold (where doubt, however, was most necessary); though they had made a solemn vow, "*de omnibus dubitandum.*"

For it may be doubted, firstly, whether antitheses exist at all; and secondly, whether the popular valuations and antitheses of value upon which metaphysicians have set their seal, are not perhaps merely superficial estimates, merely provisional perspectives, besides being probably made from some corner, perhaps from below—"frog perspectives," as it were, to borrow an expression current among painters. In spite of all the value which may belong to the true, the positive, and the unselfish, it might be possible that a higher and more fundamental value for life generally should be assigned to pretense, to the will to delusion, to selfishness, and cupidity. It might even be possible that *what* constitutes the value of those good and respected things, consists precisely in their being insidiously related, knotted, and crocheted to these evil and apparently opposed things—perhaps even in being essentially identical with them. Perhaps!

But who wishes to concern himself with such dangerous "Perhapses"! For that investigation one must await the advent of a new order of philosophers, such as will have other tastes and inclinations, the reverse of those hitherto prevalent—philosophers of the dangerous "Perhaps" in every sense of the term. And to speak in all seriousness, I see such new philosophers beginning to appear.

3

Having kept a sharp eye on philosophers, and having read between their lines long enough, I now say to myself that the greater part of conscious thinking must be counted among the instinctive functions, and it is so even in the case of philosophical thinking; one has here to learn anew, as one learned anew about heredity and "innateness." As little as the act of birth comes into consideration in the whole process and procedure of heredity, just as little is "being-conscious" *opposed* to the instinctive in any decisive sense; the greater part of the conscious thinking of a philosopher is secretly influenced by his instincts, and forced into definite channels.

And behind all logic and its seeming sovereignty of movement, there are valuations, or to speak more plainly, physiological demands, for the maintenance of a definite mode of life. For example, that the certain is worth more than the uncertain, that illusion is less valuable than "truth" such valuations, in spite of their regulative importance for *us*, might notwithstanding be only superficial valuations, special kinds of *niaiserie*, such as may be necessary for the maintenance of beings such as ourselves. Supposing, in effect, that man is not just the "measure of things."

4

The falseness of an opinion is not for us any objection to it: it is here, perhaps, that our new language sounds most strangely. The question is, how far an opinion is life-furthering, life-preserving, species-preserving, perhaps species-rearing, and we are fundamentally inclined to maintain that the falsest opinions (to which the synthetic judgments a priori belong), are the most indispensable to us, that without a recognition of logical fictions, without a comparison of reality with the purely *imagined* world of the absolute and immutable, without a constant counterfeiting of the world by means of numbers, man could not live—that the renunciation of false opinions would be a renunciation of life, a negation of life. *To recognize untruth as a condition of life*; that is certainly to impugn the traditional ideas of value in a dangerous manner, and a philosophy which ventures to do so, has thereby alone placed itself beyond good and evil.

5

That which causes philosophers to be regarded half-distrustfully and half-mockingly, is not the oft-repeated discovery how innocent they are—how often and easily they make mistakes and lose their way, in short, how childish and childlike they are,—but that there is not enough honest dealing with them, whereas they all raise a loud and virtuous outcry when the problem of truthfulness is even hinted at in the remotest manner. They all pose as though their real opinions had been discovered and attained through the self-evolving of a cold, pure, divinely indifferent dialectic (in contrast to all sorts of mystics, who, fairer and foolisher, talk of "inspiration"), whereas, in fact, a prejudiced proposition, idea, or "suggestion," which is generally their heart's desire abstracted and refined, is defended by them with arguments sought out after the event. They are all advocates who do not wish to be regarded as such, generally astute defenders, also, of their prejudices, which they dub "truths,"—and *very* far from having the conscience which bravely admits this to itself, very far from having the good taste of the courage which goes so far as to let this be understood, perhaps to warn friend or foe, or in cheerful confidence and self-ridicule.

The spectacle of the Tartuffery of old Kant, equally stiff and decent, with which he entices us into the dialectic by-ways that lead (more correctly mislead) to his "categorical imperative"—makes us fastidious ones smile, we who find no small amusement in spying out the subtle tricks of old moralists and ethical preachers. Or, still more so, the hocus-pocus in mathematical form, by means of which Spinoza has, as it were, clad his philosophy in mail and mask—in fact, the "love of *his* wisdom," to translate the term fairly and squarely—in order thereby to strike terror at once into the heart of the assailant who should dare to cast a glance on that invincible maiden, that Pallas Athene:—how much of personal timidity and vulnerability does this masquerade of a sickly recluse betray!

6

It has gradually become clear to me what every great philosophy up till now has consisted of—namely, the confession of its originator, and a species of involuntary and unconscious auto-biography; and moreover that the moral (or immoral) purpose in every philosophy has constituted the true vital germ out of which the entire plant has always grown.

Indeed, to understand how the abstrusest metaphysical assertions of a philosopher have been arrived at, it is always well (and wise) to first ask oneself: "What morality do they (or does he) aim at?" Accordingly, I do not believe that an "impulse to knowledge" is the father of philosophy; but that another impulse, here as elsewhere, has only made use of knowledge (and mistaken knowledge!) as an instrument. But whoever considers the fundamental impulses of man with a view to determining how far they may have here acted as *inspiring genii* (or as demons and cobolds), will find that they have all practiced philosophy at one time or another, and that each one of them would have been only too glad to look upon itself as the ultimate end of existence and the legitimate *lord* over all the other impulses. For every impulse is imperious, and as *such*, attempts to philosophize.

To be sure, in the case of scholars, in the case of really scientific men, it may be otherwise—"better," if you will; there may really be such a thing as an "impulse to knowledge," some kind of small, independent clock-work, which, when well wound up, works away industriously to that end, *without* the rest of the scholarly impulses taking any material part therein. The actual "interests" of the scholar, therefore, are generally in quite another direction—in the family, perhaps, or in money-making, or in politics; it is, in fact, almost indifferent at what point of research his little machine is placed, and whether the hopeful young worker becomes a good philologist, a mushroom specialist, or a chemist; he is not *characterized* by becoming this or that. In the philosopher, on the contrary, there is absolutely nothing impersonal; and above all, his morality furnishes a decided and decisive testimony as to *who he is*,—that is to say, in what order the deepest impulses of his nature stand to each other.

7

How malicious philosophers can be! I know of nothing more stinging than the joke Epicurus took the liberty of making on Plato and the Platonists; he called them Dionysiokolakes. In its original sense, and on the face of it, the word signifies "Flatterers of Dionysius"—consequently, tyrants' accessories and lick-spittles; besides this, however, it is as much as to say, "They are all *actors*, there is nothing genuine about them" (for Dionysiokolax was a popular name for an actor). And the latter is really the malignant reproach that Epicurus cast upon Plato: he was annoyed by the grandiose manner, the *mise en scène* style of which Plato and his scholars were masters—of which Epicurus was not a master! He, the old school-teacher of Samos, who sat concealed in his little garden at Athens, and wrote three hundred books, perhaps out of rage and ambitious envy of Plato, who knows!

Greece took a hundred years to find out who the garden-god Epicurus really was. Did she ever find out?

8

There is a point in every philosophy at which the "conviction" of the philosopher appears on the scene; or, to put it in the words of an ancient mystery:

> *Adventavit asinus,*
> *Pulcher et fortissimus.*

9

You desire to *live* "according to Nature"? Oh, you noble Stoics, what fraud of words! Imagine to yourselves a being like Nature, boundlessly extravagant, boundlessly indifferent, without purpose or consideration, without pity or justice, at once fruitful and barren and uncertain: imagine to yourselves *indifference* as a power—how *could* you live in accordance with such indifference? To live—is not that just endeavoring to be otherwise than this Nature? Is not living valuing, preferring, being unjust, being limited, endeavoring to be different? And granted that your imperative, "living according to Nature," means actually the same as "living according to life"—how could you do *differently?* Why should you make a principle out of what you yourselves are, and must be?

In reality, however, it is quite otherwise with you: while you pretend to read with rapture the canon of your law in Nature, you want something quite the contrary, you extraordinary stage-players and self-deluders! In your pride you wish to dictate your morals and ideals to Nature, to Nature herself, and to incorporate them therein; you insist that it shall be Nature "according to the Stoa," and would like everything to be made after your own image, as a vast, eternal glorification and generalism of Stoicism! With all your love for truth, you have forced yourselves so long, so persistently, and with such hypnotic rigidity to see Nature *falsely*, that is to say, Stoically, that you are no longer able to see it otherwise—and to crown all, some unfathomable superciliousness gives you the Bedlamite hope that *because* you are able to tyrannize over yourselves—Stoicism is self-tyranny—Nature will also allow herself to be tyrannized over: is not the Stoic a *part* of Nature?...

But this is an old and everlasting story: what happened in old times with the Stoics still happens today, as soon as ever a philosophy begins to believe in itself. It always creates the world in its own image; it cannot do otherwise; philosophy is this tyrannical impulse itself, the most spiritual Will to Power, the will to "creation of the world," the will to the causa prima.

10

The eagerness and subtlety, I should even say craftiness, with which the problem of "the real and the apparent world" is dealt with at present throughout Europe, furnishes food for thought and attention; and he who hears only a "Will to Truth" in the background, and nothing else, cannot certainly boast of the sharpest ears. In rare and isolated cases, it may really have happened that such a Will to Truth—a certain extravagant and adventurous pluck, a metaphysician's ambition of the forlorn hope—has participated therein: that which in the end always prefers a handful of "certainty" to a whole cartload of beautiful possibilities; there may even be puritanical fanatics of conscience, who prefer to put their last trust in a sure nothing, rather than in an uncertain something. But that is Nihilism, and the sign of a despairing, mortally wearied soul, notwithstanding the courageous bearing such a virtue may display.

It seems, however, to be otherwise with stronger and livelier thinkers who are still eager for life. In that they side *against* appearance, and speak superciliously of "perspective," in that they rank the credibility of their own bodies about as low as the credibility of the ocular evidence that "the earth stands still," and thus, apparently, allowing with complacency their securest possession to escape (for what does one at present believe in more firmly than in one's body?),—who knows if they are not really trying to win back something which was formerly an even securer possession, something of the old domain of the faith of former times, perhaps the "immortal soul," perhaps "the old God," in short, ideas by which they could live better, that is to say, more vigorously and more joyously, than by "modern ideas"? There is *distrust* of these modern ideas in this mode of looking at things, a disbelief in all that has been constructed yesterday and today; there is perhaps some slight admixture of satiety and scorn, which can no longer endure the *bric-a-brac* of ideas of the most varied origin, such as so-called Positivism at present throws on the market; a disgust of the more refined taste at the village-fair motleyness and patchiness of all these reality-philosophasters, in whom there is nothing either new or true, except this motleyness. Therein it seems to me that we should agree with those skeptical anti-realists and knowledge-microscopists of the present day; their instinct, which repels them from *modern* reality, is unrefuted... what do their retrograde by-paths concern us! The main thing about them is *not* that they wish to go "back," but that they wish to get *away* therefrom. A little *more* strength, swing, courage, and artistic power, and they would be *off*—and not back!

11

It seems to me that there is everywhere an attempt at present to divert attention from the actual influence which Kant exercised on German philosophy, and especially to ignore prudently the value which he set upon himself. Kant was first and foremost proud of his Table of Categories; with it in his hand he said: "This is the most difficult thing that could ever be undertaken on behalf of metaphysics." Let us only understand this "could be"! He was proud of having *discovered* a new faculty in man, the faculty of synthetic judgment a priori. Granting that he deceived himself in this matter; the development and rapid flourishing of German philosophy depended nevertheless on his pride, and on the eager rivalry of the younger generation to discover if possible something—at all events "new faculties"—of which to be still prouder!

But let us reflect for a moment—it is high time to do so. "How are synthetic judgments a priori *possible?*" Kant asks himself—and what is really his answer? "*By means of a means* (faculty)"—but unfortunately not in five words, but so circumstantially, imposingly, and with such display of German profundity and verbal flourishes, that one altogether loses sight of the comical *niaiserie allemande* involved in such an answer. People were beside themselves with delight over this new faculty, and the jubilation reached its climax when Kant further discovered a moral faculty in man—for at that time Germans were still moral, not yet dabbling in the "Politics of hard fact."

Then came the honeymoon of German philosophy. All the young theologians of the Tubingen institution went immediately into the groves—all seeking for "faculties." And what did they not find—in that innocent, rich, and still youthful period of the German spirit, to which Romanticism, the malicious fairy, piped and sang, when one could not yet distinguish between "finding" and "inventing"! Above all a faculty for the "transcendental"; Schelling christened it, intellectual intuition, and thereby gratified the most earnest longings of the naturally pious-inclined Germans. One can do no greater wrong to the whole of this exuberant and eccentric movement (which was really youthfulness, notwithstanding that it disguised itself so boldly, in hoary and senile conceptions), than to take it seriously, or even treat it with moral indignation. Enough, however—the world grew older, and the dream vanished. A time came when people rubbed their foreheads, and they still rub them today. People had been dreaming, and first and foremost—old Kant. "By means of a means (faculty)"—he had said, or at least meant to say. But, is that—an answer? An explanation? Or is it not rather merely a repetition of the question? How does opium induce sleep? "By means of a means (faculty)," namely the *virtus dormitiva*, replies the doctor in Moliere,

> *Quia est in eo virtus dormitiva,*
> *Cujus est natura sensus assoupire.*

But such replies belong to the realm of comedy, and it is high time to replace the Kantian question, "How are synthetic judgments *a priori* possible?" by another question, "Why is belief in such judgments necessary?"—in effect, it is high time that we should understand that such judgments must be believed to be true, for the sake of the preservation of creatures like ourselves; though they still might naturally be false judgments! Or, more plainly spoken, and roughly and readily—synthetic judgments a priori should not "be possible" at all; we have no right to them; in our mouths they are nothing but false judgments. Only, of course, the belief in their truth is necessary, as plausible belief and ocular evidence belonging to the perspective view of life.

And finally, to call to mind the enormous influence which "German philosophy"—I hope you understand its right to inverted commas (goosefeet)?—has exercised throughout the whole of Europe, there is no doubt that a certain *virtus dormitiva* had a share in it; thanks to German philosophy, it was a delight to the noble idlers, the virtuous, the mystics, the artiste, the three-fourths Christians, and the political obscurantists of all nations, to find an antidote to the still overwhelming sensualism which overflowed from the last century into this, in short—"*sensus assoupire.*"...

12

As regards materialistic atomism, it is one of the best-refuted theories that have been advanced, and in Europe there is now perhaps no one in the learned world so unscholarly as to attach serious signification to it, except for convenient everyday use (as an abbreviation of the means of expression)—thanks chiefly to the Pole Boscovich: he and the Pole Copernicus have hitherto been the greatest and most successful opponents of ocular evidence. For while Copernicus has persuaded us to believe, contrary to all the senses, that the earth does *not* stand fast, Boscovich has taught us to abjure the belief in the last thing that "stood fast" of the earth—the belief in "substance," in "matter," in the earth-residuum, and particle-atom: it is the greatest triumph over the senses that has hitherto been gained on earth.

One must, however, go still further, and also declare war, relentless war to the knife, against the "atomistic requirements" which still lead a dangerous after-life in places where no one suspects them, like the more celebrated "metaphysical requirements": one must also above all give the finishing stroke to that other and more portentous atomism which Christianity has taught best and longest, the *soul-atomism.* Let it be permitted to designate by this expression the belief which regards the soul as something indestructible, eternal, indivisible, as a monad, as an *atomon*: this belief ought to be expelled from science! Between ourselves, it is not at all necessary to get rid of "the soul" thereby, and thus renounce one of the oldest and most venerated hypotheses—as happens frequently to the clumsiness of naturalists, who can hardly touch on the soul without immediately losing it. But the way is open for new acceptations and refinements of the soul-hypothesis; and such conceptions as "mortal soul," and "soul of subjective multiplicity," and "soul as social structure of the instincts and passions," want henceforth to have legitimate rights in science. In that the *new* psychologist is about to put an end to the superstitions which have hitherto flourished with almost tropical luxuriance around the idea of the soul, he is really, as it were, thrusting himself into a new desert and a new distrust—it is possible that the older psychologists had a merrier and more comfortable time of it; eventually, however, he finds that precisely thereby he is also condemned to *invent*—and, who knows? perhaps to *discover* the new.

13

Psychologists should bethink themselves before putting down the instinct of self-preservation as the cardinal instinct of an organic being. A living thing seeks above all to *discharge* its strength—life itself is *will to power*; self-preservation is only one of the indirect and most frequent *results* thereof.

In short, here, as everywhere else, let us beware of *superfluous* teleological principles!—one of which is the instinct of self-preservation (we owe it to Spinoza's inconsistency). It is thus, in effect, that method ordains, which must be essentially economy of principles.

14

It is perhaps just dawning on five or six minds that natural philosophy is only a world-exposition and world-arrangement (according to us, if I may say so!) and *not* a world-explanation; but in so far as it is based on belief in the senses, it is regarded as more, and for a long time to come must be regarded as more—namely, as an explanation. It has eyes and fingers of its own, it has ocular evidence and palpableness of its own: this operates fascinatingly, persuasively, and *convincingly* upon an age with fundamentally plebeian tastes—in fact, it follows instinctively the canon of truth of eternal popular sensualism. What is clear, what is "explained"? Only that which can be seen and felt—one must pursue every problem thus far. Obversely, however, the charm of the Platonic mode of thought, which was an *aristocratic* mode, consisted precisely in *resistance* to obvious sense-evidence—perhaps among men who enjoyed even stronger and more fastidious senses than our contemporaries, but who knew how to find a higher triumph in remaining masters of them: and this by means of pale, cold, grey conceptional networks which they threw over the motley whirl of the senses—the mob of the senses, as Plato said. In this overcoming of the world, and interpreting of the world in the manner of Plato, there was an *enjoyment* different from that which the physicists of today offer us—and likewise the Darwinists and anti-teleologists among the physiological workers, with their principle of the "smallest possible effort," and the greatest possible blunder. "Where there is nothing more to see or to grasp, there is also nothing more for men to do"—that is certainly an imperative different from the Platonic one, but it may notwithstanding be the right imperative for a hardy, laborious race of machinists and bridge-builders of the future, who have nothing but *rough* work to perform.

15

To study physiology with a clear conscience, one must insist on the fact that the sense-organs are not phenomena in the sense of the idealistic philosophy; as such they certainly could not be causes! Sensualism, therefore, at least as regulative hypothesis, if not as heuristic principle.

What? And others say even that the external world is the work of our organs? But then our body, as a part of this external world, would be the work of our organs! But then our organs themselves would be the work of our organs! It seems to me that this is a complete *reductio ad absurdum*, if the conception *causa sui* is something fundamentally absurd. Consequently, the external world is *not* the work of our organs—?

16

There are still harmless self-observers who believe that there are "immediate certainties"; for instance, "I think," or as the superstition of Schopenhauer puts it, "I will"; as though cognition here got hold of its object purely and simply as "the thing in itself," without any falsification taking place either on the part of the subject or the object. I would repeat it, however, a hundred times, that "immediate certainty," as well as "absolute knowledge" and the "thing in itself," involve a *contradictio in adjecto*; we really ought to free ourselves from the misleading significance of words!

The people on their part may think that cognition is knowing all about things, but the philosopher must say to himself: "When I analyze the process that is expressed in the sentence, 'I think,' I find a whole series of daring assertions, the argumentative proof of which would be difficult, perhaps impossible: for instance, that it is *I* who think, that there must necessarily be something that thinks, that thinking is an activity and operation on the part of a being who is thought of as a cause, that there is an 'ego,' and finally, that it is already determined what is to be designated by thinking—that I *know* what thinking is. For if I had not already decided within myself what it is, by what standard could I determine whether that which is just happening is not perhaps 'willing' or 'feeling'? In short, the assertion 'I think,' assumes that I *compare* my state at the present moment with other states of myself which I know, in order to determine what it is; on account of this retrospective connection with further 'knowledge,' it has, at any rate, no immediate certainty for me."

In place of the "immediate certainty" in which the people may believe in the special case, the philosopher thus finds a series of metaphysical questions presented to him, veritable conscience questions of the intellect, to wit: "Whence did I get the notion of 'thinking'? Why do I believe in cause and effect? What gives me the right to speak of an 'ego,' and even of an 'ego' as cause, and finally of an 'ego' as cause of thought?" He who ventures to answer these metaphysical questions at once by an appeal to a sort of *intuitive* perception, like the person who says, "I think, and know that this, at least, is true, actual, and certain"—will encounter a smile and two notes of interrogation in a philosopher nowadays. "Sir," the philosopher will perhaps give him to understand, "it is improbable that you are not mistaken, but why should it be the truth?"

17

With regard to the superstitions of logicians, I shall never tire of emphasizing a small, terse fact, which is unwillingly recognized by these credulous minds—namely, that a thought comes when "it" wishes, and not when "I" wish; so that it is a *perversion* of the facts of the case to say that the subject "I" is the condition of the predicate "think." *One* thinks; but that this "one" is precisely the famous old "ego," is, to put it mildly, only a supposition, an assertion, and assuredly not an "immediate certainty." After all, one has even gone too far with this "one thinks"—even the "one" contains an *interpretation* of the process, and does not belong to the process itself. One infers here according to the usual grammatical formula—"To think is an activity; every activity requires an agency that is active; consequently"... It was pretty much on the same lines that the older atomism sought, besides the operating "power," the material particle wherein it resides and out of which it operates—the atom. More rigorous minds, however, learnt at last to get along without this "earth-residuum," and perhaps someday we shall accustom ourselves, even from the logician's point of view, to get along without the little "one" (to which the worthy old "ego" has refined itself).

18

It is certainly not the least charm of a theory that it is refutable; it is precisely thereby that it attracts the more subtle minds. It seems that the hundred-times-refuted theory of the "free will" owes its persistence to this charm alone; someone is always appearing who feels himself strong enough to refute it.

19

Philosophers are accustomed to speak of the will as though it were the best-known thing in the world; indeed, Schopenhauer has given us to understand that the will alone is really known to us, absolutely and completely known, without deduction or addition. But it again and again seems to me that in this case Schopenhauer also only did what philosophers are in the habit of doing—he seems to have adopted a *popular prejudice* and exaggerated it. Willing seems to me to be above all something *complicated*, something that is a unity only in name—and it is precisely in a name that popular prejudice lurks, which has got the mastery over the inadequate precautions of philosophers in all ages. So let us for once be more cautious, let us be "unphilosophical": let us say that in all willing there is firstly a plurality of sensations, namely, the sensation of the condition "*away from which* we go," the sensation of the condition "*towards which* we go," the sensation of this "*from*" and "*towards*" itself, and then besides, an accompanying muscular sensation, which, even without our putting in motion "arms and legs," commences its action by force of habit, directly we "will" anything.

Therefore, just as sensations (and indeed many kinds of sensations) are to be recognized as ingredients of the will, so, in the second place, thinking is also to be recognized; in every act of the will there is a ruling thought;—and let us not imagine it possible to sever this thought from the "willing," as if the will would then remain over!

In the third place, the will is not only a complex of sensation and thinking, but it is above all an *emotion*, and in fact the emotion of the command. That which is termed "freedom of the will" is essentially the emotion of supremacy in respect to him who must obey: "I am free, 'he' must obey"—this consciousness is inherent in every will; and equally so the straining of the attention, the straight look which fixes itself exclusively on one thing, the unconditional judgment that "this and nothing else is necessary now," the inward certainty that obedience will be rendered—and whatever else pertains to the position of the commander. A man who *wills* commands something within himself which renders obedience, or which he believes renders obedience.

But now let us notice what is the strangest thing about the will,—this affair so extremely complex, for which the people have only one name. Inasmuch as in the given circumstances we are at the same time the commanding *and* the obeying parties, and as the obeying party we know the sensations of constraint, impulsion, pressure, resistance, and motion, which usually commence immediately after the act of will; inasmuch as, on the other hand, we are accustomed to disregard this duality, and to deceive ourselves about it by means of the synthetic term "I": a whole series of erroneous conclusions, and consequently of false judgments about the will itself, has become attached to the act of willing—to such a degree that he who wills believes firmly that willing *suffices* for action. Since in the majority of cases there has only been exercise of will when the effect of the command—consequently obedience, and therefore action—was to be *expected*, the *appearance* has translated itself into the sentiment, as if there were a *necessity of effect*; in a word, he who wills believes with a fair amount of certainty that will and action are somehow one; he ascribes the success, the carrying out of the willing, to the will itself, and thereby enjoys an increase of the sensation of power which accompanies all success.

"Freedom of Will"—that is the expression for the complex state of delight of the person exercising volition, who commands and at the same time identifies himself with the executor of the order—who, as such, enjoys also the triumph over obstacles, but thinks within himself that it was really his own will that overcame them. In this way the person exercising volition adds the feelings of delight of his successful executive instruments, the useful "underwills" or under-souls—indeed, our body is but a social structure composed of many souls—to his feelings of delight as commander. *L'effet c'est moi.* what happens here is what happens in every well-constructed and happy commonwealth, namely, that the governing class identifies itself with the successes of the commonwealth. In all willing it is absolutely a question of commanding and obeying, on the basis, as already said, of a social structure composed of many "souls", on which account a philosopher should claim the right to include willing-as-such within the sphere of morals—regarded as the doctrine of the relations of supremacy under which the phenomenon of "life" manifests itself.

20

That the separate philosophical ideas are not anything optional or autonomously evolving, but grow up in connection and relationship with each other, that, however suddenly and arbitrarily they seem to appear in the history of thought, they nevertheless belong just as much to a system as the collective members of the fauna of a Continent—is betrayed in the end by the circumstance: how unfailingly the most diverse philosophers always fill in again a definite fundamental scheme of *possible* philosophies. Under an invisible spell, they always revolve once more in the same orbit, however independent of each other they may feel themselves with their critical or systematic wills, something within them leads them, something impels them in definite order the one after the other—to wit, the innate methodology and relationship of their ideas. Their thinking is, in fact, far less a discovery than a re-recognizing, a remembering, a return and a home-coming to a far-off, ancient common-household of the soul, out of which those ideas formerly grew: philosophizing is so far a kind of atavism of the highest order.

The wonderful family resemblance of all Indian, Greek, and German philosophizing is easily enough explained. In fact, where there is affinity of language, owing to the common philosophy of grammar—I mean owing to the unconscious domination and guidance of similar grammatical functions—it cannot but be that everything is prepared at the outset for a similar development and succession of philosophical systems, just as the way seems barred against certain other possibilities of world-interpretation. It is highly probable that philosophers within the domain of the Ural-Altaic languages (where the conception of the subject is least developed) look otherwise "into the world," and will be found on paths of thought different from those of the Indo-Germans and Mussulmans, the spell of certain grammatical functions is ultimately also the spell of *physiological* valuations and racial conditions.

So much by way of rejecting Locke's superficiality with regard to the origin of ideas.

21

The *causa sui* is the best self-contradiction that has yet been conceived, it is a sort of logical violation and unnaturalness; but the extravagant pride of man has managed to entangle itself profoundly and frightfully with this very folly. The desire for "freedom of will" in the superlative, metaphysical sense, such as still holds sway, unfortunately, in the minds of the half-educated, the desire to bear the entire and ultimate responsibility for one's actions oneself, and to absolve God, the world, ancestors, chance, and society therefrom, involves nothing less than to be precisely this *causa sui*, and, with more than Munchausen daring, to pull oneself up into existence by the hair, out of the slough of nothingness. If anyone should find out in this manner the crass stupidity of the celebrated conception of "free will" and put it out of his head altogether, I beg of him to carry his "enlightenment" a step further, and also put out of his head the contrary of this monstrous conception of "free will": I mean "non-free will," which is tantamount to a misuse of cause and effect. One should not wrongly *materialize* "cause" and "effect," as the natural philosophers do (and whoever like them naturalize in thinking at present), according to the prevailing mechanical doltishness which makes the cause press and push until it "effects" its end; one should use "cause" and "effect" only as pure *conceptions*, that is to say, as conventional fictions for the purpose of designation and mutual understanding,—*not* for explanation. In "being-in-itself" there is nothing of "casual-connection," of "necessity," or of "psychological non-freedom"; there the effect does *not* follow the cause, there "law" does not obtain. It is *we* alone who have devised cause, sequence, reciprocity, relativity, constraint, number, law, freedom, motive, and purpose; and when we interpret and intermix this symbol-world, as "being-in-itself," with things, we act once more as we have always acted—*mythologically.* The "non-free will" is mythology; in real life it is only a question of *strong* and *weak* wills.—It is almost always a symptom of what is lacking in himself, when a thinker, in every "causal-connection" and "psychological necessity," manifests something of compulsion, indigence, obsequiousness, oppression, and non-freedom; it is suspicious to have such feelings—the person betrays himself. And in general, if I have observed correctly, the "non-freedom of the will" is regarded as a problem from two entirely opposite standpoints, but always in a profoundly *personal* manner: some will not give up their "responsibility," their belief in *themselves*, the personal right to *their* merits, at any price (the vain races belong to this class); others on the contrary, do not wish to be answerable for anything, or blamed for anything, and owing to an inward self-contempt, seek to *get out of the business*, no matter how. The latter, when they write books, are in the habit at present of taking the side of criminals; a sort of socialistic sympathy is their favorite disguise. And as a matter of fact, the fatalism of the weak-willed embellishes itself surprisingly when it can pose as "*la religion de la souffrance humaine*"; that is *its* "good taste."

22

Let me be pardoned, as an old philologist who cannot desist from the mischief of putting his finger on bad modes of interpretation, but "Nature's conformity to law," of which you physicists talk so proudly, as though—why, it exists only owing to your interpretation and bad "philology." It is no matter of fact, no "text," but rather just a naively humanitarian adjustment and perversion of meaning, with which you make abundant concessions to the democratic instincts of the modern soul! "Everywhere equality before the law—Nature is not different in that respect, nor better than we": a fine instance of secret motive, in which the vulgar antagonism to everything privileged and autocratic—likewise a second and more refined atheism—is once more disguised. "*Ni dieu, ni mâtre*"— that, also, is what you want; and therefore "Cheers for natural law!"—is it not so? But, as has been said, that is interpretation, not text; and somebody might come along, who, with opposite intentions and modes of interpretation, could read out of the same "Nature," and with regard to the same phenomena, just the tyrannically inconsiderate and relentless enforcement of the claims of power—an interpreter who should so place the unexceptionalness and unconditionalness of all "Will to Power" before your eyes, that almost every word, and the word "tyranny" itself, would eventually seem unsuitable, or like a weakening and softening metaphor—as being too human; and who should, nevertheless, end by asserting the same about this world as you do, namely, that it has a "necessary" and "calculable" course, *not*, however, because laws obtain in it, but because they are absolutely *lacking*, and every power effects its ultimate consequences every moment. Granted that this also is only interpretation—and you will be eager enough to make this objection?—well, so much the better.

23

All psychology hitherto has run aground on moral prejudices and timidities, it has not dared to launch out into the depths. In so far as it is allowable to recognize in that which has hitherto been written, evidence of that which has hitherto been kept silent, it seems as if nobody had yet harbored the notion of psychology as the Morphology and *development-doctrine of the will to power*, as

I conceive of it. The power of moral prejudices has penetrated deeply into the most intellectual world, the world apparently most indifferent and unprejudiced, and has obviously operated in an injurious, obstructive, blinding, and distorting manner. A proper physio-psychology has to contend with unconscious antagonism in the heart of the investigator, it has "the heart" against it even a doctrine of the reciprocal conditionalness of the "good" and the "bad" impulses, causes (as refined immorality) distress and aversion in a still strong and manly conscience—still more so, a doctrine of the derivation of all good impulses from bad ones. If, however, a person should regard even the emotions of hatred, envy, covetousness, and imperiousness as life-conditioning emotions, as factors which must be present, fundamentally and essentially, in the general economy of life (which must, therefore, be further developed if life is to be further developed), he will suffer from such a view of things as from sea-sickness. And yet this hypothesis is far from being the strangest and most painful in this immense and almost new domain of dangerous knowledge, and there are in fact a hundred good reasons why everyone should keep away from it who *can* do so!

On the other hand, if one has once drifted hither with one's bark, well! very good! now let us set our teeth firmly! let us open our eyes and keep our hand fast on the helm! We sail away right *over* morality, we crush out, we destroy perhaps the remains of our own morality by daring to make our voyage thither—but what do *we* matter. Never yet did a *profounder* world of insight reveal itself to daring travelers and adventurers, and the psychologist who thus "makes a sacrifice"—it is not the *sacrifizio dell' intelletto*, on the contrary!—will at least be entitled to demand in return that psychology shall once more be recognized as the queen of the sciences, for whose service and equipment the other sciences exist. For psychology is once more the path to the fundamental problems.

Part Two:
The Free Spirit

24

O sancta simplicitiatas! In what strange simplification and falsification man lives! One can never cease wondering when once one has got eyes for beholding this marvel! How we have made everything around us clear and free and easy and simple! how we have been able to give our senses a passport to everything superficial, our thoughts a godlike desire for wanton pranks and wrong inferences!—how from the beginning, we have contrived to retain our ignorance in order to enjoy an almost inconceivable freedom, thoughtlessness, imprudence, heartiness, and gaiety—in order to enjoy life! And only on this solidified, granite-like foundation of ignorance could knowledge rear itself hitherto, the will to knowledge on the foundation of a far more powerful will, the will to ignorance, to the uncertain, to the untrue! Not as its opposite, but—as its refinement!

It is to be hoped, indeed, that *language*, here as elsewhere, will not get over its awkwardness, and that it will continue to talk of opposites where there are only degrees and many refinements of gradation; it is equally to be hoped that the incarnated Tartuffery of morals, which now belongs to our unconquerable "flesh and blood," will turn the words round in the mouths of us discerning ones. Here and there we understand it, and laugh at the way in which precisely the best knowledge seeks most to retain us in this *simplified*, thoroughly artificial, suitably imagined, and suitably falsified world: at the way in which, whether it will or not, it loves error, because, as living itself, it loves life!

25

After such a cheerful commencement, a serious word would fain be heard; it appeals to the most serious minds. Take care, ye philosophers and friends of knowledge, and beware of martyrdom! Of suffering "for the truth's sake"! even in your own defense! It spoils all the innocence and fine neutrality of your conscience; it makes you headstrong against objections and red rags; it stupefies, animalizes, and brutalizes, when in the struggle with danger, slander, suspicion, expulsion, and even worse consequences of enmity, ye have at last to play your last card as protectors of truth upon earth—as though "the Truth" were such an innocent and incompetent creature as to require protectors! and you of all people, ye knights of the sorrowful countenance, Messrs Loafers and Cobweb-spinners of the spirit! Finally, ye know sufficiently well that it cannot be of any consequence if *ye* just carry your point; ye know that hitherto no philosopher has carried his point, and that there might be a more laudable truthfulness in every little interrogative mark which you place after your special words and favorite doctrines (and occasionally after yourselves) than in all the solemn pantomime and trumping games before accusers and law-courts! Rather go out of the way! Flee into concealment! And have your masks and your ruses, that ye may be mistaken for what you are, or somewhat feared! And pray, don't forget the garden, the garden with golden trellis-work! And have people around you who are as a garden—or as music on the waters at eventide, when already the day becomes a memory. Choose the *good* solitude, the free, wanton, lightsome solitude, which also gives you the right still to remain good in any sense whatsoever! How poisonous, how crafty, how bad, does every long war make one, which cannot be waged openly by means of force! How *personal* does a long fear make one, a long watching of enemies, of possible enemies! These pariahs of society, these long-pursued, badly-persecuted ones—also the compulsory recluses, the Spinozas or Giordano Brunos—always become in the end, even under the most intellectual masquerade, and perhaps without being themselves aware of it, refined vengeance-seekers and poison-Brewers (just lay bare the foundation of Spinoza's ethics and theology!), not to speak of the stupidity of moral indignation, which is the unfailing sign in a philosopher that the sense of philosophical humor has left him. The martyrdom of the philosopher, his "sacrifice for the sake of truth," forces into the light whatever of the agitator and actor lurks in him; and if one has hitherto contemplated him only with artistic curiosity, with regard to many a philosopher it is easy to understand the dangerous desire to see him also in his deterioration (deteriorated into a "martyr," into a stage-and-tribune-bawler). Only, that it is necessary with such a desire to be clear *what* spectacle one will see in any case—merely a satyric play, merely an epilogue farce, merely the continued proof that the long, real tragedy *is at an end*, supposing that every philosophy has been a long tragedy in its origin.

26

Every select man strives instinctively for a citadel and a privacy, where he is *free* from the crowd, the many, the majority—where he may forget "men who are the rule," as their exception;—exclusive only of the case in which he is pushed straight to such men by a still stronger instinct, as a discerner in the great and exceptional sense. Whoever, in intercourse with men, does not occasionally glisten in all the green and grey colors of distress, owing to disgust, satiety, sympathy, gloominess, and solitariness, is assuredly not a man of elevated tastes; supposing, however, that he does not voluntarily take all this burden and disgust upon himself, that he persistently avoids it, and remains, as I said, quietly and proudly hidden in his citadel, one thing is then certain: he was not made, he was not predestined for knowledge. For as such, he would one day have to say to himself: "The devil take my good taste! but 'the rule' is more interesting than the exception—than myself, the exception!" And he would go *down*, and above all, he would go "inside."

The long and serious study of the *average* man—and consequently much disguise, self-overcoming, familiarity, and bad intercourse (all intercourse is bad intercourse except with one's equals):—that constitutes a necessary part of the life-history of every philosopher; perhaps the most disagreeable, odious, and disappointing part. If he is fortunate, however, as a favorite child of knowledge should be, he will meet with suitable auxiliaries who will shorten and lighten his task; I mean so-called cynics, those who simply recognize the animal, the commonplace and "the rule" in themselves, and at the same time have so much spirituality and ticklishness as to make them talk of themselves and their like *before witnesses*—sometimes they wallow, even in books, as on their own dung-hill.

Cynicism is the only form in which base souls approach what is called honesty; and the higher man must open his ears to all the coarser or finer cynicism, and congratulate himself when the clown becomes shameless right before him, or the scientific satyr speaks out.

There are even cases where enchantment mixes with the disgust—namely, where by a freak of nature, genius is bound to some such indiscreet billy-goat and ape, as in the case of the Abbe Galiani, the profoundest, acutest, and perhaps also filthiest man of his century—he was far profounder than Voltaire, and consequently also, a good deal more silent. It happens more frequently, as has been hinted, that a scientific head is placed on an ape's body, a fine exceptional understanding in a base soul, an occurrence by no means rare, especially among doctors and moral physiologists. And whenever anyone speaks without bitterness, or rather quite innocently, of man as a belly with two requirements, and a head with one; whenever anyone sees, seeks, and *wants* to see only hunger, sexual instinct, and vanity as the real and only motives of human actions; in short, when any one speaks "badly"—and not even "ill"—of man, then ought the lover of knowledge to hearken attentively and diligently; he ought, in general, to have an open ear wherever there is talk without indignation. For the indignant man, and he who perpetually tears and lacerates himself with his own teeth (or, in place of himself, the world, God, or society), may indeed, morally speaking, stand higher than the laughing and self-satisfied satyr, but in every other sense he is the more ordinary, more indifferent, and less instructive case. And no one is such a *liar* as the indignant man.

27

It is difficult to be understood, especially when one thinks and lives *gangasrotogati*[1] among those only who think and live otherwise—namely, *kurmagati*[2], or at best "froglike," *mandeikagati*[3] (I do everything to be "difficultly understood" myself!)—and one should be heartily grateful for the good will to some refinement of interpretation. As regards "the good friends," however, who are always too easy-going, and think that as friends they have a right to ease, one does well at the very first to grant them a play-ground and romping-place for misunderstanding—one can thus laugh still; or get rid of them altogether, these good friends—and laugh then also!

---

1 Like the river Ganges: presto
2 Like the tortoise: lento
3 Like the frog: staccato

28

What is most difficult to render from one language into another is the *tempo* of its style, which has its basis in the character of the race, or to speak more physiologically, in the average *tempo* of the assimilation of its nutriment. There are honestly meant translations, which, as involuntary vulgarizations, are almost falsifications of the original, merely because its lively and merry *tempo* (which overleaps and obviates all dangers in word and expression) could not also be rendered. A German is almost incapacitated for *presto* in his language; consequently also, as may be reasonably inferred, for many of the most delightful and daring *nuances* of free, free-spirited thought. And just as the buffoon and satyr are foreign to him in body and conscience, so Aristophanes and Petronius are untranslatable for him. Everything ponderous, viscous, and pompously clumsy, all long-winded and wearying species of style, are developed in profuse variety among Germans—pardon me for stating the fact that even Goethe's prose, in its mixture of stiffness and elegance, is no exception, as a reflection of the "good old time" to which it belongs, and as an expression of German taste at a time when there was still a "German taste," which was a rococo-taste *in moribus et artibus.*

Lessing is an exception, owing to his histrionic nature, which understood much, and was versed in many things; he who was not the translator of Bayle to no purpose, who took refuge willingly in the shadow of Diderot and Voltaire, and still more willingly among the Roman comedy-writers—Lessing loved also free-spiritism in the *tempo*, and flight out of Germany. But how could the German language, even in the prose of Lessing, imitate the *tempo* of Machiavelli, who in his *Principe* makes us breathe the dry, fine air of Florence, and cannot help presenting the most serious events in a boisterous *allegrissimo*, perhaps not without a malicious artistic sense of the contrast he ventures to present—long, heavy, difficult, dangerous thoughts, and a *tempo* of the gallop, and of the best, wantonest humor?

Finally, who would venture on a German translation of Petronius, who, more than any great musician hitherto, was a master of *presto* in invention, ideas, and words? What matter in the end about the swamps of the sick, evil world, or of the "ancient world," when like him, one has the feet of a wind, the rush, the breath, the emancipating scorn of a wind, which makes everything healthy, by making everything *run*! And with regard to Aristophanes—that transfiguring, complementary genius, for whose sake one *pardons* all Hellenism for having existed, provided one has understood in its full profundity *all* that there requires pardon and transfiguration; there is nothing that has caused me to meditate more on *Plato's* secrecy and sphinx-like nature, than the happily preserved *petit fait* that under the pillow of his death-bed there was found no "Bible," nor anything Egyptian, Pythagorean, or Platonic—but a book of Aristophanes. How could even Plato have endured life—a Greek life which he repudiated—without an Aristophanes!

29

It is the business of the very few to be independent; it is a privilege of the strong. And whoever attempts it, even with the best right, but without being *obliged* to do so, proves that he is probably not only strong, but also daring beyond measure. He enters into a labyrinth, he multiplies a thousandfold the dangers which life in itself already brings with it; not the least of which is that no one can see how and where he loses his way, becomes isolated, and is torn piecemeal by some minotaur of conscience. Supposing such a one comes to grief, it is so far from the comprehension of men that they neither feel it, nor sympathize with it. And he cannot any longer go back! He cannot even go back again to the sympathy of men!—

30

Our deepest insights must—and should—appear as follies, and under certain circumstances as crimes, when they come unauthorizedly to the ears of those who are not disposed and predestined for them. The exoteric and the esoteric, as they were formerly distinguished by philosophers—among the Indians, as among the Greeks, Persians, and Mussulmans, in short, wherever people believed in gradations of rank and *not* in equality and equal rights—are not so much in contradistinction to one another in respect to the exoteric class, standing without, and viewing, estimating, measuring, and judging from the outside, and not from the inside; the more essential distinction is that the class in question views things *from below upwards*—while the esoteric class views things *from above downwards*. There are heights of the soul from which tragedy itself no longer appears to operate tragically; and if all the woe in the world were taken together, who would dare to decide whether the sight of it would *necessarily* seduce and constrain to sympathy, and thus to a doubling of the woe?...

That which serves the higher class of men for nourishment or refreshment, must be almost poison to an entirely different and lower order of human beings. The virtues of the common man would perhaps mean vice and weakness in a philosopher; it might be possible for a highly developed man, supposing him to degenerate and go to ruin, to acquire qualities thereby alone, for the sake of which he would have to be honored as a saint in the lower world into which he had sunk. There are books which have an inverse value for the soul and the health according as the inferior soul and the lower vitality, or the higher and more powerful, make use of them. In the former case they are dangerous, disturbing, unsettling books, in the latter case they are herald-calls which summon the bravest to *their* bravery. Books for the general reader are always ill-smelling books, the odor of paltry people clings to them. Where the populace eat and drink, and even where they reverence, it is accustomed to stink. One should not go into churches if one wishes to breathe *pure* air.

31

In our youthful years we still venerate and despise without the art of *nuance*, which is the best gain of life, and we have rightly to do hard penance for having fallen upon men and things with Yea and Nay. Everything is so arranged that the worst of all tastes, *the taste for the unconditional*, is cruelly befooled and abused, until a man learns to introduce a little art into his sentiments, and prefers to try conclusions with the artificial, as do the real artists of life.

The angry and reverent spirit peculiar to youth appears to allow itself no peace, until it has suitably falsified men and things, to be able to vent its passion upon them: youth in itself even, is something falsifying and deceptive. Later on, when the young soul, tortured by continual disillusions, finally turns suspiciously against itself—still ardent and savage even in its suspicion and remorse of conscience: how it upbraids itself, how impatiently it tears itself, how it revenges itself for its long self-blinding, as though it had been a voluntary blindness! In this transition one punishes oneself by distrust of one's sentiments; one tortures one's enthusiasm with doubt, one feels even the good conscience to be a danger, as if it were the self-concealment and lassitude of a more refined uprightness; and above all, one espouses upon principle the cause *against* "youth."—A decade later, and one comprehends that all this was also still—youth!

32

Throughout the longest period of human history—one calls it the prehistoric period—the value or non-value of an action was inferred from its *consequences*; the action in itself was not taken into consideration, any more than its origin; but pretty much as in China at present, where the distinction or disgrace of a child redounds to its parents, the retro-operating power of success or failure was what induced men to think well or ill of an action. Let us call this period the *pre-moral* period of mankind; the imperative, "Know thyself!" was then still unknown.

In the last ten thousand years, on the other hand, on certain large portions of the earth, one has gradually got so far, that one no longer lets the consequences of an action, but its origin, decide with regard to its worth: a great achievement as a whole, an important refinement of vision and of criterion, the unconscious effect of the supremacy of aristocratic values and of the belief in "origin," the mark of a period which may be designated in the narrower sense as the *moral* one: the first attempt at self-knowledge is thereby made. Instead of the consequences, the origin—what an inversion of perspective! And assuredly an inversion effected only after long struggle and wavering! To be sure, an ominous new superstition, a peculiar narrowness of interpretation, attained supremacy precisely thereby: the origin of an action was interpreted in the most definite sense possible, as origin out of an *intention*; people were agreed in the belief that the value of an action lay in the value of its intention. The intention as the sole origin and antecedent history of an action: under the influence of this prejudice moral praise and blame have been bestowed, and men have judged and even philosophized almost up to the present day.

Is it not possible, however, that the necessity may now have arisen of again making up our minds with regard to the reversing and fundamental shifting of values, owing to a new self-consciousness and acuteness in man—is it not possible that we may be standing on the threshold of a period which to begin with, would be distinguished negatively as *ultra-moral*: nowadays when, at least among us immoralists, the suspicion arises that the decisive value of an action lies precisely in that which is *not intentional*, and that all its intentionalness, all that is seen, sensible, or "sensed" in it, belongs to its surface or skin—which, like every skin, betrays something, but *conceals* still more? In short, we believe that the intention is only a sign or symptom, which first requires an explanation—a sign, moreover, which has too many interpretations, and consequently hardly any meaning in itself alone: that morality, in the sense in which it has been understood hitherto, as intention-morality, has been a prejudice, perhaps a prematureness or preliminariness, probably something of the same rank as astrology and alchemy, but in any case something which must be surmounted. The surmounting of morality, in a certain sense even the self-mounting of morality—let that be the name for the long-secret labor which has been reserved for the most refined, the most upright, and also the most wicked consciences of today, as the living touchstones of the soul.

33

It cannot be helped: the sentiment of surrender, of sacrifice for one's neighbor, and all self-renunciation-morality, must be mercilessly called to account, and brought to judgment; just as the aesthetics of "disinterested contemplation," under which the emasculation of art nowadays seeks insidiously enough to create itself a good conscience. There is far too much witchery and sugar in the sentiments "for others" and "*not* for myself," for one not needing to be doubly distrustful here, and for one asking promptly: "Are they not perhaps—*deceptions?*"

That they *please*—him who has them, and him who enjoys their fruit, and also the mere spectator—that is still no argument in their *favor*, but just calls for caution. Let us therefore be cautious!

34

At whatever standpoint of philosophy one may place oneself nowadays, seen from every position, the *erroneousness* of the world in which we think we live is the surest and most certain thing our eyes can light upon: we find proof after proof thereof, which would fain allure us into surmises concerning a deceptive principle in the "nature of things." He, however, who makes thinking itself, and consequently "the spirit," responsible for the falseness of the world—an honorable exit, which every conscious or unconscious *advocatus dei* avails himself of—he who regards this world, including space, time, form, and movement, as falsely *deduced*, would have at least good reason in the end to become distrustful also of all thinking; has it not hitherto been playing upon us the worst of scurvy tricks? and what guarantee would it give that it would not continue to do what it has always been doing?

In all seriousness, the innocence of thinkers has something touching and respect-inspiring in it, which even nowadays permits them to wait upon consciousness with the request that it will give them *honest* answers: for example, whether it be "real" or not, and why it keeps the outer world so resolutely at a distance, and other questions of the same description. The belief in "immediate certainties" is a *moral naïveté* which does honor to us philosophers; but—we have now to cease being "*merely* moral" men! Apart from morality, such belief is a folly which does little honor to us! If in middle-class life an ever-ready distrust is regarded as the sign of a "bad character," and consequently as an imprudence, here among us, beyond the middle-class world and its Yeas and Nays, what should prevent our being imprudent and saying: the philosopher has at length a *right* to "bad character," as the being who has hitherto been most befooled on earth—he is now under *obligation* to distrustfulness, to the wickedest squinting out of every abyss of suspicion.

Forgive me the joke of this gloomy grimace and turn of expression; for I myself have long ago learned to think and estimate differently with regard to deceiving and being deceived, and I keep at least a couple of pokes in the ribs ready for the blind rage with which philosophers struggle against being deceived. Why *not?* It is nothing more than a moral prejudice that truth is worth more than semblance; it is, in fact, the worst proved supposition in the world. So much must be conceded: there could have been no life at all except upon the basis of perspective estimates and semblances; and if, with the virtuous enthusiasm and stupidity of many philosophers, one wished to do away altogether with the "seeming world"—well, granted that *you* could do that,—at least nothing of your "truth" would thereby remain! Indeed, what is it that forces us in general to the supposition that there is an essential opposition of "true" and "false"? Is it not enough to suppose degrees of seemingness, and as it were lighter and darker shades and tones of semblance—different *valeurs*, as the painters say? Why might not the world *which concerns us*—be a fiction? And to anyone who suggested: "But to a fiction belongs an originator?"—might it not be bluntly replied: *why?* May not this "belong" also belong to the fiction? Is it not at length permitted to be a little ironical towards the subject, just as towards the predicate and object? Might not the philosopher elevate himself above faith in grammar? All respect to governesses, but is it not time that philosophy should renounce governess-faith?

35

O Voltaire! O humanity! O idiocy! There is something ticklish in "the truth," and in the *search* for the truth; and if man goes about it too humanely— "*il ne cherche le vrai que pour faire le bien*"—I wager he finds nothing!

36

Supposing that nothing else is "given" as real but our world of desires and passions, that we cannot sink or rise to any other "reality" but just that of our impulses—for thinking is only a relation of these impulses to one another:— are we not permitted to make the attempt and to ask the question whether this which is "given" does not *suffice*, by means of our counterparts, for the understanding even of the so-called mechanical (or "material") world? I do not mean as an illusion, a "semblance," a "representation" (in the Berkeleyan and Schopenhauerian sense), but as possessing the same degree of reality as our emotions themselves—as a more primitive form of the world of emotions, in which everything still lies locked in a mighty unity, which afterwards branches off and develops itself in organic processes (naturally also, refines and debilitates)—as a kind of instinctive life in which all organic functions, including self-regulation, assimilation, nutrition, secretion, and change of matter, are still synthetically united with one another—as a *primary form* of life?

In the end, it is not only permitted to make this attempt, it is commanded by the conscience of *logical method*. Not to assume several kinds of causality, so long as the attempt to get along with a single one has not been pushed to its furthest extent (to absurdity, if I may be allowed to say so): that is a morality of method which one may not repudiate nowadays—it follows "from its definition," as mathematicians say. The question is ultimately whether we really recognize the will as *operating*, whether we believe in the causality of the will; if we do so—and fundamentally our belief *in this* is just our belief in causality itself—we *must* make the attempt to posit hypothetically the causality of the will as the only causality. "Will" can naturally only operate on "will"—and not on "matter" (not on "nerves," for instance): in short, the hypothesis must be hazarded, whether will does not operate on will wherever "effects" are recognized—and whether all mechanical action, inasmuch as a power operates therein, is not just the power of will, the effect of will.

Granted, finally, that we succeeded in explaining our entire instinctive life as the development and ramification of one fundamental form of will—namely, the Will to Power, as my thesis puts it; granted that all organic functions could be traced back to this Will to Power, and that the solution of the problem of generation and nutrition—it is one problem—could also be found therein: one would thus have acquired the right to define *all* active force unequivocally as *will to power*. The world seen from within, the world defined and designated according to its "intelligible character"—it would simply be "Will to Power," and nothing else.

37

"What? Does not that mean in popular language: God is disproved, but not the devil?"—On the contrary! On the contrary, my friends! And who the devil also compels you to speak popularly!

38

As happened finally in all the enlightenment of modern times with the French Revolution (that terrible farce, quite superfluous when judged close at hand, into which, however, the noble and visionary spectators of all Europe have interpreted from a distance their own indignation and enthusiasm so long and passionately, *until the text has disappeared under the interpretation*), so a noble posterity might once more misunderstand the whole of the past, and perhaps only thereby make *its* aspect endurable.

Or rather, has not this already happened? Have not we ourselves been— that "noble posterity"? And, in so far as we now comprehend this, is it not— thereby already past?

39

Nobody will very readily regard a doctrine as true merely because it makes people happy or virtuous—excepting, perhaps, the amiable "Idealists," who are enthusiastic about the good, true, and beautiful, and let all kinds of motley, coarse, and good-natured desirabilities swim about promiscuously in their pond. Happiness and virtue are no arguments. It is willingly forgotten, however, even on the part of thoughtful minds, that to make unhappy and to make bad are just as little counter-arguments. A thing could be *true*, although it were in the highest degree injurious and dangerous; indeed, the fundamental constitution of existence might be such that one succumbed by a full knowledge of it—so that the strength of a mind might be measured by the amount of "truth" it could endure—or to speak more plainly, by the extent to which it *required* truth attenuated, veiled, sweetened, damped, and falsified.

But there is no doubt that for the discovery of certain *portions* of truth the wicked and unfortunate are more favorably situated and have a greater likelihood of success; not to speak of the wicked who are happy—a species about whom moralists are silent. Perhaps severity and craft are more favorable conditions for the development of strong, independent spirits and philosophers than the gentle, refined, yielding good-nature, and habit of taking things easily, which are prized, and rightly prized in a learned man. Presupposing always, to begin with, that the term "philosopher" be not confined to the philosopher who writes books, or even introduces *his* philosophy into books!

Stendhal furnishes a last feature of the portrait of the free-spirited philosopher, which for the sake of German taste I will not omit to underline—for it is *opposed* to German taste. *"Pour être bon philosophe,"* says this last great psychologist, *"il faut être sec, clair, sans illusion. Un banquier, qui a fait fortune, a une partie du caractère requis pour faire des découvertes en philosophie, c'est-à-dire pour voir clair dans ce qui est."*

40

Everything that is profound loves the mask: the profoundest things have a hatred even of figure and likeness. Should not the *contrary* only be the right disguise for the shame of a God to go about in? A question worth asking!—it would be strange if some mystic has not already ventured on the same kind of thing. There are proceedings of such a delicate nature that it is well to overwhelm them with coarseness and make them unrecognizable; there are actions of love and of an extravagant magnanimity after which nothing can be wiser than to take a stick and thrash the witness soundly: one thereby obscures his recollection. Many a one is able to obscure and abuse his own memory, in order at least to have vengeance on this sole party in the secret: shame is inventive.

They are not the worst things of which one is most ashamed: there is not only deceit behind a mask—there is so much goodness in craft. I could imagine that a man with something costly and fragile to conceal, would roll through life clumsily and rotundly like an old, green, heavily-hooped wine-cask: the refinement of his shame requiring it to be so.

A man who has depths in his shame meets his destiny and his delicate decisions upon paths which few ever reach, and with regard to the existence of which his nearest and most intimate friends may be ignorant; his mortal danger conceals itself from their eyes, and equally so his regained security. Such a hidden nature, which instinctively employs speech for silence and concealment, and is inexhaustible in evasion of communication, *desires* and insists that a mask of himself shall occupy his place in the hearts and heads of his friends; and supposing he does not desire it, his eyes will someday be opened to the fact that there is nevertheless a mask of him there—and that it is well to be so. Every profound spirit needs a mask; nay, more, around every profound spirit there continually grows a mask, owing to the constantly false, that is to say, *superficial* interpretation of every word he utters, every step he takes, every sign of life he manifests.

41

One must subject oneself to one's own tests that one is destined for independence and command, and do so at the right time. One must not avoid one's tests, although they constitute perhaps the most dangerous game one can play, and are in the end tests made only before ourselves and before no other judge.

Not to cleave to any person, be it even the dearest—every person is a prison and also a recess. Not to cleave to a fatherland, be it even the most suffering and necessitous—it is even less difficult to detach one's heart from a victorious fatherland. Not to cleave to a sympathy, be it even for higher men, into whose peculiar torture and helplessness chance has given us an insight. Not to cleave to a science, though it tempt one with the most valuable discoveries, apparently specially reserved for us. Not to cleave to one's own liberation, to the voluptuous distance and remoteness of the bird, which always flies further aloft in order always to see more under it—the danger of the flier. Not to cleave to our own virtues, nor become as a whole a victim to any of our specialties, to our "hospitality" for instance, which is the danger of dangers for highly developed and wealthy souls, who deal prodigally, almost indifferently with themselves, and push the virtue of liberality so far that it becomes a vice. One must know *how to conserve oneself*—the best test of independence.

42

A new order of philosophers is appearing; I shall venture to baptize them by a name not without danger. As far as I understand them, as far as they allow themselves to be understood—for it is their nature to *wish* to remain something of a puzzle—these philosophers of the future might rightly, perhaps also wrongly, claim to be designated as "tempters." This name itself is after all only an attempt, or, if it be preferred, a temptation.

43

Will they be new friends of "truth," these coming philosophers? Very probably, for all philosophers hitherto have loved their truths. But assuredly they will not be dogmatists. It must be contrary to their pride, and also contrary to their taste, that their truth should still be truth for every one—that which has hitherto been the secret wish and ultimate purpose of all dogmatic efforts. "My opinion is *my* opinion: another person has not easily a right to it"—such a philosopher of the future will say, perhaps.

One must renounce the bad taste of wishing to agree with many people. "Good" is no longer good when one's neighbor takes it into his mouth. And how could there be a "common good"! The expression contradicts itself; that which can be common is always of small value. In the end things must be as they are and have always been—the great things remain for the great, the abysses for the profound, the delicacies and thrills for the refined, and, to sum up shortly, everything rare for the rare.

44

Need I say expressly after all this that they will be free, *very* free spirits, these philosophers of the future—as certainly also they will not be merely free spirits, but something more, higher, greater, and fundamentally different, which does not wish to be misunderstood and mistaken? But while I say this, I feel under *obligation* almost as much to them as to ourselves (we free spirits who are their heralds and forerunners), to sweep away from ourselves altogether a stupid old prejudice and misunderstanding, which, like a fog, has too long made the conception of "free spirit" obscure.

In every country of Europe, and the same in America, there is at present something which makes an abuse of this name a very narrow, prepossessed, enchained class of spirits, who desire almost the opposite of what our intentions and instincts prompt—not to mention that in respect to the *new* philosophers who are appearing, they must still more be closed windows and bolted doors. Briefly and regrettably, they belong to the *levelers*, these wrongly named "free spirits"—as glib-tongued and scribe-fingered slaves of the democratic taste and its "modern ideas" all of them men without solitude, without personal solitude, blunt honest fellows to whom neither courage nor honorable conduct ought to be denied, only, they are not free, and are ludicrously superficial, especially in their innate partiality for seeing the cause of almost *all* human misery and failure in the old forms in which society has hitherto existed—a notion which happily inverts the truth entirely! What they would fain attain with all their strength, is the universal, green-meadow happiness of the herd, together with security, safety, comfort, and alleviation of life for everyone, their two most frequently chanted songs and doctrines are called "Equality of Rights" and "Sympathy with All Sufferers"—and suffering itself is looked upon by them as something which must be *done away with.*

We opposite ones, however, who have opened our eye and conscience to the question how and where the plant "man" has hitherto grown most vigorously, believe that this has always taken place under the opposite conditions, that for this end the dangerousness of his situation had to be increased enormously, his inventive faculty and dissembling power (his "spirit") had to develop into subtlety and daring under long oppression and compulsion, and his Will to Life had to be increased to the unconditioned Will to Power—we believe that severity, violence, slavery, danger in the street and in the heart, secrecy, stoicism, tempter's art and devilry of every kind,—that everything wicked, terrible, tyrannical, predatory, and serpentine in man, serves as well for the elevation of the human species as its opposite—we do not even say enough when we only say *this much*, and in any case we find ourselves here, both with our speech and our silence, at the *other* extreme of all modern ideology and gregarious desirability, as their antipodes perhaps?

What wonder that we "free spirits" are not exactly the most communicative spirits? that we do not wish to betray in every respect *what* a spirit can free itself from, and *where* perhaps it will then be driven? And as to the import of the dangerous formula, "Beyond Good and Evil," with which we at least avoid confusion, we *are* something else than "*libres-penseurs,*" "*liben pensatori*" "freethinkers," and whatever these honest advocates of "modern ideas" like to call themselves.

Having been at home, or at least guests, in many realms of the spirit, having escaped again and again from the gloomy, agreeable nooks in which preferences and prejudices, youth, origin, the accident of men and books, or even the weariness of travel seemed to confine us, full of malice against the seductions of dependency which he concealed in honours, money, positions, or exaltation of the senses, grateful even for distress and the vicissitudes of illness, because they always free us from some rule, and its "prejudice," grateful to the God, devil, sheep, and worm in us, inquisitive to a fault, investigators to the point of cruelty, with unhesitating fingers for the intangible, with teeth and stomachs for the most indigestible, ready for any business that requires sagacity and acute senses, ready for every adventure, owing to an excess of "free will", with anterior and posterior souls, into the ultimate intentions of which it is difficult to pry, with foregrounds and backgrounds to the end of which no foot may run, hidden ones under the mantles of light, appropriators, although we resemble heirs and spendthrifts, arrangers and collectors from morning till night, misers of our wealth and our full-crammed drawers, economical in learning and forgetting, inventive in scheming, sometimes proud of tables of categories, sometimes pedants, sometimes night-owls of work even in full day, yea, if necessary, even scarecrows—and it is necessary nowadays, that is to say, inasmuch as we are the born, sworn, jealous friends of *solitude*, of our own profoundest midnight and midday solitude—such kind of men are we, we free spirits! And perhaps ye are also something of the same kind, ye coming ones? ye *new* philosophers?

Part Three:
The Religious Mood

45

The human soul and its limits, the range of man's inner experiences hitherto attained, the heights, depths, and distances of these experiences, the entire history of the soul *up to the present time*, and its still unexhausted possibilities: this is the preordained hunting-domain for a born psychologist and lover of a "big hunt". But how often must he say despairingly to himself: "A single individual! alas, only a single individual! and this great forest, this virgin forest!" So he would like to have some hundreds of hunting assistants, and fine trained hounds, that he could send into the history of the human soul, to drive HIS game together. In vain: again and again he experiences, profoundly and bitterly, how difficult it is to find assistants and dogs for all the things that directly excite his curiosity. The evil of sending scholars into new and dangerous hunting-domains, where courage, sagacity, and subtlety in every sense are required, is that they are no longer serviceable just when the "*big* hunt," and also the great danger commences,—it is precisely then that they lose their keen eye and nose.

In order, for instance, to divine and determine what sort of history the problem of *knowledge and conscience* has hitherto had in the souls of *homines religiosi*, a person would perhaps himself have to possess as profound, as bruised, as immense an experience as the intellectual conscience of Pascal; and then he would still require that wide-spread heaven of clear, wicked spirituality, which, from above, would be able to oversee, arrange, and effectively formulize this mass of dangerous and painful experiences.

But who could do me this service! And who would have time to wait for such servants!—they evidently appear too rarely, they are so improbable at all times! Eventually one must do everything *oneself* in order to know something; which means that one has *much* to do!

But a curiosity like mine is once for all the most agreeable of vices—pardon me! I mean to say that the love of truth has its reward in heaven, and already upon earth.

46

Faith, such as early Christianity desired, and not infrequently achieved in the midst of a skeptical and southernly free-spirited world, which had centuries of struggle between philosophical schools behind it and in it, counting besides the education in tolerance which the *Imperium Romanum* gave—this faith is *not* that sincere, austere slave-faith by which perhaps a Luther or a Cromwell, or some other northern barbarian of the spirit remained attached to his God and Christianity, it is much rather the faith of Pascal, which resembles in a terrible manner a continuous suicide of reason—a tough, long-lived, worm-like reason, which is not to be slain at once and with a single blow.

The Christian faith from the beginning, is sacrifice the sacrifice of all freedom, all pride, all self-confidence of spirit, it is at the same time subjection, self-derision, and self-mutilation. There is cruelty and religious Phoenicianism in this faith, which is adapted to a tender, many-sided, and very fastidious conscience, it takes for granted that the subjection of the spirit is indescribably *painful*, that all the past and all the habits of such a spirit resist the *absurdissimum*, in the form of which "faith" comes to it.

Modern men, with their obtuseness as regards all Christian nomenclature, have no longer the sense for the terribly superlative conception which was implied to an antique taste by the paradox of the formula, "God on the Cross". Hitherto there had never and nowhere been such boldness in inversion, nor anything at once so dreadful, questioning, and questionable as this formula: it promised a transvaluation of all ancient values.

It was the Orient, the *profound* Orient, it was the Oriental slave who thus took revenge on Rome and its noble, light-minded toleration, on the Roman "Catholicism" of non-faith, and it was always not the faith, but the freedom from the faith, the half-stoical and smiling indifference to the seriousness of the faith, which made the slaves indignant at their masters and revolt against them. "Enlightenment" causes revolt, for the slave desires the unconditioned, he understands nothing but the tyrannous, even in morals, he loves as he hates, without *nuance*, to the very depths, to the point of pain, to the point of sickness— his many *hidden* sufferings make him revolt against the noble taste which seems to *deny* suffering. The skepticism with regard to suffering, fundamentally only an attitude of aristocratic morality, was not the least of the causes, also, of the last great slave-insurrection which began with the French Revolution.

47

Wherever the religious neurosis has appeared on the earth so far, we find it connected with three dangerous prescriptions as to regimen: solitude, fasting, and sexual abstinence—but without its being possible to determine with certainty which is cause and which is effect, or *if* any relation at all of cause and effect exists there. This latter doubt is justified by the fact that one of the most regular symptoms among savage as well as among civilized peoples is the most sudden and excessive sensuality, which then with equal suddenness transforms into penitential paroxysms, world-renunciation, and will-renunciation, both symptoms perhaps explainable as disguised epilepsy? But nowhere is it *more* obligatory to put aside explanations around no other type has there grown such a mass of absurdity and superstition, no other type seems to have been more interesting to men and even to philosophers—perhaps it is time to become just a little indifferent here, to learn caution, or, better still, to look *away, to go away.*

Yet in the background of the most recent philosophy, that of Schopenhauer, we find almost as the problem in itself, this terrible note of interrogation of the religious crisis and awakening. How is the negation of will *possible?* how is the saint possible?—that seems to have been the very question with which Schopenhauer made a start and became a philosopher. And thus it was a genuine Schopenhauerian consequence, that his most convinced adherent (perhaps also his last, as far as Germany is concerned), namely, Richard Wagner, should bring his own life-work to an end just here, and should finally put that terrible and eternal type upon the stage as Kundry, *type vécu,* and as it loved and lived, at the very time that the mad-doctors in almost all European countries had an opportunity to study the type close at hand, wherever the religious neurosis—or as I call it, "the religious mood"—made its latest epidemical outbreak and display as the "Salvation Army."

If it be a question, however, as to what has been so extremely interesting to men of all sorts in all ages, and even to philosophers, in the whole phenomenon of the saint, it is undoubtedly the appearance of the miraculous therein—namely, the immediate *succession of opposites*, of states of the soul regarded as morally antithetical: it was believed here to be self-evident that a "bad man" was all at once turned into a "saint," a good man. The hitherto existing psychology was wrecked at this point, is it not possible it may have happened principally because psychology had placed itself under the dominion of morals, because it *believed* in oppositions of moral values, and saw, read, and *interpreted* these oppositions into the text and facts of the case?

What? "Miracle" only an error of interpretation? A lack of philology?

48

It seems that the Latin races are far more deeply attached to their Catholicism than we Northerners are to Christianity generally, and that consequently unbelief in Catholic countries means something quite different from what it does among Protestants—namely, a sort of revolt against the spirit of the race, while with us it is rather a return to the spirit (or non-spirit) of the race. We Northerners undoubtedly derive our origin from barbarous races, even as regards our talents for religion—we have *poor* talents for it. One may make an exception in the case of the Celts, who have theretofore furnished also the best soil for Christian infection in the North: the Christian ideal blossomed forth in France as much as ever the pale sun of the north would allow it. How strangely pious for our taste are still these later French skeptics, whenever there is any Celtic blood in their origin! How Catholic, how un-German does Auguste Comte's Sociology seem to us, with the Roman logic of its instincts! How Jesuitical, that amiable and shrewd cicerone of Port Royal, Sainte-Beuve, in spite of all his hostility to Jesuits! And even Ernest Renan: how inaccessible to us Northerners does the language of such a Renan appear, in whom every instant the merest touch of religious thrill throws his refined voluptuous and comfortably couching soul off its balance! Let us repeat after him these fine sentences—and what wickedness and haughtiness is immediately aroused by way of answer in our probably less beautiful but harder souls, that is to say, in our more German souls!

"*Disons donc hardiment que la religion est un produit de l'homme normal, que l'homme est le plus dans le vrai quant il est le plus religieux et le plus assuré d'une destinée infinie.... C'est quand il est bon qu'il veut que la virtu corresponde à un order éternal, c'est quand il contemple les choses d'une manière désintéressée qu'il trouve la mort révoltante et absurde. Comment ne pas supposer que c'est dans ces moments-là, que l'homme voit le mieux?"*

These sentences are so extremely *antipodal* to my ears and habits of thought, that in my first impulse of rage on finding them, I wrote on the margin, *"la niaiserie religieuse par excellence!"*—until in my later rage I even took a fancy to them, these sentences with their truth absolutely inverted! It is so nice and such a distinction to have one's own antipodes!

49

That which is so astonishing in the religious life of the ancient Greeks is the irrestrainable stream of *gratitude* which it pours forth—it is a very superior kind of man who takes *such* an attitude towards nature and life.

Later on, when the populace got the upper hand in Greece, *fear* became rampant also in religion; and Christianity was preparing itself.

50

The passion for God: there are churlish, honest-hearted, and importunate kinds of it, like that of Luther—the whole of Protestantism lacks the southern *delicatezza.* There is an Oriental exaltation of the mind in it, like that of an undeservedly favored or elevated slave, as in the case of St. Augustine, for instance, who lacks in an offensive manner, all nobility in bearing and desires. There is a feminine tenderness and sensuality in it, which modestly and unconsciously longs for a *unio mystica et physica,* as in the case of Madame de Guyon. In many cases it appears, curiously enough, as the disguise of a girl's or youth's puberty; here and there even as the hysteria of an old maid, also as her last ambition. The Church has frequently canonized the woman in such a case.

51

The mightiest men have hitherto always bowed reverently before the saint, as the enigma of self-subjugation and utter voluntary privation—why did they thus bow? They divined in him—and as it were behind the questionableness of his frail and wretched appearance—the superior force which wished to test itself by such a subjugation; the strength of will, in which they recognized their own strength and love of power, and knew how to honor it: they honored something in themselves when they honored the saint. In addition to this, the contemplation of the saint suggested to them a suspicion: such an enormity of self-negation and anti-naturalness will not have been coveted for nothing—they have said, inquiringly. There is perhaps a reason for it, some very great danger, about which the ascetic might wish to be more accurately informed through his secret interlocutors and visitors? In a word, the mighty ones of the world learned to have a new fear before him, they divined a new power, a strange, still unconquered enemy:—it was the "Will to Power" which obliged them to halt before the saint. They had to question him.

52

In the Jewish "Old Testament," the book of divine justice, there are men, things, and sayings on such an immense scale, that Greek and Indian literature has nothing to compare with it. One stands with fear and reverence before those stupendous remains of what man was formerly, and one has sad thoughts about old Asia and its little out-pushed peninsula Europe, which would like, by all means, to figure before Asia as the "Progress of Mankind." To be sure, he who is himself only a slender, tame house-animal, and knows only the wants of a house-animal (like our cultured people of today, including the Christians of "cultured" Christianity), need neither be amazed nor even sad amid those ruins—the taste for the Old Testament is a touchstone with respect to "great" and "small": perhaps he will find that the New Testament, the book of grace, still appeals more to his heart (there is much of the odor of the genuine, tender, stupid beadsman and petty soul in it). To have bound up this New Testament (a kind of *rococo* of taste in every respect) along with the Old Testament into one book, as the "Bible," as "The Book in Itself," is perhaps the greatest audacity and "sin against the Spirit" which literary Europe has upon its conscience.

53

Why Atheism nowadays? "The father" in God is thoroughly refuted; equally so "the judge," "the rewarder." Also his "free will": he does not hear— and even if he did, he would not know how to help. The worst is that he seems incapable of communicating himself clearly; is he uncertain?

This is what I have made out (by questioning and listening at a variety of conversations) to be the cause of the decline of European theism; it appears to me that though the religious instinct is in vigorous growth,—it rejects the theistic satisfaction with profound distrust.

54

What does all modern philosophy mainly do? Since Descartes—and indeed more in defiance of him than on the basis of his procedure—an *attentat* has been made on the part of all philosophers on the old conception of the soul, under the guise of a criticism of the subject and predicate conception—that is to say, an *attentat* on the fundamental presupposition of Christian doctrine. Modern philosophy, as epistemological skepticism, is secretly or openly *anti-Christian*, although (for keener ears, be it said) by no means anti-religious.

Formerly, in effect, one believed in "the soul" as one believed in grammar and the grammatical subject: one said, "I" is the condition, "think" is the predicate and is conditioned—to think is an activity for which one *must* suppose a subject as cause. The attempt was then made, with marvelous tenacity and subtlety, to see if one could not get out of this net,—to see if the opposite was not perhaps true: "think" the condition, and "I" the conditioned; "I," therefore, only a synthesis which has been *made* by thinking itself. *Kant* really wished to prove that, starting from the subject, the subject could not be proved—nor the object either: the possibility of an *apparent existence* of the subject, and therefore of "the soul," may not always have been strange to him,—the thought which once had an immense power on earth as the Vedanta philosophy.

55

There is a great ladder of religious cruelty, with many rounds; but three of these are the most important.

Once on a time men sacrificed human beings to their God, and perhaps just those they loved the best—to this category belong the firstling sacrifices of all primitive religions, and also the sacrifice of the Emperor Tiberius in the Mithra-Grotto on the Island of Capri, that most terrible of all Roman anachronisms.

Then, during the moral epoch of mankind, they sacrificed to their God the strongest instincts they possessed, their "nature"; *this* festal joy shines in the cruel glances of ascetics and "anti-natural" fanatics.

Finally, what still remained to be sacrificed? Was it not necessary in the end for men to sacrifice everything comforting, holy, healing, all hope, all faith in hidden harmonies, in future blessedness and justice? Was it not necessary to sacrifice God himself, and out of cruelty to themselves to worship stone, stupidity, gravity, fate, nothingness? To sacrifice God for nothingness—this paradoxical mystery of the ultimate cruelty has been reserved for the rising generation; we all know something thereof already.

56

Whoever, like myself, prompted by some enigmatical desire, has long endeavored to go to the bottom of the question of pessimism and free it from the half-Christian, half-German narrowness and stupidity in which it has finally presented itself to this century, namely, in the form of Schopenhauer's philosophy; whoever, with an Asiatic and super-Asiatic eye, has actually looked inside, and into the most world-renouncing of all possible modes of thought—beyond good and evil, and no longer like Buddha and Schopenhauer, under the dominion and delusion of morality,—whoever has done this, has perhaps just thereby, without really desiring it, opened his eyes to behold the opposite ideal: the ideal of the most world-approving, exuberant, and vivacious man, who has not only learnt to compromise and arrange with that which was and is, but wishes to have it again *as it was and is*, for all eternity, insatiably calling out *da capo*, not only to himself, but to the whole piece and play; and not only the play, but actually to him who requires the play—and makes it necessary; because he always requires himself anew—and makes himself necessary.—What? And this would not be—*circulus vitiosus deus?*

57

The distance, and as it were the space around man, grows with the strength of his intellectual vision and insight: his world becomes profounder; new stars, new enigmas, and notions are ever coming into view. Perhaps everything on which the intellectual eye has exercised its acuteness and profundity has just been an occasion for its exercise, something of a game, something for children and childish minds. Perhaps the most solemn conceptions that have caused the most fighting and suffering, the conceptions "God" and "sin," will one day seem to us of no more importance than a child's plaything or a child's pain seems to an old man;—and perhaps another plaything and another pain will then be necessary once more for "the old man"—always childish enough, an eternal child!

58

Has it been observed to what extent outward idleness, or semi-idleness, is necessary to a real religious life (alike for its favorite microscopic labor of self-examination, and for its soft placidity called "prayer," the state of perpetual readiness for the "coming of God"), I mean the idleness with a good conscience, the idleness of olden times and of blood, to which the aristocratic sentiment that work is *dishonoring*—that it vulgarizes body and soul—is not quite unfamiliar? And that consequently the modern, noisy, time-engrossing, conceited, foolishly proud laboriousness educates and prepares for "unbelief" more than anything else?

Among these, for instance, who are at present living apart from religion in Germany, I find "free-thinkers" of diversified species and origin, but above all a majority of those in whom laboriousness from generation to generation has dissolved the religious instincts; so that they no longer know what purpose religions serve, and only note their existence in the world with a kind of dull astonishment. They feel themselves already fully occupied, these good people, be it by their business or by their pleasures, not to mention the "Fatherland," and the newspapers, and their "family duties"; it seems that they have no time whatever left for religion; and above all, it is not obvious to them whether it is a question of a new business or a new pleasure—for it is impossible, they say to themselves, that people should go to church merely to spoil their tempers. They are by no means enemies of religious customs; should certain circumstances, State affairs perhaps, require their participation in such customs, they do what is required, as so many things are done—with a patient and unassuming seriousness, and without much curiosity or discomfort;—they live too much apart and outside to feel even the necessity for a *for* or *against* in such matters.

Among those indifferent persons may be reckoned nowadays the majority of German Protestants of the middle classes, especially in the great laborious centers of trade and commerce; also the majority of laborious scholars, and the entire University personnel (with the exception of the theologians, whose existence and possibility there always gives psychologists new and more subtle puzzles to solve). On the part of pious, or merely church-going people, there is seldom any idea of *how much* good-will, one might say arbitrary will, is now necessary for a German scholar to take the problem of religion seriously; his whole profession (and as I have said, his whole workmanlike laboriousness, to which he is compelled by his modern conscience) inclines him to a lofty and almost charitable serenity as regards religion, with which is occasionally mingled a slight disdain for the "uncleanliness" of spirit which he takes for granted wherever any one still professes to belong to the Church. It is only with the help of history (*not* through his own personal experience, therefore) that the scholar succeeds in bringing himself to a respectful seriousness, and to a certain timid deference in presence of religions; but even when his sentiments have reached the stage of gratitude towards them, he has not personally advanced one step nearer to that which still maintains itself as Church or as piety; perhaps even the contrary. The practical indifference to religious matters in the midst of which he has been born and brought up, usually sublimates itself in his case into circumspection and cleanliness, which shuns contact with religious men and things; and it may be just the depth of his tolerance and humanity which prompts him to avoid the delicate trouble which tolerance itself brings with it.

Every age has its own divine type of naïveté, for the discovery of which other ages may envy it: and how much naïveté—adorable, childlike, and boundlessly foolish naïveté is involved in this belief of the scholar in his superiority, in the good conscience of his tolerance, in the unsuspecting, simple certainty with which his instinct treats the religious man as a lower and less valuable type, beyond, before, and *above* which he himself has developed—he, the little arrogant dwarf and mob-man, the sedulously alert, head-and-hand drudge of "ideas," of "modern ideas"!

59

Whoever has seen deeply into the world has doubtless divined what wisdom there is in the fact that men are superficial. It is their preservative instinct which teaches them to be flighty, lightsome, and false. Here and there one finds a passionate and exaggerated adoration of "pure forms" in philosophers as well as in artists: it is not to be doubted that whoever has *need* of the cult of the superficial to that extent, has at one time or another made an unlucky dive *beneath* it.

Perhaps there is even an order of rank with respect to those burnt children, the born artists who find the enjoyment of life only in trying to *falsify* its image (as if taking wearisome revenge on it), one might guess to what degree life has disgusted them, by the extent to which they wish to see its image falsified, attenuated, ultrified, and deified,—one might reckon the *homines religiosi* among the artists, as their *highest* rank.

It is the profound, suspicious fear of an incurable pessimism which compels whole centuries to fasten their teeth into a religious interpretation of existence: the fear of the instinct which divines that truth might be attained *too* soon, before man has become strong enough, hard enough, artist enough....

Piety, the "Life in God," regarded in this light, would appear as the most elaborate and ultimate product of the *fear* of truth, as artist-adoration and artist-intoxication in presence of the most logical of all falsifications, as the will to the inversion of truth, to untruth at any price. Perhaps there has hitherto been no more effective means of beautifying man than piety, by means of it man can become so artful, so superficial, so iridescent, and so good, that his appearance no longer offends.

60

To love mankind *for God's sake*—this has so far been the noblest and remotest sentiment to which mankind has attained. That love to mankind, without any redeeming intention in the background, is only an *additional* folly and brutishness, that the inclination to this love has first to get its proportion, its delicacy, its gram of salt and sprinkling of ambergris from a higher inclination— whoever first perceived and "experienced" this, however his tongue may have stammered as it attempted to express such a delicate matter, let him for all time be holy and respected, as the man who has so far flown highest and gone astray in the finest fashion!

61

The philosopher, as *we* free spirits understand him—as the man of the greatest responsibility, who has the conscience for the general development of mankind,—will use religion for his disciplining and educating work, just as he will use the contemporary political and economic conditions. The selecting and disciplining influence—destructive, as well as creative and fashioning—which can be exercised by means of religion is manifold and varied, according to the sort of people placed under its spell and protection. For those who are strong and independent, destined and trained to command, in whom the judgment and skill of a ruling race is incorporated, religion is an additional means for overcoming resistance in the exercise of authority—as a bond which binds rulers and subjects in common, betraying and surrendering to the former the conscience of the latter, their inmost heart, which would fain escape obedience. And in the case of the unique natures of noble origin, if by virtue of superior spirituality they should incline to a more retired and contemplative life, reserving to themselves only the more refined forms of government (over chosen disciples or members of an order), religion itself may be used as a means for obtaining peace from the noise and trouble of managing *grosser* affairs, and for securing immunity from the *unavoidable* filth of all political agitation. The Brahmins, for instance, understood this fact. With the help of a religious organization, they secured to themselves the power of nominating kings for the people, while their sentiments prompted them to keep apart and outside, as men with a higher and super-regal mission.

At the same time religion gives inducement and opportunity to some of the subjects to qualify themselves for future ruling and commanding the slowly ascending ranks and classes, in which, through fortunate marriage customs, volitional power and delight in self-control are on the increase. To them religion offers sufficient incentives and temptations to aspire to higher intellectuality, and to experience the sentiments of authoritative self-control, of silence, and of solitude. Asceticism and Puritanism are almost indispensable means of educating and ennobling a race which seeks to rise above its hereditary baseness and work itself upwards to future supremacy.

And finally, to ordinary men, to the majority of the people, who exist for service and general utility, and are only so far entitled to exist, religion gives invaluable contentedness with their lot and condition, peace of heart, ennoblement of obedience, additional social happiness and sympathy, with something of transfiguration and embellishment, something of justification of all the commonplaceness, all the meanness, all the semi-animal poverty of their souls. Religion, together with the religious significance of life, sheds sunshine over such perpetually harassed men, and makes even their own aspect endurable to them, it operates upon them as the Epicurean philosophy usually operates upon sufferers of a higher order, in a refreshing and refining manner, almost *turning* suffering *to account*, and in the end even hallowing and vindicating it. There is perhaps nothing so admirable in Christianity and Buddhism as their art of teaching even the lowest to elevate themselves by piety to a seemingly higher order of things, and thereby to retain their satisfaction with the actual world in which they find it difficult enough to live—this very difficulty being necessary.

62

To be sure—to make also the bad counter-reckoning against such religions, and to bring to light their secret dangers—the cost is always excessive and terrible when religions do *not* operate as an educational and disciplinary medium in the hands of the philosopher, but rule voluntarily and *paramountly*, when they wish to be the final end, and not a means along with other means. Among men, as among all other animals, there is a surplus of defective, diseased, degenerating, infirm, and necessarily suffering individuals; the successful cases, among men also, are always the exception; and in view of the fact that man is *the animal not yet properly adapted to his environment,* the rare exception. But worse still. The higher the type a man represents, the greater is the improbability that he will *succeed;* the accidental, the law of irrationality in the general constitution of mankind, manifests itself most terribly in its destructive effect on the higher orders of men, the conditions of whose lives are delicate, diverse, and difficult to determine.

What, then, is the attitude of the two greatest religions above-mentioned to the *surplus* of failures in life? They endeavor to preserve and keep alive whatever can be preserved; in fact, as the religions *for sufferers,* they take the part of these upon principle; they are always in favor of those who suffer from life as from a disease, and they would fain treat every other experience of life as false and impossible. However highly we may esteem this indulgent and preservative care (inasmuch as in applying to others, it has applied, and applies also to the highest and usually the most suffering type of man), the hitherto *paramount* religions—to give a general appreciation of them—are among the principal causes which have kept the type of "man" upon a lower level—they have preserved too much *that which should have perished.* One has to thank them for invaluable services; and who is sufficiently rich in gratitude not to feel poor at the contemplation of all that the "spiritual men" of Christianity have done for Europe hitherto! But when they had given comfort to the sufferers, courage to the oppressed and despairing, a staff and support to the helpless, and when they had allured from society into convents and spiritual penitentiaries the broken-hearted and distracted: what else had they to do in order to work systematically in that fashion, and with a good conscience, for the preservation of all the sick and suffering, which means, in deed and in truth, to work for the *deterioration of the European race?* To *reverse* all estimates of value—*that* is what they had to do! And to shatter the strong, to spoil great hopes, to cast suspicion on the delight in beauty, to break down everything autonomous, manly, conquering, and imperious—all instincts which are natural to the highest and most successful type of "man"—into uncertainty, distress of conscience, and self-destruction; forsooth, to invert all love of the earthly and of supremacy over the earth, into hatred of the earth and earthly things—*that* is the task the Church imposed on itself, and was obliged to impose, until, according to its standard of value, "unworldliness," "unsensuousness," and "higher man" fused into one sentiment.

If one could observe the strangely painful, equally coarse and refined comedy of European Christianity with the derisive and impartial eye of an Epicurean god, I should think one would never cease marveling and laughing; does it not actually seem that some single will has ruled over Europe for eighteen centuries in order to make *a sublime abortion* of man? He, however, who, with opposite requirements (no longer Epicurean) and with some divine hammer in his hand, could approach this almost voluntary degeneration and stunting of mankind, as exemplified in the European Christian (Pascal, for instance), would he not have to cry aloud with rage, pity, and horror: "Oh, you bunglers, presumptuous pitiful bunglers, what have you done! Was that a work for your hands? How you have hacked and botched my finest stone! What have you presumed to do!"

I should say that Christianity has hitherto been the most portentous of presumptions. Men, not great enough, nor hard enough, to be entitled as artists to take part in fashioning *man*; men, not sufficiently strong and far-sighted to *allow*, with sublime self-constraint, the obvious law of the thousandfold failures and perishings to prevail; men, not sufficiently noble to see the radically different grades of rank and intervals of rank that separate man from man:—*such* men, with their "equality before God," have hitherto swayed the destiny of Europe; until at last a dwarfed, almost ludicrous species has been produced, a gregarious animal, something obliging, sickly, mediocre, the European of the present day.

Part Four:
Apophthegms and Interludes

63

He who is a thorough teacher takes things seriously—and even himself—only in relation to his pupils.

64

"Knowledge for its own sake"—that is the last snare laid by morality: we are thereby completely entangled in morals once more.

65

The charm of knowledge would be small, were it not so much shame has to be overcome on the way to it.

65A

We are most dishonorable towards our God: he is not *permitted* to sin.

66

The tendency of a person to allow himself to be degraded, robbed, deceived, and exploited might be the diffidence of a God among men.

67

Love to one only is a barbarity, for it is exercised at the expense of all others. Love to God also!

68

"I did that," says my memory. "I could not have done that," says my pride, and remains inexorable. Eventually—the memory yields.

69

One has regarded life carelessly, if one has failed to see the hand that—kills with leniency.

70

If a man has character, he has also his typical experience, which always recurs.

71

The sage as astronomer.—So long as thou feelest the stars as an "above thee," thou lackest the eye of the discerning one.

72

It is not the strength, but the duration of great sentiments that makes great men.

73

He who attains his ideal, precisely thereby surpasses it.

74A

Many a peacock hides his tail from every eye—and calls it his pride.

74

A man of genius is unbearable, unless he possess at least two things besides: gratitude and purity.

75

The degree and nature of a man's sensuality extends to the highest altitudes of his spirit.

76

Under peaceful conditions the militant man attacks himself.

77

With his principles a man seeks either to dominate, or justify, or honor, or reproach, or conceal his habits: two men with the same principles probably seek fundamentally different ends therewith.

78

He who despises himself, nevertheless esteems himself thereby, as a despiser.

79

A soul which knows that it is loved, but does not itself love, betrays its sediment: its dregs come up.

80

A thing that is explained ceases to concern us—What did the God mean who gave the advice, "Know thyself!" Did it perhaps imply "Cease to be concerned about thyself! Become objective!"—And Socrates?—And the "scientific man"?

81

It is terrible to die of thirst at sea. Is it necessary that you should so salt your truth that it will no longer—quench thirst?

82

"Sympathy for all"—would be harshness and tyranny for *thee*, my good neighbor.

83

Instinct—When the house is on fire one forgets even the dinner—Yes, but one recovers it from among the ashes.

84

Woman learns how to hate in proportion as she—forgets how to charm.

85

The same emotions are in man and woman, but in different *tempo*, on that account man and woman never cease to misunderstand each other.

86

In the background of all their personal vanity, women themselves have still their impersonal scorn—for "woman".

87

Fettered heart, free spirit—When one firmly fetters one's heart and keeps it prisoner, one can allow one's spirit many liberties: I said this once before. But people do not believe it when I say so, unless they know it already.

88

One begins to distrust very clever persons when they become embarrassed.

89

Dreadful experiences raise the question whether he who experiences them is not something dreadful also.

90

Heavy, melancholy men turn lighter, and come temporarily to their surface, precisely by that which makes others heavy—by hatred and love.

91

So cold, so icy, that one burns one's finger at the touch of him! Every hand that lays hold of him shrinks back!—And for that very reason many think him red-hot.

92

Who has not, at one time or another—sacrificed himself for the sake of his good name?

93

In affability there is no hatred of men, but precisely on that account a great deal too much contempt of men.

94

The maturity of man—that means, to have reacquired the seriousness that one had as a child at play.

95

To be ashamed of one's immorality is a step on the ladder at the end of which one is ashamed also of one's morality.

96

One should part from life as Ulysses parted from Nausicaa—blessing it rather than in love with it.

97

What? A great man? I always see merely the play-actor of his own ideal.

98

When one trains one's conscience, it kisses one while it bites.

99

The disappointed one speaks—"I listened for the echo and I heard only praise."

100

We all feign to ourselves that we are simpler than we are, we thus relax ourselves away from our fellows.

101

A discerning one might easily regard himself at present as the animalization of God.

102

Discovering reciprocal love should really disenchant the lover with regard to the beloved. "What! She is modest enough to love even you? Or stupid enough? Or—or—"

103

The danger in happiness.—"Everything now turns out best for me, I now love every fate:—who would like to be my fate?"

104

Not their love of humanity, but the impotence of their love, prevents the Christians of today—burning us.

105

The *pia fraus* is still more repugnant to the taste (the "piety") of the free spirit (the "pious man of knowledge") than the *impia fraus*. Hence the profound lack of judgment, in comparison with the Church, characteristic of the type "free spirit"—as *its* non-freedom.

106

By means of music the very passions enjoy themselves.

107

A sign of strong character, when once the resolution has been taken, to shut the ear even to the best counter-arguments. Occasionally, therefore, a will to stupidity.

108

There is no such thing as moral phenomena, but only a moral interpretation of phenomena.

109

The criminal is often enough not equal to his deed: he extenuates and maligns it.

110

The advocates of a criminal are seldom artists enough to turn the beautiful terribleness of the deed to the advantage of the doer.

111

Our vanity is most difficult to wound just when our pride has been wounded.

112

To him who feels himself preordained to contemplation and not to belief, all believers are too noisy and obtrusive; he guards against them.

113

"You want to prepossess him in your favor? Then you must be embarrassed before him."

114

The immense expectation with regard to sexual love, and the coyness in this expectation, spoils all the perspectives of women at the outset.

115

Where there is neither love nor hatred in the game, woman's play is mediocre.

116

The great epochs of our life are at the points when we gain courage to rebaptize our badness as the best in us.

117

The will to overcome an emotion, is ultimately only the will of another, or of several other, emotions.

118

There is an innocence of admiration: it is possessed by him to whom it has not yet occurred that he himself may be admired someday.

119

Our loathing of dirt may be so great as to prevent our cleaning ourselves— "justifying" ourselves.

120

Sensuality often forces the growth of love too much, so that its root remains weak, and is easily torn up.

121

It is a curious thing that God learned Greek when he wished to turn author—and that he did not learn it better.

122

To rejoice on account of praise is in many cases merely politeness of heart—and the very opposite of vanity of spirit.

123

Even concubinage has been corrupted—by marriage.

124

He who exults at the stake, does not triumph over pain, but because of the fact that he does not feel pain where he expected it. A parable.

125

When we have to change an opinion about any one, we charge heavily to his account the inconvenience he thereby causes us.

126

A nation is a detour of nature to arrive at six or seven great men.—Yes, and then to get round them.

127

In the eyes of all true women science is hostile to the sense of shame. They feel as if one wished to peep under their skin with it—or worse still! under their dress and finery.

128

The more abstract the truth you wish to teach, the more must you allure the senses to it.

129

The devil has the most extensive perspectives for God; on that account he keeps so far away from him:—the devil, in effect, as the oldest friend of knowledge.

130

What a person *is* begins to betray itself when his talent decreases,—when he ceases to show what he *can* do. Talent is also an adornment; an adornment is also a concealment.

131

The sexes deceive themselves about each other: the reason is that in reality they honor and love only themselves (or their own ideal, to express it more agreeably). Thus man wishes woman to be peaceable: but in fact woman is *essentially* unpeaceable, like the cat, however well she may have assumed the peaceable demeanor.

132

One is punished best for one's virtues.

133

He who cannot find the way to *his* ideal, lives more frivolously and shamelessly than the man without an ideal.

134

From the senses originate all trustworthiness, all good conscience, all evidence of truth.

135

Pharisaism is not a deterioration of the good man; a considerable part of it is rather an essential condition of being good.

136

The one seeks an accoucheur for his thoughts, the other seeks someone whom he can assist: a good conversation thus originates.

137

In intercourse with scholars and artists one readily makes mistakes of opposite kinds: in a remarkable scholar one not infrequently finds a mediocre man; and often, even in a mediocre artist, one finds a very remarkable man.

138

We do the same when awake as when dreaming: we only invent and imagine him with whom we have intercourse—and forget it immediately.

139

In revenge and in love woman is more barbarous than man.

140

Advice as a riddle.—"If the band is not to break, bite it first—secure to make!"

141

The belly is the reason why man does not so readily take himself for a God.

142

The chastest utterance I ever heard: "*Dans le véritable amour c'est l'âme qui enveloppe le corps.*"

143

Our vanity would like what we do best to pass precisely for what is most difficult to us.—Concerning the origin of many systems of morals.

144

When a woman has scholarly inclinations there is generally something wrong with her sexual nature. Barrenness itself conduces to a certain virility of taste; man, indeed, if I may say so, is "the barren animal."

145

Comparing man and woman generally, one may say that woman would not have the genius for adornment, if she had not the instinct for the *secondary* role.

146

He who fights with monsters should be careful lest he thereby become a monster. And if thou gaze long into an abyss, the abyss will also gaze into thee.

147

From old Florentine novels—moreover, from life: *Buona femmina e mala femmina vuol bastone.*—Sacchetti, Nov. 86.

148

To seduce their neighbor to a favorable opinion, and afterwards to believe implicitly in this opinion of their neighbor—who can do this conjuring trick so well as women?

149

That which an age considers evil is usually an unseasonable echo of what was formerly considered good—the atavism of an old ideal.

150

Around the hero everything becomes a tragedy; around the demigod everything becomes a satyr-play; and around God everything becomes—what? perhaps a "world"?

151

It is not enough to possess a talent: one must also have your permission to possess it;—eh, my friends?

152

"Where there is the tree of knowledge, there is always Paradise": so say the most ancient and the most modern serpents.

153

What is done out of love always takes place beyond good and evil.

154

Objection, evasion, joyous distrust, and love of irony are signs of health; everything absolute belongs to pathology.

155

The sense of the tragic increases and declines with sensuousness.

156

Insanity in individuals is something rare—but in groups, parties, nations, and epochs it is the rule.

157

The thought of suicide is a great consolation: by means of it one gets successfully through many a bad night.

158

Not only our reason, but also our conscience, truckles to our strongest impulse— the tyrant in us.

159

One *must* repay good and ill; but why just to the person who did us good or ill?

160

One no longer loves one's knowledge sufficiently after one has communicated it.

161

Poets act shamelessly towards their experiences: they exploit them.

162

"Our fellow-creature is not our neighbor, but our neighbor's neighbor":—so thinks every nation.

163

Love brings to light the noble and hidden qualities of a lover—his rare and exceptional traits: it is thus liable to be deceptive as to his normal character.

164

Jesus said to his Jews: "The law was for servants;—love God as I love him, as his Son! What have we Sons of God to do with morals!"

165

In sight of every party.—A shepherd has always need of a bell-wether—or he has himself to be a wether occasionally.

166

One may indeed lie with the mouth; but with the accompanying grimace one nevertheless tells the truth.

167

To vigorous men intimacy is a matter of shame—and something precious.

168

Christianity gave Eros poison to drink; he did not die of it, certainly, but degenerated to Vice.

169

To talk much about oneself may also be a means of concealing oneself.

170

In praise there is more obtrusiveness than in blame.

171

Pity has an almost ludicrous effect on a man of knowledge, like tender hands on a Cyclops.

172

One occasionally embraces someone or other, out of love to mankind (because one cannot embrace all); but this is what one must never confess to the individual.

173

One does not hate as long as one disesteems, but only when one esteems equal or superior.

174

Ye Utilitarians—ye, too, love the *utile* only as a *vehicle* for your inclinations,—ye, too, really find the noise of its wheels insupportable!

175

One loves ultimately one's desires, not the thing desired.

176

The vanity of others is only counter to our taste when it is counter to our vanity.

177

With regard to what "truthfulness" is, perhaps nobody has ever been sufficiently truthful.

178

One does not believe in the follies of clever men: what a forfeiture of the rights of man!

179

The consequences of our actions seize us by the forelock, very indifferent to the fact that we have meanwhile "reformed."

180

There is an innocence in lying which is the sign of good faith in a cause.

181

It is inhuman to bless when one is being cursed.

182

The familiarity of superiors embitters one, because it may not be returned.

183

"I am affected, not because you have deceived me, but because I can no longer believe in you."

184

There is a haughtiness of kindness which has the appearance of wickedness.

185

"I dislike him."—Why?—"I am not a match for him."—Did anyone ever answer so?

Part Five:
The Natural History of Morals

186

The moral sentiment in Europe at present is perhaps as subtle, belated, diverse, sensitive, and refined, as the "Science of Morals" belonging thereto is recent, initial, awkward, and coarse-fingered:—an interesting contrast, which sometimes becomes incarnate and obvious in the very person of a moralist. Indeed, the expression, "Science of Morals" is, in respect to what is designated thereby, far too presumptuous and counter to *good* taste,—which is always a foretaste of more modest expressions. One ought to avow with the utmost fairness *what* is still necessary here for a long time, *what* is alone proper for the present: namely, the collection of material, the comprehensive survey and classification of an immense domain of delicate sentiments of worth, and distinctions of worth, which live, grow, propagate, and perish—and perhaps attempts to give a clear idea of the recurring and more common forms of these living crystallizations—as preparation for a *theory of types* of morality.

To be sure, people have not hitherto been so modest. All the philosophers, with a pedantic and ridiculous seriousness, demanded of themselves something very much higher, more pretentious, and ceremonious, when they concerned themselves with morality as a science: they wanted to *give a basic* to morality— and every philosopher hitherto has believed that he has given it a basis; morality itself, however, has been regarded as something "given." How far from their awkward pride was the seemingly insignificant problem—left in dust and decay—of a description of forms of morality, notwithstanding that the finest hands and senses could hardly be fine enough for it!

It was precisely owing to moral philosophers' knowing the moral facts imperfectly, in an arbitrary epitome, or an accidental abridgement—perhaps as the morality of their environment, their position, their church, their Zeitgeist, their climate and zone—it was precisely because they were badly instructed with regard to nations, eras, and past ages, and were by no means eager to know about these matters, that they did not even come in sight of the real problems of morals—problems which only disclose themselves by a comparison of *many* kinds of morality. In every "Science of Morals" hitherto, strange as it may sound, the problem of morality itself has been *omitted*: there has been no suspicion that there was anything problematic there! That which philosophers called "giving a basis to morality," and endeavored to realize, has, when seen in a right light, proved merely a learned form of good *faith* in prevailing morality, a new means of its *expression*, consequently just a matter-of-fact within the sphere of a definite morality, yea, in its ultimate motive, a sort of denial that it is *lawful* for this morality to be called in question—and in any case the reverse of the testing, analyzing, doubting, and vivisecting of this very faith.

Hear, for instance, with what innocence—almost worthy of honor—Schopenhauer represents his own task, and draw your conclusions concerning the scientificness of a "Science" whose latest master still talks in the strain of children and old wives: "The principle," he says (page 136 of the *Grundprobleme der Ethik*),[4] "the axiom about the purport of which all moralists are *practically* agreed: *neminem laede, immo omnes quantum potes juva*—is *really* the proposition which all moral teachers strive to establish, ... the *real* basis of ethics which has been sought, like the philosopher's stone, for centuries."

The difficulty of establishing the proposition referred to may indeed be great—it is well known that Schopenhauer also was unsuccessful in his efforts; and whoever has thoroughly realized how absurdly false and sentimental this proposition is, in a world whose essence is Will to Power, may be reminded that Schopenhauer, although a pessimist, *actually*—played the flute... daily after dinner: one may read about the matter in his biography. A question by the way: a pessimist, a repudiator of God and of the world, who *makes a halt* at morality—who assents to morality, and plays the flute to *laede-neminem* morals, what? Is that really—a pessimist?

187

Apart from the value of such assertions as "there is a categorical imperative in us," one can always ask: What does such an assertion indicate about him who makes it? There are systems of morals which are meant to justify their author in

---

4   Pages 54-55 of Schopenhauer's *Basis of Morality*, translated by Arthur B. Bullock, M.A. (1903).

the eyes of other people; other systems of morals are meant to tranquilize him, and make him self-satisfied; with other systems he wants to crucify and humble himself, with others he wishes to take revenge, with others to conceal himself, with others to glorify himself and gave superiority and distinction,—this system of morals helps its author to forget, that system makes him, or something of him, forgotten, many a moralist would like to exercise power and creative arbitrariness over mankind, many another, perhaps, Kant especially, gives us to understand by his morals that "what is estimable in me, is that I know how to obey—and with you it *shall* not be otherwise than with me!" In short, systems of morals are only a *sign-language of the emotions.*

188

In contrast to *laisser-aller,* every system of morals is a sort of tyranny against "nature" and also against "reason", that is, however, no objection, unless one should again decree by some system of morals, that all kinds of tyranny and unreasonableness are unlawful What is essential and invaluable in every system of morals, is that it is a long constraint. In order to understand Stoicism, or Port Royal, or Puritanism, one should remember the constraint under which every language has attained to strength and freedom—the metrical constraint, the tyranny of rhyme and rhythm.

How much trouble have the poets and orators of every nation given themselves!—not excepting some of the prose writers of today, in whose ear dwells an inexorable conscientiousness—"for the sake of a folly," as utilitarian bunglers say, and thereby deem themselves wise—"from submission to arbitrary laws," as the anarchists say, and thereby fancy themselves "free," even free-spirited. The singular fact remains, however, that everything of the nature of freedom, elegance, boldness, dance, and masterly certainty, which exists or has existed, whether it be in thought itself, or in administration, or in speaking and persuading, in art just as in conduct, has only developed by means of the tyranny of such arbitrary law, and in all seriousness, it is not at all improbable that precisely this is "nature" and "natural"—and not *laisser-aller!*

Every artist knows how different from the state of letting himself go, is his "most natural" condition, the free arranging, locating, disposing, and constructing in the moments of "inspiration"—and how strictly and delicately he then obeys a thousand laws, which, by their very rigidness and precision, defy all formulation by means of ideas (even the most stable idea has, in comparison therewith, something floating, manifold, and ambiguous in it).

The essential thing "in heaven and in earth" is, apparently (to repeat it once more), that there should be long *obedience* in the same direction, there thereby results, and has always resulted in the long run, something which has made life worth living; for instance, virtue, art, music, dancing, reason, spirituality—anything whatever that is transfiguring, refined, foolish, or divine. The long bondage of the spirit, the distrustful constraint in the communicability of ideas, the discipline which the thinker imposed on himself to think in accordance with the rules of a church or a court, or conformable to Aristotelian premises, the persistent spiritual will to interpret everything that happened according to a Christian scheme, and in every occurrence to rediscover and justify the Christian God:—all this violence, arbitrariness, severity, dreadfulness, and unreasonableness, has proved itself the disciplinary means whereby the European spirit has attained its strength, its remorseless curiosity and subtle mobility; granted also that much irrecoverable strength and spirit had to be stifled, suffocated, and spoilt in the process (for here, as everywhere, "nature" shows herself as she is, in all her extravagant and *indifferent* magnificence, which is shocking, but nevertheless noble).

That for centuries European thinkers only thought in order to prove something—nowadays, on the contrary, we are suspicious of every thinker who "wishes to prove something"—that it was always settled beforehand what *was to be* the result of their strictest thinking, as it was perhaps in the Asiatic astrology of former times, or as it is still at the present day in the innocent, Christian-moral explanation of immediate personal events "for the glory of God," or "for the good of the soul":—this tyranny, this arbitrariness, this severe and magnificent stupidity, has *educated* the spirit; slavery, both in the coarser and the finer sense, is apparently an indispensable means even of spiritual education and discipline. One may look at every system of morals in this light: it is "nature" therein which teaches to hate the *laisser-aller*, the too great freedom, and implants the need for limited horizons, for immediate duties—it teaches the *narrowing of perspectives*, and thus, in a certain sense, that stupidity is a condition of life and development.

"Thou must obey someone, and for a long time; *otherwise* thou wilt come to grief, and lose all respect for thyself"—this seems to me to be the moral imperative of nature, which is certainly neither "categorical," as old Kant wished (consequently the "otherwise"), nor does it address itself to the individual (what does nature care for the individual!), but to nations, races, ages, and ranks; above all, however, to the animal "man" generally, to *mankind*.

189

Industrious races find it a great hardship to be idle: it was a master stroke of *English* instinct to hallow and begloom Sunday to such an extent that the Englishman unconsciously hankers for his week—and work-day again:—as a kind of cleverly devised, cleverly intercalated *fast*, such as is also frequently found in the ancient world (although, as is appropriate in southern nations, not precisely with respect to work). Many kinds of fasts are necessary; and wherever powerful influences and habits prevail, legislators have to see that intercalary days are appointed, on which such impulses are fettered, and learn to hunger anew. Viewed from a higher standpoint, whole generations and epochs, when they show themselves infected with any moral fanaticism, seem like those intercalated periods of restraint and fasting, during which an impulse learns to humble and submit itself—at the same time also to *purify* and *sharpen* itself; certain philosophical sects likewise admit of a similar interpretation (for instance, the Stoa, in the midst of Hellenic culture, with the atmosphere rank and overcharged with Aphrodisiacal odors).

Here also is a hint for the explanation of the paradox, why it was precisely in the most Christian period of European history, and in general only under the pressure of Christian sentiments, that the sexual impulse sublimated into love (*amour-passion*).

190

There is something in the morality of Plato which does not really belong to Plato, but which only appears in his philosophy, one might say, in spite of him: namely, Socratism, for which he himself was too noble. "No one desires to injure himself, hence all evil is done unwittingly. The evil man inflicts injury on himself; he would not do so, however, if he knew that evil is evil. The evil man, therefore, is only evil through error; if one free him from error one will necessarily make him—good."

This mode of reasoning savors of the *populace*, who perceive only the unpleasant consequences of evil-doing, and practically judge that "it is *stupid* to do wrong"; while they accept "good" as identical with "useful and pleasant," without further thought. As regards every system of utilitarianism, one may at once assume that it has the same origin, and follow the scent: one will seldom err.

Plato did all he could to interpret something refined and noble into the tenets of his teacher, and above all to interpret himself into them—he, the most daring of all interpreters, who lifted the entire Socrates out of the street, as a popular theme and song, to exhibit him in endless and impossible modifications—namely, in all his own disguises and multiplicities. In jest, and in Homeric language as well, what is the Platonic Socrates, if not *prosthe Platon opithen te Platon messe te chimaera.* [Plato in front and Plato behind, in the middle the Chimera.]

191

The old theological problem of "Faith" and "Knowledge," or more plainly, of instinct and reason—the question whether, in respect to the valuation of things, instinct deserves more authority than rationality, which wants to appreciate and act according to motives, according to a "Why," that is to say, in conformity to purpose and utility—it is always the old moral problem that first appeared in the person of Socrates, and had divided men's minds long before Christianity. Socrates himself, following, of course, the taste of his talent—that of a surpassing dialectician—took first the side of reason; and, in fact, what did he do all his life but laugh at the awkward incapacity of the noble Athenians, who were men of instinct, like all noble men, and could never give satisfactory answers concerning the motives of their actions? In the end, however, though silently and secretly, he laughed also at himself: with his finer conscience and introspection, he found in himself the same difficulty and incapacity. "But why"—he said to himself—"should one on that account separate oneself from the instincts! One must set them right, and the reason *also*—one must follow the instincts, but at the same time persuade the reason to support them with good arguments." This was the real *falseness* of that great and mysterious ironist; he brought his conscience up to the point that he was satisfied with a kind of self-outwitting: in fact, he perceived the irrationality in the moral judgment.

Plato, more innocent in such matters, and without the craftiness of the plebeian, wished to prove to himself, at the expenditure of all his strength—the greatest strength a philosopher had ever expended—that reason and instinct lead spontaneously to one goal, to the good, to "God"; and since Plato, all theologians and philosophers have followed the same path—which means that in matters of morality, instinct (or as Christians call it, "Faith," or as I call it, "the herd") has hitherto triumphed. Unless one should make an exception in the case of Descartes, the father of rationalism (and consequently the grandfather of the Revolution), who recognized only the authority of reason: but reason is only a tool, and Descartes was superficial.

192

Whoever has followed the history of a single science, finds in its development a clue to the understanding of the oldest and commonest processes of all "knowledge and cognizance": there, as here, the premature hypotheses, the fictions, the good stupid will to "belief," and the lack of distrust and patience are first developed—our senses learn late, and never learn completely, to be subtle, reliable, and cautious organs of knowledge. Our eyes find it easier on a given occasion to produce a picture already often produced, than to seize upon the divergence and novelty of an impression: the latter requires more force, more "morality." It is difficult and painful for the ear to listen to anything new; we hear strange music badly. When we hear another language spoken, we involuntarily attempt to form the sounds into words with which we are more familiar and conversant—it was thus, for example, that the Germans modified the spoken word *arcubalista* into *armbrust* (cross-bow). Our senses are also hostile and averse to the new; and generally, even in the "simplest" processes of sensation, the emotions *dominate*—such as fear, love, hatred, and the passive emotion of indolence.

As little as a reader nowadays reads all the single words (not to speak of syllables) of a page—he rather takes about five out of every twenty words at random, and "guesses" the probably appropriate sense to them—just as little do we see a tree correctly and completely in respect to its leaves, branches, color, and shape; we find it so much easier to fancy the chance of a tree. Even in the midst of the most remarkable experiences, we still do just the same; we fabricate the greater part of the experience, and can hardly be made to contemplate any event, *except* as "inventors" thereof. All this goes to prove that from our fundamental nature and from remote ages we have been—*accustomed to lying.* Or, to express it more politely and hypocritically, in short, more pleasantly—one is much more of an artist than one is aware of.

In an animated conversation, I often see the face of the person with whom I am speaking so clearly and sharply defined before me, according to the thought he expresses, or which I believe to be evoked in his mind, that the degree of distinctness far exceeds the *strength* of my visual faculty—the delicacy of the play of the muscles and of the expression of the eyes *must* therefore be imagined by me. Probably the person put on quite a different expression, or none at all.

193

Quidquid luce fuit, tenebris agit: but also contrariwise. What we experience in dreams, provided we experience it often, pertains at last just as much to the general belongings of our soul as anything "actually" experienced; by virtue thereof we are richer or poorer, we have a requirement more or less, and finally, in broad daylight, and even in the brightest moments of our waking life, we are ruled to some extent by the nature of our dreams.

Supposing that someone has often flown in his dreams, and that at last, as soon as he dreams, he is conscious of the power and art of flying as his privilege and his peculiarly enviable happiness; such a person, who believes that on the slightest impulse, he can actualize all sorts of curves and angles, who knows the sensation of a certain divine levity, an "upwards" without effort or constraint, a "downwards" without descending or lowering—without *trouble.*—how could the man with such dream-experiences and dream-habits fail to find "happiness" differently colored and defined, even in his waking hours! How could he fail—to long *differently* for happiness? "Flight," such as is described by poets, must, when compared with his own "flying," be far too earthly, muscular, violent, far too "troublesome" for him.

194

The difference among men does not manifest itself only in the difference of their lists of desirable things—in their regarding different good things as worth striving for, and being disagreed as to the greater or less value, the order of rank, of the commonly recognized desirable things:—it manifests itself much more in what they regard as actually *having* and *possessing* a desirable thing.

As regards a woman, for instance, the control over her body and her sexual gratification serves as an amply sufficient sign of ownership and possession to the more modest man; another with a more suspicious and ambitious thirst for possession, sees the "questionableness," the mere apparentness of such ownership, and wishes to have finer tests in order to know especially whether the woman not only gives herself to him, but also gives up for his sake what she has or would like to have—only *then* does he look upon her as "possessed." A third, however, has not even here got to the limit of his distrust and his desire for possession: he asks himself whether the woman, when she gives up everything for him, does not perhaps do so for a phantom of him; he wishes first to be thoroughly, indeed, profoundly well known; in order to be loved at all he ventures to let himself be found out. Only then does he feel the beloved one fully in his possession, when she no longer deceives herself about him, when she loves him just as much for the sake of his devilry and concealed insatiability, as for his goodness, patience, and spirituality.

One man would like to possess a nation, and he finds all the higher arts of Cagliostro and Catalina suitable for his purpose. Another, with a more refined thirst for possession, says to himself: "One may not deceive where one desires to possess"—he is irritated and impatient at the idea that a mask of him should rule in the hearts of the people: "I must, therefore, *make* myself known, and first of all learn to know myself!"

Among helpful and charitable people, one almost always finds the awkward craftiness which first gets up suitably him who has to be helped, as though, for instance, he should "merit" help, seek just *their* help, and would show himself deeply grateful, attached, and subservient to them for all help. With these conceits, they take control of the needy as a property, just as in general they are charitable and helpful out of a desire for property. One finds them jealous when they are crossed or forestalled in their charity.

Parents involuntarily make something like themselves out of their children—they call that "education"; no mother doubts at the bottom of her heart that the child she has borne is thereby her property, no father hesitates about his right to *his own* ideas and notions of worth. Indeed, in former times fathers deemed it right to use their discretion concerning the life or death of the newly born (as among the ancient Germans). And like the father, so also do the teacher, the class, the priest, and the prince still see in every new individual an unobjectionable opportunity for a new possession. The consequence is...

195

The Jews—a people "born for slavery," as Tacitus and the whole ancient world say of them; "the chosen people among the nations," as they themselves say and believe—the Jews performed the miracle of the inversion of valuations, by means of which life on earth obtained a new and dangerous charm for a couple of millenniums. Their prophets fused into one the expressions "rich," "godless," "wicked," "violent," "sensual," and for the first time coined the word "world" as a term of reproach. In this inversion of valuations (in which is also included the use of the word "poor" as synonymous with "saint" and "friend") the significance of the Jewish people is to be found; it is with *them* that the *slave-insurrection in morals* commences.

196

It is to be *inferred* that there are countless dark bodies near the sun—such as we shall never see. Among ourselves, this is an allegory; and the psychologist of morals reads the whole star-writing merely as an allegorical and symbolic language in which much may be unexpressed.

197

The beast of prey and the man of prey (for instance, Caesar Borgia) are fundamentally misunderstood, "nature" is misunderstood, so long as one seeks a "morbidness" in the constitution of these healthiest of all tropical monsters and growths, or even an innate "hell" in them—as almost all moralists have done hitherto. Does it not seem that there is a hatred of the virgin forest and of the tropics among moralists? And that the "tropical man" must be discredited at all costs, whether as disease and deterioration of mankind, or as his own hell and self-torture? And why? In favor of the "temperate zones"? In favor of the temperate men? The "moral"? The mediocre?—This for the chapter: "Morals as Timidity."

198

All the systems of morals which address themselves with a view to their "happiness," as it is called—what else are they but suggestions for behavior adapted to the degree of *danger* from themselves in which the individuals live; recipes for their passions, their good and bad propensities, insofar as such have the Will to Power and would like to play the master; small and great expediencies and elaborations, permeated with the musty odor of old family medicines and old-wife wisdom; all of them grotesque and absurd in their form—because they address themselves to "all," because they generalize where generalization is not authorized; all of them speaking unconditionally, and taking themselves unconditionally; all of them flavored not merely with one grain of salt, but rather endurable only, and sometimes even seductive, when they are over-spiced and begin to smell dangerously, especially of "the other world." That is all of little value when estimated intellectually, and is far from being "science," much less "wisdom"; but, repeated once more, and three times repeated, it is expediency, expediency, expediency, mixed with stupidity, stupidity, stupidity—whether it be the indifference and statuesque coldness towards the heated folly of the emotions, which the Stoics advised and fostered; or the no-more-laughing and no-more-weeping of Spinoza, the destruction of the emotions by their analysis and vivisection, which he recommended so naively; or the lowering of the emotions to an innocent mean at which they may be satisfied, the Aristotelianism of morals; or even morality as the enjoyment of the emotions in a voluntary attenuation and spiritualization by the symbolism of art, perhaps as music, or as love of God, and of mankind for God's sake—for in religion the passions are once more enfranchised, provided that...; or, finally, even the complaisant and wanton surrender to the emotions, as has been taught by Hafis and Goethe, the bold letting-go of the reins, the spiritual and corporeal *licentia morum* in the exceptional cases of wise old codgers and drunkards, with whom it "no longer has much danger."—This also for the chapter: "Morals as Timidity."

199

Inasmuch as in all ages, as long as mankind has existed, there have also been human herds (family alliances, communities, tribes, peoples, states, churches), and always a great number who obey in proportion to the small number who command—in view, therefore, of the fact that obedience has been most practiced and fostered among mankind hitherto, one may reasonably suppose that, generally speaking, the need thereof is now innate in every one, as a kind of *formal conscience* which gives the command "Thou shalt unconditionally do something, unconditionally refrain from something", in short, "Thou shalt". This need tries to satisfy itself and to fill its form with a content, according to its strength, impatience, and eagerness, it at once seizes as an omnivorous appetite with little selection, and accepts whatever is shouted into its ear by all sorts of commanders—parents, teachers, laws, class prejudices, or public opinion.

The extraordinary limitation of human development, the hesitation, protractedness, frequent retrogression, and turning thereof, is attributable to the fact that the herd-instinct of obedience is transmitted best, and at the cost of the art of command. If one imagines this instinct increasing to its greatest extent, commanders and independent individuals will finally be lacking altogether, or they will suffer inwardly from a bad conscience, and will have to impose a deception on themselves in the first place in order to be able to command just as if they also were only obeying. This condition of things actually exists in Europe at present—I call it the moral hypocrisy of the commanding class. They know no other way of protecting themselves from their bad conscience than by playing the role of executors of older and higher orders (of predecessors, of the constitution, of justice, of the law, or of God himself), or they even justify themselves by maxims from the current opinions of the herd, as "first servants of their people," or "instruments of the public weal".

On the other hand, the gregarious European man nowadays assumes an air as if he were the only kind of man that is allowable, he glorifies his qualities, such as public spirit, kindness, deference, industry, temperance, modesty, indulgence, sympathy, by virtue of which he is gentle, endurable, and useful to the herd, as the peculiarly human virtues. In cases, however, where it is believed that the leader and bell-wether cannot be dispensed with, attempt after attempt is made nowadays to replace commanders by the summing together of clever gregarious men all representative constitutions, for example, are of this origin. In spite of all, what a blessing, what a deliverance from a weight becoming unendurable, is the appearance of an absolute ruler for these gregarious Europeans—of this fact the effect of the appearance of Napoleon was the last great proof the history of the influence of Napoleon is almost the history of the higher happiness to which the entire century has attained in its worthiest individuals and periods.

200

The man of an age of dissolution which mixes the races with one another, who has the inheritance of a diversified descent in his body—that is to say, contrary, and often not only contrary, instincts and standards of value, which struggle with one another and are seldom at peace—such a man of late culture and broken lights, will, on an average, be a weak man. His fundamental desire is that the war which is *in him* should come to an end; happiness appears to him in the character of a soothing medicine and mode of thought (for instance, Epicurean or Christian); it is above all things the happiness of repose, of undisturbedness, of repletion, of final unity—it is the "Sabbath of Sabbaths," to use the expression of the holy rhetorician, St. Augustine, who was himself such a man.

Should, however, the contrariety and conflict in such natures operate as an *additional* incentive and stimulus to life—and if, on the other hand, in addition to their powerful and irreconcilable instincts, they have also inherited and indoctrinated into them a proper mastery and subtlety for carrying on the conflict with themselves (that is to say, the faculty of self-control and self-deception), there then arise those marvelously incomprehensible and inexplicable beings, those enigmatical men, predestined for conquering and circumventing others, the finest examples of which are Alcibiades and Caesar (with whom I should like to associate the *first* of Europeans according to my taste, the Hohenstaufen, Frederick the Second), and among artists, perhaps Leonardo da Vinci. They appear precisely in the same periods when that weaker type, with its longing for repose, comes to the front; the two types are complementary to each other, and spring from the same causes.

201

As long as the utility which determines moral estimates is only gregarious utility, as long as the preservation of the community is only kept in view, and the immoral is sought precisely and exclusively in what seems dangerous to the maintenance of the community, there can be no "morality of love to one's neighbor." Granted even that there is already a little constant exercise of consideration, sympathy, fairness, gentleness, and mutual assistance, granted that even in this condition of society all those instincts are already active which are latterly distinguished by honorable names as "virtues," and eventually almost coincide with the conception "morality": in that period they do not as yet belong to the domain of moral valuations—they are still *ultra-moral.* A sympathetic action, for instance, is neither called good nor bad, moral nor immoral, in the best period of the Romans; and should it be praised, a sort of resentful disdain is compatible with this praise, even at the best, directly the sympathetic action is compared with one which contributes to the welfare of the whole, to the *res publica.*

After all, "love to our neighbor" is always a secondary matter, partly conventional and arbitrarily manifested in relation to our *fear of our neighbor.* After the fabric of society seems on the whole established and secured against external dangers, it is this fear of our neighbor which again creates new perspectives of moral valuation. Certain strong and dangerous instincts, such as the love of enterprise, foolhardiness, revengefulness, astuteness, rapacity, and love of power, which up till then had not only to be honored from the point of view of general utility—under other names, of course, than those here given—but had to be fostered and cultivated (because they were perpetually required in the common danger against the common enemies), are now felt in their dangerousness to be doubly strong—when the outlets for them are lacking—and are gradually branded as immoral and given over to calumny.

The contrary instincts and inclinations now attain to moral honor, the gregarious instinct gradually draws its conclusions. How much or how little dangerousness to the community or to equality is contained in an opinion, a condition, an emotion, a disposition, or an endowment—that is now the moral perspective, here again fear is the mother of morals.

It is by the loftiest and strongest instincts, when they break out passionately and carry the individual far above and beyond the average, and the low level of the gregarious conscience, that the self-reliance of the community is destroyed, its belief in itself, its backbone, as it were, breaks, consequently these very instincts will be most branded and defamed. The lofty independent spirituality, the will to stand alone, and even the cogent reason, are felt to be dangers, everything that elevates the individual above the herd, and is a source of fear to the neighbor, is henceforth called *evil*, the tolerant, unassuming, self-adapting, self-equalizing disposition, the *mediocrity* of desires, attains to moral distinction and honor. Finally, under very peaceful circumstances, there is always less opportunity and necessity for training the feelings to severity and rigor, and now every form of severity, even in justice, begins to disturb the conscience, a lofty and rigorous nobleness and self-responsibility almost offends, and awakens distrust, "the lamb," and still more "the sheep," wins respect.

There is a point of diseased mellowness and effeminacy in the history of society, at which society itself takes the part of him who injures it, the part of the *criminal*, and does so, in fact, seriously and honestly. To punish, appears to it to be somehow unfair—it is certain that the idea of "punishment" and "the obligation to punish" are then painful and alarming to people. "Is it not sufficient if the criminal be rendered *harmless*? Why should we still punish? Punishment itself is terrible!"—with these questions gregarious morality, the morality of fear, draws its ultimate conclusion. If one could at all do away with danger, the cause of fear, one would have done away with this morality at the same time, it would no longer be necessary, it *would not consider itself* any longer necessary!

Whoever examines the conscience of the present-day European, will always elicit the same imperative from its thousand moral folds and hidden recesses, the imperative of the timidity of the herd "we wish that some time or other there may be *nothing more to fear!*" Some time or other—the will and the way *thereto* is nowadays called "progress" all over Europe.

202

Let us at once say again what we have already said a hundred times, for people's ears nowadays are unwilling to hear such truths—*our* truths. We know well enough how offensive it sounds when any one plainly, and without metaphor, counts man among the animals, but it will be accounted to us almost a *crime*, that it is precisely in respect to men of "modern ideas" that we have constantly applied the terms "herd," "herd-instincts," and such like expressions. What avail is it? We cannot do otherwise, for it is precisely here that our new insight is. We have found that in all the principal moral judgments, Europe has become unanimous, including likewise the countries where European influence prevails in Europe people evidently *know* what Socrates thought he did not know, and what the famous serpent of old once promised to teach—they "know" today what is good and evil.

It must then sound hard and be distasteful to the ear, when we always insist that that which here thinks it knows, that which here glorifies itself with praise and blame, and calls itself good, is the instinct of the herding human animal, the instinct which has come and is ever coming more and more to the front, to preponderance and supremacy over other instincts, according to the increasing physiological approximation and resemblance of which it is the symptom. *Morality in Europe at present is herding-animal morality,* and therefore, as we understand the matter, only one kind of human morality, beside which, before which, and after which many other moralities, and above all *higher* moralities, are or should be possible. Against such a "possibility," against such a "should be," however, this morality defends itself with all its strength, it says obstinately and inexorably "I am morality itself and nothing else is morality!" Indeed, with the help of a religion which has humored and flattered the sublimest desires of the herding-animal, things have reached such a point that we always find a more visible expression of this morality even in political and social arrangements:

the *democratic* movement is the inheritance of the Christian movement. That its *tempo*, however, is much too slow and sleepy for the more impatient ones, for those who are sick and distracted by the herding-instinct, is indicated by the increasingly furious howling, and always less disguised teeth-gnashing of the anarchist dogs, who are now roving through the highways of European culture. Apparently in opposition to the peacefully industrious democrats and Revolution-ideologues, and still more so to the awkward philosophasters and fraternity-visionaries who call themselves Socialists and want a "free society," those are really at one with them all in their thorough and instinctive hostility to every form of society other than that of the *autonomous* herd (to the extent even of repudiating the notions "master" and "servant"—*ni dieu ni mâitre*, says a socialist formula); at one in their tenacious opposition to every special claim, every special right and privilege (this means ultimately opposition to *every* right, for when all are equal, no one needs "rights" any longer); at one in their distrust of punitive justice (as though it were a violation of the weak, unfair to the *necessary* consequences of all former society); but equally at one in their religion of sympathy, in their compassion for all that feels, lives, and suffers (down to the very animals, up even to "God"—the extravagance of "sympathy for God" belongs to a democratic age); altogether at one in the cry and impatience of their sympathy, in their deadly hatred of suffering generally, in their almost feminine incapacity for witnessing it or *allowing* it; at one in their involuntary beglooming and heart-softening, under the spell of which Europe seems to be threatened with a new Buddhism; at one in their belief in the morality of *mutual* sympathy, as though it were morality in itself, the climax, the *attained* climax of mankind, the sole hope of the future, the consolation of the present, the great discharge from all the obligations of the past; altogether at one in their belief in the community as the *deliverer*, in the herd, and therefore in "themselves."

203

We, who hold a different belief—we, who regard the democratic movement, not only as a degenerating form of political organization, but as equivalent to a degenerating, a waning type of man, as involving his mediocrizing and depreciation: where have *we* to fix our hopes?

In *new philosophers*—there is no other alternative: in minds strong and original enough to initiate opposite estimates of value, to transvalue and invert "eternal valuations"; in forerunners, in men of the future, who in the present shall fix the constraints and fasten the knots which will compel millenniums to take *new* paths. To teach man the future of humanity as his *will*, as depending on human will, and to make preparation for vast hazardous enterprises and collective attempts in rearing and educating, in order thereby to put an end to the frightful rule of folly and chance which has hitherto gone by the name of "history" (the folly of the "greatest number" is only its last form)—for that purpose a new type of philosopher and commander will some time or other be needed, at the very idea of which everything that has existed in the way of occult, terrible, and benevolent beings might look pale and dwarfed. The image of such leaders hovers before *our* eyes:—is it lawful for me to say it aloud, ye free spirits? The conditions which one would partly have to create and partly utilize for their genesis; the presumptive methods and tests by virtue of which a soul should grow up to such an elevation and power as to feel a *constraint* to these tasks; a transvaluation of values, under the new pressure and hammer of which a conscience should be steeled and a heart transformed into brass, so as to bear the weight of such responsibility; and on the other hand the necessity for such leaders, the dreadful danger that they might be lacking, or miscarry and degenerate:—these are *our* real anxieties and glooms, ye know it well, ye free spirits! these are the heavy distant thoughts and storms which sweep across the heaven of *our* life.

There are few pains so grievous as to have seen, divined, or experienced how an exceptional man has missed his way and deteriorated; but he who has the rare eye for the universal danger of "man" himself *deteriorating*, he who like us has recognized the extraordinary fortuitousness which has hitherto played its game in respect to the future of mankind—a game in which neither the hand, nor even a "finger of God" has participated!—he who divines the fate that is hidden under the idiotic unwariness and blind confidence of "modern ideas," and still more under the whole of Christo-European morality—suffers from an anguish with which no other is to be compared. He sees at a glance all that could still *be made out of man* through a favorable accumulation and augmentation of human powers and arrangements; he knows with all the knowledge of his conviction how unexhausted man still is for the greatest possibilities, and how often in the past the type man has stood in presence of mysterious decisions and new paths:—he knows still better from his painfulest recollections on what wretched obstacles promising developments of the highest rank have hitherto usually gone to pieces, broken down, sunk, and become contemptible.

The *universal degeneracy of mankind* to the level of the "man of the future"—as idealized by the socialistic fools and shallow-pates—this degeneracy and dwarfing of man to an absolutely gregarious animal (or as they call it, to a man of "free society"), this brutalizing of man into a pigmy with equal rights and claims, is undoubtedly *possible*! He who has thought out this possibility to its ultimate conclusion knows *another* loathing unknown to the rest of mankind—and perhaps also a new *mission*!

Part Six:
We Scholars

204

At the risk that moralizing may also reveal itself here as that which it has always been—namely, resolutely *montrer ses plaies*, according to Balzac—I would venture to protest against an improper and injurious alteration of rank, which quite unnoticed, and as if with the best conscience, threatens nowadays to establish itself in the relations of science and philosophy. I mean to say that one must have the right out of one's own *experience*—experience, as it seems to me, always implies unfortunate experience?—to treat of such an important question of rank, so as not to speak of color like the blind, or *against* science like women and artists ("Ah! this dreadful science!" sigh their instinct and their shame, "it always *finds things out!*").

The declaration of independence of the scientific man, his emancipation from philosophy, is one of the subtler after-effects of democratic organization and disorganization: the self-glorification and self-conceitedness of the learned man is now everywhere in full bloom, and in its best springtime—which does not mean to imply that in this case self-praise smells sweet. Here also the instinct of the populace cries, "Freedom from all masters!" and after science has, with the happiest results, resisted theology, whose "hand-maid" it had been too long, it now proposes in its wantonness and indiscretion to lay down laws for philosophy, and in its turn to play the "master"—what am I saying! to play the *philosopher* on its own account.

My memory—the memory of a scientific man, if you please!—teems with the naïvetés of insolence which I have heard about philosophy and philosophers from young naturalists and old physicians (not to mention the most cultured and most conceited of all learned men, the philologists and schoolmasters, who are both the one and the other by profession). On one occasion it was the specialist and the Jack Horner who instinctively stood on the defensive against all synthetic tasks and capabilities; at another time it was the industrious worker who had got a scent of *otium* and refined luxuriousness in the internal economy of the philosopher, and felt himself aggrieved and belittled thereby. On another occasion it was the color-blindness of the utilitarian, who sees nothing in philosophy but a series of *refuted* systems, and an extravagant expenditure which "does nobody any good". At another time the fear of disguised mysticism and of the boundary-adjustment of knowledge became conspicuous, at another time the disregard of individual philosophers, which had involuntarily extended to disregard of philosophy generally.

In fine, I found most frequently, behind the proud disdain of philosophy in young scholars, the evil after-effect of some particular philosopher, to whom on the whole obedience had been foresworn, without, however, the spell of his scornful estimates of other philosophers having been got rid of—the result being a general ill-will to all philosophy. (Such seems to me, for instance, the after-effect of Schopenhauer on the most modern Germany: by his unintelligent rage against Hegel, he has succeeded in severing the whole of the last generation of Germans from its connection with German culture, which culture, all things considered, has been an elevation and a divining refinement of the *historical sense*, but precisely at this point Schopenhauer himself was poor, irreceptive, and un-German to the extent of ingeniousness.)

On the whole, speaking generally, it may just have been the humanness, all-too-humanness of the modern philosophers themselves, in short, their contemptibleness, which has injured most radically the reverence for philosophy and opened the doors to the instinct of the populace. Let it but be acknowledged to what an extent our modern world diverges from the whole style of the world of Heraclitus, Plato, Empedocles, and whatever else all the royal and magnificent anchorites of the spirit were called, and with what justice an honest man of science *may* feel himself of a better family and origin, in view of such representatives of philosophy, who, owing to the fashion of the present day, are just as much aloft as they are down below—in Germany, for instance, the two lions of Berlin, the anarchist Eugen Duhring and the amalgamist Eduard von Hartmann. It is especially the sight of those hotch-potch philosophers, who call themselves "realists," or "positivists," which is calculated to implant a dangerous distrust in the soul of a young and ambitious scholar those philosophers, at the best, are themselves but scholars and specialists, that is very evident! All of them are persons who have been vanquished and *brought back again* under the dominion of science, who at one time or another claimed more from themselves, without having a right to the "more" and its responsibility—and who now, creditably, rancorously, and vindictively, represent in word and deed, *disbelief* in the master-task and supremacy of philosophy.

After all, how could it be otherwise? Science flourishes nowadays and has the good conscience clearly visible on its countenance, while that to which the entire modern philosophy has gradually sunk, the remnant of philosophy of the present day, excites distrust and displeasure, if not scorn and pity Philosophy reduced to a "theory of knowledge," no more in fact than a diffident science of epochs and doctrine of forbearance a philosophy that never even gets beyond the threshold, and rigorously *denies* itself the right to enter—that is philosophy in its last throes, an end, an agony, something that awakens pity. How could such a philosophy—*rule*!

205

The dangers that beset the evolution of the philosopher are, in fact, so manifold nowadays, that one might doubt whether this fruit could still come to maturity. The extent and towering structure of the sciences have increased enormously, and therewith also the probability that the philosopher will grow tired even as a learner, or will attach himself somewhere and "specialize" so that he will no longer attain to his elevation, that is to say, to his superspection, his circumspection, and his *despection*. Or he gets aloft too late, when the best of his maturity and strength is past, or when he is impaired, coarsened, and deteriorated, so that his view, his general estimate of things, is no longer of much importance. It is perhaps just the refinement of his intellectual conscience that makes him hesitate and linger on the way, he dreads the temptation to become a dilettante, a millepede, a milleantenna, he knows too well that as a discerner, one who has lost his self-respect no longer commands, no longer *leads*, unless he should aspire to become a great play-actor, a philosophical Cagliostro and spiritual rat-catcher—in short, a misleader. This is in the last instance a question of taste, if it has not really been a question of conscience.

To double once more the philosopher's difficulties, there is also the fact that he demands from himself a verdict, a Yea or Nay, not concerning science, but concerning life and the worth of life—he learns unwillingly to believe that it is his right and even his duty to obtain this verdict, and he has to seek his way to the right and the belief only through the most extensive (perhaps disturbing and destroying) experiences, often hesitating, doubting, and dumbfounded.

In fact, the philosopher has long been mistaken and confused by the multitude, either with the scientific man and ideal scholar, or with the religiously elevated, desensualized, desecularized visionary and God-intoxicated man; and even yet when one hears anybody praised, because he lives "wisely," or "as a philosopher," it hardly means anything more than "prudently and apart." Wisdom: that seems to the populace to be a kind of flight, a means and artifice for withdrawing successfully from a bad game; but the *genuine* philosopher— does it not seem so to *us*, my friends?—lives "unphilosophically" and "unwisely," above all, *imprudently*, and feels the obligation and burden of a hundred attempts and temptations of life—he risks *himself* constantly, he plays *this* bad game.

206

In relation to the genius, that is to say, a being who either *engenders* or *produces*—both words understood in their fullest sense—the man of learning, the scientific average man, has always something of the old maid about him; for, like her, he is not conversant with the two principal functions of man. To both, of course, to the scholar and to the old maid, one concedes respectability, as if by way of indemnification—in these cases one emphasizes the respectability— and yet, in the compulsion of this concession, one has the same admixture of vexation.

Let us examine more closely: what is the scientific man? Firstly, a commonplace type of man, with commonplace virtues: that is to say, a non-ruling, non-authoritative, and non-self-sufficient type of man; he possesses industry, patient adaptableness to rank and file, equability and moderation in capacity and requirement; he has the instinct for people like himself, and for that which they require—for instance: the portion of independence and green meadow without which there is no rest from labor, the claim to honor and consideration (which first and foremost presupposes recognition and recognizability), the sunshine of a good name, the perpetual ratification of his value and usefulness, with which the inward *distrust* which lies at the bottom of the heart of all dependent men and gregarious animals, has again and again to be overcome.

The learned man, as is appropriate, has also maladies and faults of an ignoble kind: he is full of petty envy, and has a lynx-eye for the weak points in those natures to whose elevations he cannot attain. He is confiding, yet only as one who lets himself go, but does not *flow*; and precisely before the man of the great current he stands all the colder and more reserved—his eye is then like a smooth and irresponsive lake, which is no longer moved by rapture or sympathy. The worst and most dangerous thing of which a scholar is capable results from the instinct of mediocrity of his type, from the Jesuitism of mediocrity, which labors instinctively for the destruction of the exceptional man, and endeavors to break—or still better, to relax—every bent bow To relax, of course, with consideration, and naturally with an indulgent hand—to *relax* with confiding sympathy that is the real art of Jesuitism, which has always understood how to introduce itself as the religion of sympathy.

207

However gratefully one may welcome the *objective* spirit—and who has not been sick to death of all subjectivity and its confounded *ipsisimosity!*—in the end, however, one must learn caution even with regard to one's gratitude, and put a stop to the exaggeration with which the unselfing and depersonalizing of the spirit has recently been celebrated, as if it were the goal in itself, as if it were salvation and glorification—as is especially accustomed to happen in the pessimist school, which has also in its turn good reasons for paying the highest honors to "disinterested knowledge."

The objective man, who no longer curses and scolds like the pessimist, the *ideal* man of learning in whom the scientific instinct blossoms forth fully after a thousand complete and partial failures, is assuredly one of the most costly instruments that exist, but his place is in the hand of one who is more powerful. He is only an instrument, we may say, he is a *mirror*—he is no "purpose in himself." The objective man is in truth a mirror accustomed to prostration before everything that wants to be known, with such desires only as knowing or "reflecting" implies—he waits until something comes, and then expands himself sensitively, so that even the light footsteps and gliding-past of spiritual beings may not be lost on his surface and film.

Whatever "personality" he still possesses seems to him accidental, arbitrary, or still oftener, disturbing, so much has he come to regard himself as the passage and reflection of outside forms and events. He calls up the recollection of "himself" with an effort, and not infrequently wrongly, he readily confounds himself with other persons, he makes mistakes with regard to his own needs, and here only is he unrefined and negligent. Perhaps he is troubled about the health, or the pettiness and confined atmosphere of wife and friend, or the lack of companions and society—indeed, he sets himself to reflect on his suffering, but in vain! His thoughts already rove away to the *more general* case, and tomorrow he knows as little as he knew yesterday how to help himself. He does not now take himself seriously and devote time to himself he is serene, *not* from lack of trouble, but from lack of capacity for grasping and dealing with *his* trouble. The habitual complaisance with respect to all objects and experiences, the radiant and impartial hospitality with which he receives everything that comes his way, his habit of inconsiderate good-nature, of dangerous indifference as to Yea and Nay: alas! there are enough of cases in which he has to atone for these virtues of his!—and as man generally, he becomes far too easily the *caput mortuum* of such virtues.

Should one wish love or hatred from him—I mean love and hatred as God, woman, and animal understand them—he will do what he can, and furnish what he can. But one must not be surprised if it should not be much—if he should show himself just at this point to be false, fragile, questionable, and deteriorated. His love is constrained, his hatred is artificial, and rather *un tour de force*, a slight ostentation and exaggeration. He is only genuine so far as he can be objective; only in his serene totality is he still "nature" and "natural." His mirroring and eternally self-polishing soul no longer knows how to affirm, no longer how to deny; he does not command; neither does he destroy. "*Je ne méprise presque rien*"—he says, with Leibniz: let us not overlook nor undervalue the *presque*!

Neither is he a model man; he does not go in advance of any one, nor after, either; he places himself generally too far off to have any reason for espousing the cause of either good or evil. If he has been so long confounded with the *philosopher*, with the Caesarian trainer and dictator of civilization, he has had far too much honor, and what is more essential in him has been overlooked—he is an instrument, something of a slave, though certainly the sublimest sort of slave, but nothing in himself—*presque rien*! The objective man is an instrument, a costly, easily injured, easily tarnished measuring instrument and mirroring apparatus, which is to be taken care of and respected; but he is no goal, not outgoing nor upgoing, no complementary man in whom the *rest* of existence justifies itself, no termination—and still less a commencement, an engendering, or primary cause, nothing hardy, powerful, self-centered, that wants to be master; but rather only a soft, inflated, delicate, movable potter's-form, that must wait for some kind of content and frame to "shape" itself thereto—for the most part a man without frame and content, a "selfless" man. Consequently, also, nothing for women, *in parenthesi.*

208

When a philosopher nowadays makes known that he is not a skeptic—I hope that has been gathered from the foregoing description of the objective spirit?—people all hear it impatiently; they regard him on that account with some apprehension, they would like to ask so many, many questions... indeed among timid hearers, of whom there are now so many, he is henceforth said to be dangerous. With his repudiation of skepticism, it seems to them as if they heard some evil-threatening sound in the distance, as if a new kind of explosive were being tried somewhere, a dynamite of the spirit, perhaps a newly discovered Russian *nihiline*, a pessimism *bonae voluntatis*, that not only denies, means denial, but—dreadful thought! *practises* denial.

Against this kind of "good-will"—a will to the veritable, actual negation of life—there is, as is generally acknowledged nowadays, no better soporific and sedative than skepticism, the mild, pleasing, lulling poppy of skepticism; and Hamlet himself is now prescribed by the doctors of the day as an antidote to the "spirit," and its underground noises. "Are not our ears already full of bad sounds?" say the skeptics, as lovers of repose, and almost as a kind of safety police; "this subterranean Nay is terrible! Be still, ye pessimistic moles!"

The skeptic, in effect, that delicate creature, is far too easily frightened; his conscience is schooled so as to start at every Nay, and even at that sharp, decided Yea, and feels something like a bite thereby. Yea! and Nay!—they seem to him opposed to morality; he loves, on the contrary, to make a festival to his virtue by a noble aloofness, while perhaps he says with Montaigne: "What do I know?" Or with Socrates: "I know that I know nothing." Or: "Here I do not trust myself, no door is open to me." Or: "Even if the door were open, why should I enter immediately?" Or: "What is the use of any hasty hypotheses? It might quite well be in good taste to make no hypotheses at all. Are you absolutely obliged to straighten at once what is crooked? to stuff every hole with some kind of oakum? Is there not time enough for that? Has not the time leisure? Oh, ye demons, can ye not at all *wait*? The uncertain also has its charms, the Sphinx, too, is a Circe, and Circe, too, was a philosopher."

Thus does a skeptic console himself; and in truth he needs some consolation. For skepticism is the most spiritual expression of a certain many-sided physiological temperament, which in ordinary language is called nervous debility and sickliness; it arises whenever races or classes which have been long separated, decisively and suddenly blend with one another. In the new generation, which has inherited as it were different standards and valuations in its blood, everything is disquiet, derangement, doubt, and tentativeness; the best powers operate restrictively, the very virtues prevent each other growing and becoming strong, equilibrium, ballast, and perpendicular stability are lacking in body and soul. That, however, which is most diseased and degenerated in such nondescripts is the *will*; they are no longer familiar with independence of decision, or the courageous feeling of pleasure in willing—they are doubtful of the "freedom of the will" even in their dreams.

Our present-day Europe, the scene of a senseless, precipitate attempt at a radical blending of classes, and *consequently* of races, is therefore skeptical in all its heights and depths, sometimes exhibiting the mobile skepticism which springs impatiently and wantonly from branch to branch, sometimes with gloomy aspect, like a cloud over-charged with interrogative signs—and often sick unto death of its will! Paralysis of will, where do we not find this cripple sitting nowadays! And yet how bedecked oftentimes' How seductively ornamented! There are the finest gala dresses and disguises for this disease, and that, for instance, most of what places itself nowadays in the show-cases as "objectiveness," "the scientific spirit," "*l'art pour l'art*," and "pure voluntary knowledge," is only decked-out skepticism and paralysis of will—I am ready to answer for this diagnosis of the European disease.

The disease of the will is diffused unequally over Europe, it is worst and most varied where civilization has longest prevailed, it decreases according as "the barbarian" still—or again—asserts his claims under the loose drapery of Western culture It is therefore in the France of today, as can be readily disclosed and comprehended, that the will is most infirm, and France, which has always had a masterly aptitude for converting even the portentous crises of its spirit into something charming and seductive, now manifests emphatically its intellectual ascendancy over Europe, by being the school and exhibition of all the charms of skepticism.

The power to will and to persist, moreover, in a resolution, is already somewhat stronger in Germany, and again in the North of Germany it is stronger than in Central Germany, it is considerably stronger in England, Spain, and Corsica, associated with phlegm in the former and with hard skulls in the latter—not to mention Italy, which is too young yet to know what it wants, and must first show whether it can exercise will, but it is strongest and most surprising of all in that immense middle empire where Europe as it were flows back to Asia—namely, in Russia There the power to will has been long stored up and accumulated, there the will—uncertain whether to be negative or affirmative—waits threateningly to be discharged (to borrow their pet phrase from our physicists) Perhaps not only Indian wars and complications in Asia would be necessary to free Europe from its greatest danger, but also internal subversion, the shattering of the empire into small states, and above all the introduction of parliamentary imbecility, together with the obligation of every one to read his newspaper at breakfast.

I do not say this as one who desires it, in my heart I should rather prefer the contrary—I mean such an increase in the threatening attitude of Russia, that Europe would have to make up its mind to become equally threatening—namely, *to acquire one will*, by means of a new caste to rule over the Continent, a persistent, dreadful will of its own, that can set its aims thousands of years ahead; so that the long spun-out comedy of its petty-statism, and its dynastic as well as its democratic many-willed-ness, might finally be brought to a close. The time for petty politics is past; the next century will bring the struggle for the dominion of the world—the *compulsion* to great politics.

209

As to how far the new warlike age on which we Europeans have evidently entered may perhaps favor the growth of another and stronger kind of skepticism, I should like to express myself preliminarily merely by a parable, which the lovers of German history will already understand. That unscrupulous enthusiast for big, handsome grenadiers (who, as King of Prussia, brought into being a military and skeptical genius—and therewith, in reality, the new and now triumphantly emerged type of German), the problematic, crazy father of Frederick the Great, had on one point the very knack and lucky grasp of the genius: he knew what was then lacking in Germany, the want of which was a hundred times more alarming and serious than any lack of culture and social form—his ill-will to the young Frederick resulted from the anxiety of a profound instinct. *men were lacking*, and he suspected, to his bitterest regret, that his own son was not man enough. There, however, he deceived himself; but who would not have deceived himself in his place? He saw his son lapsed to atheism, to the *esprit*, to the pleasant frivolity of clever Frenchmen—he saw in the background the great bloodsucker, the spider skepticism; he suspected the incurable wretchedness of a heart no longer hard enough either for evil or good, and of a broken will that no longer commands, is no longer *able* to command. Meanwhile, however, there grew up in his son that new kind of harder and more dangerous skepticism—who knows *to what extent* it was encouraged just by his father's hatred and the icy melancholy of a will condemned to solitude?—the skepticism of daring manliness, which is closely related to the genius for war and conquest, and made its first entrance into Germany in the person of the great Frederick.

This skepticism despises and nevertheless grasps; it undermines and takes possession; it does not believe, but it does not thereby lose itself; it gives the spirit a dangerous liberty, but it keeps strict guard over the heart. It is the *German* form of skepticism, which, as a continued Fredericianism, risen to the highest spirituality, has kept Europe for a considerable time under the dominion of the German spirit and its critical and historical distrust. Owing to the insuperably strong and tough masculine character of the great German philologists and historical critics (who, rightly estimated, were also all of them artists of destruction and dissolution), a *new* conception of the German spirit gradually established itself—in spite of all Romanticism in music and philosophy—in which the leaning towards masculine skepticism was decidedly prominent whether, for instance, as fearlessness of gaze, as courage and sternness of the dissecting hand, or as resolute will to dangerous voyages of discovery, to spiritualized North Pole expeditions under barren and dangerous skies.

There may be good grounds for it when warm-blooded and superficial humanitarians cross themselves before this spirit, *cet esprit fataliste, ironique, méphistophélique*, as Michelet calls it, not without a shudder. But if one would realize how characteristic is this fear of the "man" in the German spirit which awakened Europe out of its "dogmatic slumber," let us call to mind the former conception which had to be overcome by this new one—and that it is not so very long ago that a masculinized woman could dare, with unbridled presumption, to recommend the Germans to the interest of Europe as gentle, good-hearted, weak-willed, and poetical fools. Finally, let us only understand profoundly enough Napoleon's astonishment when he saw Goethe it reveals what had been regarded for centuries as the "German spirit" "*Voilà un homme!*"—that was as much as to say "But this is a *man*! And I only expected to see a German!"

210

Supposing, then, that in the picture of the philosophers of the future, some trait suggests the question whether they must not perhaps be skeptics in the last-mentioned sense, something in them would only be designated thereby—and not they themselves. With equal right they might call themselves critics, and assuredly they will be men of experiments. By the name with which I ventured to baptize them, I have already expressly emphasized their attempting and their love of attempting is this because, as critics in body and soul, they will love to make use of experiments in a new, and perhaps wider and more dangerous sense? In their passion for knowledge, will they have to go further in daring and painful attempts than the sensitive and pampered taste of a democratic century can approve of?

There is no doubt these coming ones will be least able to dispense with the serious and not unscrupulous qualities which distinguish the critic from the skeptic. I mean the certainty as to standards of worth, the conscious employment of a unity of method, the wary courage, the standing-alone, and the capacity for self-responsibility, indeed, they will avow among themselves a *delight* in denial and dissection, and a certain considerate cruelty, which knows how to handle the knife surely and deftly, even when the heart bleeds. They will be *sterner* (and perhaps not always towards themselves only) than humane people may desire, they will not deal with the "truth" in order that it may "please" them, or "elevate" and "inspire" them—they will rather have little faith in "*truth*" bringing with it such revels for the feelings.

They will smile, those rigorous spirits, when any one says in their presence "That thought elevates me, why should it not be true?" or "That work enchants me, why should it not be beautiful?" or "That artist enlarges me, why should he not be great?" Perhaps they will not only have a smile, but a genuine disgust for all that is thus rapturous, idealistic, feminine, and hermaphroditic, and if anyone could look into their inmost hearts, he would not easily find therein the intention to reconcile "Christian sentiments" with "antique taste," or even with "modern parliamentarism" (the kind of reconciliation necessarily found even among philosophers in our very uncertain and consequently very conciliatory century).

Critical discipline, and every habit that conduces to purity and rigor in intellectual matters, will not only be demanded from themselves by these philosophers of the future, they may even make a display thereof as their special adornment—nevertheless they will not want to be called critics on that account. It will seem to them no small indignity to philosophy to have it decreed, as is so welcome nowadays, that "philosophy itself is criticism and critical science—and nothing else whatever!" Though this estimate of philosophy may enjoy the approval of all the Positivists of France and Germany (and possibly it even flattered the heart and taste of *Kant*: let us call to mind the titles of his principal works), our new philosophers will say, notwithstanding, that critics are instruments of the philosopher, and just on that account, as instruments, they are far from being philosophers themselves! Even the great Chinaman of Konigsberg was only a great critic.

211

I insist upon it that people finally cease confounding philosophical workers, and in general scientific men, with philosophers—that precisely here one should strictly give "each his own," and not give those far too much, these far too little.

It may be necessary for the education of the real philosopher that he himself should have once stood upon all those steps upon which his servants, the scientific workers of philosophy, remain standing, and *must* remain standing he himself must perhaps have been critic, and dogmatist, and historian, and besides, poet, and collector, and traveler, and riddle-reader, and moralist, and seer, and "free spirit," and almost everything, in order to traverse the whole range of human values and estimations, and that he may *be able* with a variety of eyes and consciences to look from a height to any distance, from a depth up to any height, from a nook into any expanse. But all these are only preliminary conditions for his task; this task itself demands something else—it requires him *to create values.*

The philosophical workers, after the excellent pattern of Kant and Hegel, have to fix and formalize some great existing body of valuations—that is to say, former *determinations of value,* creations of value, which have become prevalent, and are for a time called "truths"—whether in the domain of the *logical,* the *political* (moral), or the *artistic.* It is for these investigators to make whatever has happened and been esteemed hitherto, conspicuous, conceivable, intelligible, and manageable, to shorten everything long, even "time" itself, and to *subjugate* the entire past: an immense and wonderful task, in the carrying out of which all refined pride, all tenacious will, can surely find satisfaction. *The real philosophers, however, are commanders and law-givers;* they say: "Thus *shall* it be!" They determine first the Whither and the Why of mankind, and thereby set aside the previous labor of all philosophical workers, and all subjugators of the past— they grasp at the future with a creative hand, and whatever is and was, becomes for them thereby a means, an instrument, and a hammer. Their "knowing" is *creating,* their creating is a law-giving, their will to truth is—*will to power.*

Are there at present such philosophers? Have there ever been such philosophers? *must* there not be such philosophers some day? ...

212

It is always more obvious to me that the philosopher, as a man *indispensable* for the morrow and the day after the morrow, has ever found himself, and *has been obliged* to find himself, in contradiction to the day in which he lives; his enemy has always been the ideal of his day. Hitherto all those extraordinary furtherers of humanity whom one calls philosophers—who rarely regarded themselves as lovers of wisdom, but rather as disagreeable fools and dangerous interrogators—have found their mission, their hard, involuntary, imperative mission (in the end, however, the greatness of their mission), in being the bad conscience of their age.

In putting the vivisector's knife to the breast of the very *virtues of their age*, they have betrayed their own secret; it has been for the sake of a *new* greatness of man, a new untrodden path to his aggrandizement. They have always disclosed how much hypocrisy, indolence, self-indulgence, and self-neglect, how much falsehood was concealed under the most venerated types of contemporary morality, how much virtue was *outlived*, they have always said "We must remove hence to where *you* are least at home."

In the face of a world of "modern ideas," which would like to confine everyone in a corner, in a "specialty," a philosopher, if there could be philosophers nowadays, would be compelled to place the greatness of man, the conception of "greatness," precisely in his comprehensiveness and multifariousness, in his all-roundness, he would even determine worth and rank according to the amount and variety of that which a man could bear and take upon himself, according to the *extent* to which a man could stretch his responsibility.

Nowadays the taste and virtue of the age weaken and attenuate the will, nothing is so adapted to the spirit of the age as weakness of will consequently, in the ideal of the philosopher, strength of will, sternness, and capacity for prolonged resolution, must specially be included in the conception of "greatness", with as good a right as the opposite doctrine, with its ideal of a silly, renouncing, humble, selfless humanity, was suited to an opposite age—such as the sixteenth century, which suffered from its accumulated energy of will, and from the wildest torrents and floods of selfishness.

In the time of Socrates, among men only of worn-out instincts, old conservative Athenians who let themselves go—"for the sake of happiness," as they said, for the sake of pleasure, as their conduct indicated—and who had continually on their lips the old pompous words to which they had long forfeited the right by the life they led, *irony* was perhaps necessary for greatness of soul, the wicked Socratic assurance of the old physician and plebeian, who cut ruthlessly into his own flesh, as into the flesh and heart of the "noble," with a look that said plainly enough: "Do not dissemble before me! here—we are equal!"

At present, on the contrary, when throughout Europe the herding-animal alone attains to honors, and dispenses honors, when "equality of right" can too readily be transformed into equality in wrong—I mean to say into general war against everything rare, strange, and privileged, against the higher man, the higher soul, the higher duty, the higher responsibility, the creative plenipotence and lordliness—at present it belongs to the conception of "greatness" to be noble, to wish to be apart, to be capable of being different, to stand alone, to have to live by personal initiative, and the philosopher will betray something of his own ideal when he asserts "He shall be the greatest who can be the most solitary, the most concealed, the most divergent, the man beyond good and evil, the master of his virtues, and of super-abundance of will; precisely this shall be called *greatness*: as diversified as can be entire, as ample as can be full." And to ask once more the question: Is greatness *possible*—nowadays?

213

It is difficult to learn what a philosopher is, because it cannot be taught: one must "know" it by experience—or one should have the pride *not* to know it. The fact that at present people all talk of things of which they *cannot* have any experience, is true more especially and unfortunately as concerns the philosopher and philosophical matters:—the very few know them, are permitted to know them, and all popular ideas about them are false.

Thus, for instance, the truly philosophical combination of a bold, exuberant spirituality which runs at presto pace, and a dialectic rigor and necessity which makes no false step, is unknown to most thinkers and scholars from their own experience, and therefore, should any one speak of it in their presence, it is incredible to them. They conceive of every necessity as troublesome, as a painful compulsory obedience and state of constraint; thinking itself is regarded by them as something slow and hesitating, almost as a trouble, and often enough as "worthy of the *sweat* of the noble"—but not at all as something easy and divine, closely related to dancing and exuberance! "To think" and to take a matter "seriously," "arduously"—that is one and the same thing to them; such only has been their "experience."

Artists have here perhaps a finer intuition; they who know only too well that precisely when they no longer do anything "arbitrarily," and everything of necessity, their feeling of freedom, of subtlety, of power, of creatively fixing, disposing, and shaping, reaches its climax—in short, that necessity and "freedom of will" are then the same thing with them.

There is, in fine, a gradation of rank in psychical states, to which the gradation of rank in the problems corresponds; and the highest problems repel ruthlessly everyone who ventures too near them, without being predestined for their solution by the loftiness and power of his spirituality. Of what use is it for nimble, everyday intellects, or clumsy, honest mechanics and empiricists to press, in their plebeian ambition, close to such problems, and as it were into this "holy of holies"—as so often happens nowadays! But coarse feet must never tread upon such carpets: this is provided for in the primary law of things; the doors remain closed to those intruders, though they may dash and break their heads thereon.

People have always to be born to a high station, or, more definitely, they have to be *bred* for it: a person has only a right to philosophy—taking the word in its higher significance—in virtue of his descent; the ancestors, the "blood," decide here also. Many generations must have prepared the way for the coming of the philosopher; each of his virtues must have been separately acquired, nurtured, transmitted, and embodied; not only the bold, easy, delicate course and current of his thoughts, but above all the readiness for great responsibilities, the majesty of ruling glance and contemning look, the feeling of separation from the multitude with their duties and virtues, the kindly patronage and defense of whatever is misunderstood and calumniated, be it God or devil, the delight and practice of supreme justice, the art of commanding, the amplitude of will, the lingering eye which rarely admires, rarely looks up, rarely loves....

Part Seven:
Our Virtues

214

Our virtues?—It is probable that we, too, have still our virtues, although naturally they are not those sincere and massive virtues on account of which we hold our grandfathers in esteem and also at a little distance from us. We Europeans of the day after tomorrow, we firstlings of the twentieth century—with all our dangerous curiosity, our multifariousness and art of disguising, our mellow and seemingly sweetened cruelty in sense and spirit—we shall presumably, *if* we must have virtues, have those only which have come to agreement with our most secret and heartfelt inclinations, with our most ardent requirements: well, then, let us look for them in our labyrinths!—where, as we know, so many things lose themselves, so many things get quite lost! And is there anything finer than to *search* for one's own virtues? Is it not almost to *believe* in one's own virtues? But this "believing in one's own virtues"—is it not practically the same as what was formerly called one's "good conscience," that long, respectable pigtail of an idea, which our grandfathers used to hang behind their heads, and often enough also behind their understandings? It seems, therefore, that however little we may imagine ourselves to be old-fashioned and grandfatherly respectable in other respects, in one thing we are nevertheless the worthy grandchildren of our grandfathers, we last Europeans with good consciences: we also still wear their pigtail.—Ah! if you only knew how soon, so very soon—it will be different!

215

As in the stellar firmament there are sometimes two suns which determine the path of one planet, and in certain cases suns of different colors shine around a single planet, now with red light, now with green, and then simultaneously illumine and flood it with motley colors: so we modern men, owing to the complicated mechanism of our "firmament," are determined by *different* moralities; our actions shine alternately in different colors, and are seldom unequivocal—and there are often cases, also, in which our actions are *motley-colored*.

216

To love one's enemies? I think that has been well learnt: it takes place thousands of times at present on a large and small scale; indeed, at times the higher and sublimer thing takes place:—we learn to *despise* when we love, and precisely when we love best; all of it, however, unconsciously, without noise, without ostentation, with the shame and secrecy of goodness, which forbids the utterance of the pompous word and the formula of virtue. Morality as attitude— is opposed to our taste nowadays. This is *also* an advance, as it was an advance in our fathers that religion as an attitude finally became opposed to their taste, including the enmity and Voltairean bitterness against religion (and all that formerly belonged to freethinker-pantomime). It is the music in our conscience, the dance in our spirit, to which Puritan litanies, moral sermons, and goody-goodness won't chime.

217

Let us be careful in dealing with those who attach great importance to being credited with moral tact and subtlety in moral discernment! They never forgive us if they have once made a mistake *before* us (or even with *regard* to us)—they inevitably become our instinctive calumniators and detractors, even when they still remain our "friends."

Blessed are the forgetful: for they "get the better" even of their blunders.

218

The psychologists of France—and where else are there still psychologists nowadays?—have never yet exhausted their bitter and manifold enjoyment of the *bêtise bourgeoise*, just as though... in short, they betray something thereby. Flaubert, for instance, the honest citizen of Rouen, neither saw, heard, nor tasted anything else in the end; it was his mode of self-torment and refined cruelty. As this is growing wearisome, I would now recommend for a change something else for a pleasure—namely, the unconscious astuteness with which good, fat, honest mediocrity always behaves towards loftier spirits and the tasks they have to perform, the subtle, barbed, Jesuitical astuteness, which is a thousand times subtler than the taste and understanding of the middle-class in its best moments—subtler even than the understanding of its victims:—a repeated proof that "instinct" is the most intelligent of all kinds of intelligence which have hitherto been discovered. In short, you psychologists, study the philosophy of the "rule" in its struggle with the "exception": there you have a spectacle fit for Gods and godlike malignity! Or, in plainer words, practice vivisection on "good people," on the "*homo bonae voluntatis*," on *yourselves!*

219

The practice of judging and condemning morally, is the favorite revenge of the intellectually shallow on those who are less so, it is also a kind of indemnity for their being badly endowed by nature, and finally, it is an opportunity for acquiring spirit and *becoming* subtle—malice spiritualizes. They are glad in their inmost heart that there is a standard according to which those who are over-endowed with intellectual goods and privileges, are equal to them, they contend for the "equality of all before God," and almost *need* the belief in God for this purpose. It is among them that the most powerful antagonists of atheism are found. If any one were to say to them "A lofty spirituality is beyond all comparison with the honesty and respectability of a merely moral man"—it would make them furious, I shall take care not to say so. I would rather flatter them with my theory that lofty spirituality itself exists only as the ultimate product of moral qualities, that it is a synthesis of all qualities attributed to the "merely moral" man, after they have been acquired singly through long training and practice, perhaps during a whole series of generations, that lofty spirituality is precisely the spiritualizing of justice, and the beneficent severity which knows that it is authorized to maintain *gradations of rank* in the world, even among things—and not only among men.

220

Now that the praise of the "disinterested person" is so popular one must—probably not without some danger—get an idea of *what* people actually take an interest in, and what are the things generally which fundamentally and profoundly concern ordinary men—including the cultured, even the learned, and perhaps philosophers also, if appearances do not deceive. The fact thereby becomes obvious that the greater part of what interests and charms higher natures, and more refined and fastidious tastes, seems absolutely "uninteresting" to the average man—if, notwithstanding, he perceives devotion to these interests, he calls it *désintéressé*, and wonders how it is possible to act "disinterestedly." There have been philosophers who could give this popular astonishment a seductive and mystical, other-worldly expression (perhaps because they did not know the higher nature by experience?), instead of stating the naked and candidly reasonable truth that "disinterested" action is very interesting and "interested" action, provided that...

"And love?"—What! Even an action for love's sake shall be "unegoistic"? But you fools—! "And the praise of the self-sacrificer?"—But whoever has really offered sacrifice knows that he wanted and obtained something for it—perhaps something from himself for something from himself; that he relinquished here in order to have more there, perhaps in general to be more, or even feel himself "more." But this is a realm of questions and answers in which a more fastidious spirit does not like to stay: for here truth has to stifle her yawns so much when she is obliged to answer. And after all, truth is a woman; one must not use force with her.

221

"It sometimes happens," said a moralistic pedant and trifle-retailer, "that I honor and respect an unselfish man: not, however, because he is unselfish, but because I think he has a right to be useful to another man at his own expense. In short, the question is always who *he* is, and who *the other* is. For instance, in a person created and destined for command, self-denial and modest retirement, instead of being virtues, would be the waste of virtues: so it seems to me. Every system of unegoistic morality which takes itself unconditionally and appeals to everyone, not only sins against good taste, but is also an incentive to sins of omission, an *additional* seduction under the mask of philanthropy—and precisely a seduction and injury to the higher, rarer, and more privileged types of men. Moral systems must be compelled first of all to bow before the *gradations of rank*; their presumption must be driven home to their conscience—until they thoroughly understand at last that it is *immoral* to say that 'what is right for one is proper for another.'"

So said my moralistic pedant and *bonhomme*. Did he perhaps deserve to be laughed at when he thus exhorted systems of morals to practice morality? But one should not be too much in the right if one wishes to have the laughers on *one's own* side; a grain of wrong pertains even to good taste.

222

Wherever sympathy (fellow-suffering) is preached nowadays—and, if I gather rightly, no other religion is any longer preached—let the psychologist have his ears open through all the vanity, through all the noise which is natural to these preachers (as to all preachers), he will hear a hoarse, groaning, genuine note of *self-contempt*. It belongs to the overshadowing and uglifying of Europe, which has been on the increase for a century (the first symptoms of which are already specified documentarily in a thoughtful letter of Galiani to Madame d'Epinay)—*if it is not really the cause thereof!* The man of "modern ideas," the conceited ape, is excessively dissatisfied with himself—this is perfectly certain. He suffers, and his vanity wants him only "to suffer with his fellows."

223

The hybrid European—a tolerably ugly plebeian, taken all in all—absolutely requires a costume: he needs history as a storeroom of costumes. To be sure, he notices that none of the costumes fit him properly—he changes and changes. Let us look at the nineteenth century with respect to these hasty preferences and changes in its masquerades of style, and also with respect to its moments of desperation on account of "nothing suiting" us. It is in vain to get ourselves up as romantic, or classical, or Christian, or Florentine, or barocco, or "national," *in moribus et artibus*: it does not "clothe us"! But the "spirit," especially the "historical spirit," profits even by this desperation: once and again a new sample of the past or of the foreign is tested, put on, taken off, packed up, and above all studied—we are the first studious age in puncto of "costumes," I mean as concerns morals, articles of belief, artistic tastes, and religions; we are prepared as no other age has ever been for a carnival in the grand style, for the most spiritual festival—laughter and arrogance, for the transcendental height of supreme folly and Aristophanic ridicule of the world. Perhaps we are still discovering the domain of our invention just here, the domain where even we can still be original, probably as parodists of the world's history and as God's Merry-Andrews,—perhaps, though nothing else of the present have a future, our laughter itself may have a future!

224

The historical sense (or the capacity for divining quickly the order of rank of the valuations according to which a people, a community, or an individual has lived, the "divining instinct" for the relationships of these valuations, for the relation of the authority of the valuations to the authority of the operating forces),—this historical sense, which we Europeans claim as our specialty, has come to us in the train of the enchanting and mad semi-barbarity into which Europe has been plunged by the democratic mingling of classes and races—it is only the nineteenth century that has recognized this faculty as its sixth sense. Owing to this mingling, the past of every form and mode of life, and of cultures which were formerly closely contiguous and superimposed on one another, flows forth into us "modern souls"; our instincts now run back in all directions, we ourselves are a kind of chaos: in the end, as we have said, the spirit perceives its advantage therein.

By means of our semi-barbarity in body and in desire, we have secret access everywhere, such as a noble age never had; we have access above all to the labyrinth of imperfect civilizations, and to every form of semi-barbarity that has at any time existed on earth; and in so far as the most considerable part of human civilization hitherto has just been semi-barbarity, the "historical sense" implies almost the sense and instinct for everything, the taste and tongue for everything: whereby it immediately proves itself to be an *ignoble* sense. For instance, we enjoy Homer once more: it is perhaps our happiest acquisition that we know how to appreciate Homer, whom men of distinguished culture (as the French of the seventeenth century, like Saint-Evremond, who reproached him for his *esprit vaste*, and even Voltaire, the last echo of the century) cannot and could not so easily appropriate—whom they scarcely permitted themselves to enjoy. The very decided Yea and Nay of their palate, their promptly ready disgust, their hesitating reluctance with regard to everything strange, their horror of the bad taste even of lively curiosity, and in general the averseness of every distinguished and self-sufficing culture to avow a new desire, a dissatisfaction with its own condition, or an admiration of what is strange: all this determines and disposes them unfavorably even towards the best things of the world which are not their property or could not become their prey—and no faculty is more unintelligible to such men than just this historical sense, with its truckling, plebeian curiosity.

The case is not different with Shakespeare, that marvelous Spanish-Moorish-Saxon synthesis of taste, over whom an ancient Athenian of the circle of Aeschylus would have half-killed himself with laughter or irritation: but we—accept precisely this wild motleyness, this medley of the most delicate, the most coarse, and the most artificial, with a secret confidence and cordiality; we enjoy it as a refinement of art reserved expressly for us, and allow ourselves to be as little disturbed by the repulsive fumes and the proximity of the English populace in which Shakespeare's art and taste lives, as perhaps on the Chiaja of Naples, where, with all our senses awake, we go our way, enchanted and voluntarily, in spite of the drain-odor of the lower quarters of the town.

That as men of the "historical sense" we have our virtues, is not to be disputed:—we are unpretentious, unselfish, modest, brave, habituated to self-control and self-renunciation, very grateful, very patient, very complaisant—but with all this we are perhaps not very "tasteful." Let us finally confess it, that what is most difficult for us men of the "historical sense" to grasp, feel, taste, and love, what finds us fundamentally prejudiced and almost hostile, is precisely the perfection and ultimate maturity in every culture and art, the essentially noble in works and men, their moment of smooth sea and halcyon self-sufficiency, the goldenness and coldness which all things show that have perfected themselves.

Perhaps our great virtue of the historical sense is in necessary contrast to *good* taste, at least to the very bad taste; and we can only evoke in ourselves imperfectly, hesitatingly, and with compulsion the small, short, and happy godsends and glorifications of human life as they shine here and there: those moments and marvelous experiences when a great power has voluntarily come to a halt before the boundless and infinite,—when a super-abundance of refined delight has been enjoyed by a sudden checking and petrifying, by standing firmly and planting oneself fixedly on still trembling ground. *Proportionateness* is strange to us, let us confess it to ourselves; our itching is really the itching for the infinite, the immeasurable. Like the rider on his forward panting horse, we let the reins fall before the infinite, we modern men, we semi-barbarians—and are only in *our* highest bliss when we—*are in most danger.*

225

Whether it be hedonism, pessimism, utilitarianism, or eudaemonism, all those modes of thinking which measure the worth of things according to *pleasure* and *pain*, that is, according to accompanying circumstances and secondary considerations, are plausible modes of thought and naïvetés, which everyone conscious of *creative* powers and an artist's conscience will look down upon with scorn, though not without sympathy. Sympathy for you!—to be sure, that is not sympathy as you understand it: it is not sympathy for social "distress," for "society" with its sick and misfortuned, for the hereditarily vicious and defective who lie on the ground around us; still less is it sympathy for the grumbling, vexed, revolutionary slave-classes who strive after power—they call it "freedom." *Our* sympathy is a loftier and further-sighted sympathy:—we see how *man* dwarfs himself, how *you* dwarf him! and there are moments when we view *your* sympathy with an indescribable anguish, when we resist it,—when we regard your seriousness as more dangerous than any kind of levity. You want, if possible—and there is not a more foolish "if possible"—*to do away with suffering,* and we?—it really seems that *we* would rather have it increased and made worse than it has ever been! Well-being, as you understand it—is certainly not a goal; it seems to us an *end*; a condition which at once renders man ludicrous and contemptible—and makes his destruction *desirable!*

The discipline of suffering, of *great* suffering—know ye not that it is only *this* discipline that has produced all the elevations of humanity hitherto? The tension of soul in misfortune which communicates to it its energy, its shuddering in view of rack and ruin, its inventiveness and bravery in undergoing, enduring, interpreting, and exploiting misfortune, and whatever depth, mystery, disguise, spirit, artifice, or greatness has been bestowed upon the soul—has it not been bestowed through suffering, through the discipline of great suffering? In man *creature* and *creator* are united: in man there is not only matter, shred, excess, clay, mire, folly, chaos; but there is also the creator, the sculptor, the hardness of the hammer, the divinity of the spectator, and the seventh day—do ye understand this contrast? And that *your* sympathy for the "creature in man" applies to that which has to be fashioned, bruised, forged, stretched, roasted, annealed, refined—to that which must necessarily *suffer*, and *is meant* to suffer? And our sympathy—do ye not understand what our *reverse* sympathy applies to, when it resists your sympathy as the worst of all pampering and enervation?

So it is sympathy *against* sympathy!

But to repeat it once more, there are higher problems than the problems of pleasure and pain and sympathy; and all systems of philosophy which deal only with these are naïvetés.

226

We immoralists.—This world with which *we* are concerned, in which we have to fear and love, this almost invisible, inaudible world of delicate command and delicate obedience, a world of "almost" in every respect, captious, insidious, sharp, and tender—yes, it is well protected from clumsy spectators and familiar curiosity! We are woven into a strong net and garment of duties, and *cannot* disengage ourselves—precisely here, we are "men of duty," even we! Occasionally, it is true, we dance in our "chains" and betwixt our "swords"; it is none the less true that more often we gnash our teeth under the circumstances, and are impatient at the secret hardship of our lot. But do what we will, fools and appearances say of us: "These are men *without* duty,"—we have always fools and appearances against us!

227

Honesty, granting that it is the virtue of which we cannot rid ourselves, we free spirits—well, we will labor at it with all our perversity and love, and not tire of "perfecting" ourselves in *our* virtue, which alone remains: may its glance someday overspread like a gilded, blue, mocking twilight this aging civilization with its dull gloomy seriousness! And if, nevertheless, our honesty should one day grow weary, and sigh, and stretch its limbs, and find us too hard, and would fain have it pleasanter, easier, and gentler, like an agreeable vice, let us remain *hard*, we latest Stoics, and let us send to its help whatever devilry we have in us:—our disgust at the clumsy and undefined, our "*nitimur in vetitum*," our love of adventure, our sharpened and fastidious curiosity, our most subtle, disguised, intellectual Will to Power and universal conquest, which rambles and roves avidiously around all the realms of the future—let us go with all our "devils" to the help of our "God"!

It is probable that people will misunderstand and mistake us on that account: what does it matter! They will say: "Their 'honesty'—that is their devilry, and nothing else!" What does it matter! And even if they were right— have not all Gods hitherto been such sanctified, re-baptized devils? And after all, what do we know of ourselves? And what the spirit that leads us wants *to be called*? (It is a question of names.) And how many spirits we harbor?

Our honesty, we free spirits—let us be careful lest it become our vanity, our ornament and ostentation, our limitation, our stupidity! Every virtue inclines to stupidity, every stupidity to virtue; "stupid to the point of sanctity," they say in Russia,—let us be careful lest out of pure honesty we eventually become saints and bores! Is not life a hundred times too short for us—to bore ourselves? One would have to believe in eternal life in order to...

228

I hope to be forgiven for discovering that all moral philosophy hitherto has been tedious and has belonged to the soporific appliances—and that "virtue," in my opinion, has been *more* injured by the *tediousness* of its advocates than by anything else; at the same time, however, I would not wish to overlook their general usefulness. It is desirable that as few people as possible should reflect upon morals, and consequently it is very desirable that morals should not someday become interesting! But let us not be afraid! Things still remain today as they have always been: I see no one in Europe who has (or *discloses*) an idea of the fact that philosophizing concerning morals might be conducted in a dangerous, captious, and ensnaring manner—that *calamity* might be involved therein.

Observe, for example, the indefatigable, inevitable English utilitarians: how ponderously and respectably they stalk on, stalk along (a Homeric metaphor expresses it better) in the footsteps of Bentham, just as he had already stalked in the footsteps of the respectable Helvetius! (no, he was not a dangerous man, Helvetius, *ce sénateur Pococurante*, to use an expression of Galiani). No new thought, nothing of the nature of a finer turning or better expression of an old thought, not even a proper history of what has been previously thought on the subject: an *impossible* literature, taking it all in all, unless one knows how to leaven it with some mischief.

In effect, the old English vice called *cant*, which is *moral Tartuffism*, has insinuated itself also into these moralists (whom one must certainly read with an eye to their motives if one *must* read them), concealed this time under the new form of the scientific spirit; moreover, there is not absent from them a secret struggle with the pangs of conscience, from which a race of former Puritans must naturally suffer, in all their scientific tinkering with morals. (Is not a moralist the opposite of a Puritan? That is to say, as a thinker who regards morality as questionable, as worthy of interrogation, in short, as a problem? Is moralizing not-immoral?) In the end, they all want English morality to be recognized as authoritative, inasmuch as mankind, or the "general utility," or "the happiness of the greatest number,"—no! the happiness of *England*, will be best served thereby. They would like, by all means, to convince themselves that the striving after English happiness, I mean after *comfort* and *fashion* (and in the highest instance, a seat in Parliament), is at the same time the true path of virtue; in fact, that in so far as there has been virtue in the world hitherto, it has just consisted in such striving. Not one of those ponderous, conscience-stricken herding-animals (who undertake to advocate the cause of egoism as conducive to the general welfare) wants to have any knowledge or inkling of the facts that the "general welfare" is no ideal, no goal, no notion that can be at all grasped, but is only a nostrum,— that what is fair to one *may not* at all be fair to another, that the requirement of one morality for all is really a detriment to higher men, in short, that there is a *distinction of rank* between man and man, and consequently between morality and morality. They are an unassuming and fundamentally mediocre species of men, these utilitarian Englishmen, and, as already remarked, in so far as they are tedious, one cannot think highly enough of their utility. One ought even to *encourage* them, as has been partially attempted in the following rhymes:—

> Hail, ye worthies, barrow-wheeling,
> "Longer—better," aye revealing,
>
> Stiffer aye in head and knee;
> Unenraptured, never jesting,
> Mediocre everlasting,
> *sans génie et sans esprit!*

229

In these later ages, which may be proud of their humanity, there still remains so much fear, so much *superstition* of the fear, of the "cruel wild beast," the mastering of which constitutes the very pride of these humaner ages—that even obvious truths, as if by the agreement of centuries, have long remained unuttered, because they have the appearance of helping the finally slain wild beast back to life again. I perhaps risk something when I allow such a truth to escape; let others capture it again and give it so much "milk of pious sentiment"[5] to drink, that it will lie down quiet and forgotten, in its old corner.

One ought to learn anew about cruelty, and open one's eyes; one ought at last to learn impatience, in order that such immodest gross errors—as, for instance, have been fostered by ancient and modern philosophers with regard to tragedy—may no longer wander about virtuously and boldly. Almost everything that we call "higher culture" is based upon the spiritualizing and intensifying of *cruelty*—this is my thesis; the "wild beast" has not been slain at all, it lives, it flourishes, it has only been—transfigured.

---

5   An expression from Schiller's *William Tell*, Act IV, Scene 3.

That which constitutes the painful delight of tragedy is cruelty; that which operates agreeably in so-called tragic sympathy, and at the basis even of everything sublime, up to the highest and most delicate thrills of metaphysics, obtains its sweetness solely from the intermingled ingredient of cruelty. What the Roman enjoys in the arena, the Christian in the ecstasies of the cross, the Spaniard at the sight of the faggot and stake, or of the bull-fight, the present-day Japanese who presses his way to the tragedy, the workman of the Parisian suburbs who has a homesickness for bloody revolutions, the Wagnerienne who, with unhinged will, "undergoes" the performance of *Tristan and Isolde*—what all these enjoy, and strive with mysterious ardor to drink in, is the *philtre* of the great Circe "cruelty."

Here, to be sure, we must put aside entirely the blundering psychology of former times, which could only teach with regard to cruelty that it originated at the sight of the suffering of *others*: there is an abundant, super-abundant enjoyment even in one's own suffering, in causing one's own suffering—and wherever man has allowed himself to be persuaded to self-denial in the *religious* sense, or to self-mutilation, as among the Phoenicians and ascetics, or in general, to desensualization, decarnalization, and contrition, to Puritanical repentance-spasms, to vivisection of conscience and to Pascal-like *sacrifizia dell' intelleto*, he is secretly allured and impelled forwards by his cruelty, by the dangerous thrill of cruelty *towards himself.*

Finally, let us consider that even the seeker of knowledge operates as an artist and glorifier of cruelty, in that he compels his spirit to perceive *against* its own inclination, and often enough against the wishes of his heart:—he forces it to say Nay, where he would like to affirm, love, and adore; indeed, every instance of taking a thing profoundly and fundamentally, is a violation, an intentional injuring of the fundamental will of the spirit, which instinctively aims at appearance and superficiality,—even in every desire for knowledge there is a drop of cruelty.

230

Perhaps what I have said here about a "fundamental will of the spirit" may not be understood without further details; I may be allowed a word of explanation.

That imperious something which is popularly called "the spirit," wishes to be master internally and externally, and to feel itself master; it has the will of a multiplicity for a simplicity, a binding, taming, imperious, and essentially ruling will. Its requirements and capacities here, are the same as those assigned by physiologists to everything that lives, grows, and multiplies. The power of the spirit to appropriate foreign elements reveals itself in a strong tendency to assimilate the new to the old, to simplify the manifold, to overlook or repudiate the absolutely contradictory; just as it arbitrarily re-underlines, makes prominent, and falsifies for itself certain traits and lines in the foreign elements, in every portion of the "outside world." Its object thereby is the incorporation of new "experiences," the assortment of new things in the old arrangements—in short, growth; or more properly, the *feeling* of growth, the feeling of increased power—is its object.

This same will has at its service an apparently opposed impulse of the spirit, a suddenly adopted preference of ignorance, of arbitrary shutting out, a closing of windows, an inner denial of this or that, a prohibition to approach, a sort of defensive attitude against much that is knowable, a contentment with obscurity, with the shutting-in horizon, an acceptance and approval of ignorance: as that which is all necessary according to the degree of its appropriating power, its "digestive power," to speak figuratively (and in fact "the spirit" resembles a stomach more than anything else).

Here also belong an occasional propensity of the spirit to let itself be deceived (perhaps with a waggish suspicion that it is *not* so and so, but is only allowed to pass as such), a delight in uncertainty and ambiguity, an exulting enjoyment of arbitrary, out-of-the-way narrowness and mystery, of the too-near, of the foreground, of the magnified, the diminished, the misshapen, the beautified—an enjoyment of the arbitrariness of all these manifestations of power.

Finally, in this connection, there is the not unscrupulous readiness of the spirit to deceive other spirits and dissemble before them—the constant pressing and straining of a creating, shaping, changeable power: the spirit enjoys therein its craftiness and its variety of disguises, it enjoys also its feeling of security therein—it is precisely by its Protean arts that it is best protected and concealed!—*counter to* this propensity for appearance, for simplification, for a disguise, for a cloak, in short, for an outside—for every outside is a cloak—there operates the sublime tendency of the man of knowledge, which takes, and *insists* on taking things profoundly, variously, and thoroughly; as a kind of cruelty of the intellectual conscience and taste, which every courageous thinker will acknowledge in himself, provided, as it ought to be, that he has sharpened and hardened his eye sufficiently long for introspection, and is accustomed to severe discipline and even severe words. He will say: "There is something cruel in the tendency of my spirit": let the virtuous and amiable try to convince him that it is not so!

In fact, it would sound nicer, if, instead of our cruelty, perhaps our "extravagant honesty" were talked about, whispered about, and glorified—we free, *very* free spirits—and some day perhaps *such* will actually be our—posthumous glory! Meanwhile—for there is plenty of time until then—we should be least inclined to deck ourselves out in such florid and fringed moral verbiage; our whole former work has just made us sick of this taste and its sprightly exuberance. They are beautiful, glistening, jingling, festive words: honesty, love of truth, love of wisdom, sacrifice for knowledge, heroism of the truthful—there is something in them that makes one's heart swell with pride. But we anchorites and marmots have long ago persuaded ourselves in all the secrecy of an anchorite's conscience, that this worthy parade of verbiage also belongs to the old false adornment, frippery, and gold-dust of unconscious human vanity, and that even under such flattering color and repainting, the terrible original text *homo natura* must again be recognized.

In effect, to translate man back again into nature; to master the many vain and visionary interpretations and subordinate meanings which have hitherto been scratched and daubed over the eternal original text, *homo natura*; to bring it about that man shall henceforth stand before man as he now, hardened by the discipline of science, stands before the *other* forms of nature, with fearless Oedipus-eyes, and stopped Ulysses-ears, deaf to the enticements of old metaphysical bird-catchers, who have piped to him far too long: "Thou art more! thou art higher! thou hast a different origin!"—this may be a strange and foolish task, but that it is a *task*, who can deny! Why did we choose it, this foolish task?

Or, to put the question differently: "Why knowledge at all?"

Everyone will ask us about this. And thus pressed, we, who have asked ourselves the question a hundred times, have not found and cannot find any better answer....

231

Learning alters us, it does what all nourishment does that does not merely "conserve"—as the physiologist knows. But at the bottom of our souls, quite "down below," there is certainly something unteachable, a granite of spiritual fate, of predetermined decision and answer to predetermined, chosen questions. In each cardinal problem there speaks an unchangeable "I am this"; a thinker cannot learn anew about man and woman, for instance, but can only learn fully—he can only follow to the end what is "fixed" about them in himself. Occasionally we find certain solutions of problems which make strong beliefs for us; perhaps they are henceforth called "convictions." Later on—one sees in them only footsteps to self-knowledge, guide-posts to the problem which we ourselves *are*—or more correctly to the great stupidity which we embody, our spiritual fate, the *unteachable* in us, quite "down below."

In view of this liberal compliment which I have just paid myself, permission will perhaps be more readily allowed me to utter some truths about "woman as she is," provided that it is known at the outset how literally they are merely—*my* truths.

232

Woman wishes to be independent, and therefore she begins to enlighten men about "woman as she is"—*this* is one of the worst developments of the general *uglifying* of Europe. For what must these clumsy attempts of feminine scientificality and self-exposure bring to light! Woman has so much cause for shame; in woman there is so much pedantry, superficiality, schoolmasterliness, petty presumption, unbridledness, and indiscretion concealed—study only woman's behavior towards children!—which has really been best restrained and dominated hitherto by the *fear* of man. Alas, if ever the "eternally tedious in woman"—she has plenty of it!—is allowed to venture forth! if she begins radically and on principle to unlearn her wisdom and art-of charming, of playing, of frightening away sorrow, of alleviating and taking easily; if she forgets her delicate aptitude for agreeable desires!

Female voices are already raised, which, by Saint Aristophanes! make one afraid:—with medical explicitness it is stated in a threatening manner what woman first and last *requires* from man. Is it not in the very worst taste that woman thus sets herself up to be scientific? Enlightenment hitherto has fortunately been men's affair, men's gift—we remained therewith "among ourselves"; and in the end, in view of all that women write about "woman," we may well have considerable doubt as to whether woman really *desires* enlightenment about herself—and *can* desire it.

If woman does not thereby seek a new *ornament* for herself—I believe ornamentation belongs to the eternally feminine?—why, then, she wishes to make herself feared: perhaps she thereby wishes to get the mastery. But she does not want truth—what does woman care for truth? From the very first, nothing is more foreign, more repugnant, or more hostile to woman than truth—her great art is falsehood, her chief concern is appearance and beauty. Let us confess it, we men: we honor and love this very art and this very instinct in woman: we who have the hard task, and for our recreation gladly seek the company of beings under whose hands, glances, and delicate follies, our seriousness, our gravity, and profundity appear almost like follies to us.

Finally, I ask the question: Did a woman herself ever acknowledge profundity in a woman's mind, or justice in a woman's heart? And is it not true that on the whole "woman" has hitherto been most despised by woman herself, and not at all by us?

We men desire that woman should not continue to compromise herself by enlightening us; just as it was man's care and the consideration for woman, when the church decreed: *mulier taceat in ecclesia.* It was to the benefit of woman when Napoleon gave the too eloquent Madame de Staël to understand: *mulier taceat in politicis!*—and in my opinion, he is a true friend of woman who calls out to women today: *mulier taceat de mulierel.*

233

It betrays corruption of the instincts—apart from the fact that it betrays bad taste—when a woman refers to Madame Roland, or Madame de Staël, or Monsieur George Sand, as though something were proved thereby in favor of "woman as she is." Among men, these are the three comical women as they are—nothing more!—and just the best involuntary counter-arguments against feminine emancipation and autonomy.

234

Stupidity in the kitchen; woman as cook; the terrible thoughtlessness with which the feeding of the family and the master of the house is managed! Woman does not understand what food means, and she insists on being cook! If woman had been a thinking creature, she should certainly, as cook for thousands of years, have discovered the most important physiological facts, and should likewise have got possession of the healing art! Through bad female cooks—through the entire lack of reason in the kitchen—the development of mankind has been longest retarded and most interfered with: even today matters are very little better. A word to High School girls.

235

There are turns and casts of fancy, there are sentences, little handfuls of words, in which a whole culture, a whole society suddenly crystallizes itself. Among these is the incidental remark of Madame de Lambert to her son: "*mon ami, ne vous permettez jamais que des folies, qui vous feront grand plaisir*"—the motherliest and wisest remark, by the way, that was ever addressed to a son.

236

I have no doubt that every noble woman will oppose what Dante and Goethe believed about woman—the former when he sang, "*ella guardava suso, ed io in lei,*" and the latter when he interpreted it, "the eternally feminine draws us *aloft*"; for *this* is just what she believes of the eternally masculine.

237

SEVEN APOPHTHEGMS FOR WOMEN

How the longest ennui flees, When a man comes to our knees!

Age, alas! and science staid, Furnish even weak virtue aid.

Somber garb and silence meet: Dress for every dame—discreet.

Whom I thank when in my bliss? God!—and my good tailoress!

Young, a flower-decked cavern home; Old, a dragon thence doth roam.

Noble title, leg that's fine, Man as well: Oh, were *he* mine!

Speech in brief and sense in mass—Slippery for the jenny-ass!

237A

Woman has hitherto been treated by men like birds, which, losing their way, have come down among them from an elevation: as something delicate, fragile, wild, strange, sweet, and animating—but as something also which must be cooped up to prevent it flying away.

238

To be mistaken in the fundamental problem of "man and woman," to deny here the profoundest antagonism and the necessity for an eternally hostile tension, to dream here perhaps of equal rights, equal training, equal claims and obligations: that is a *typical* sign of shallow-mindedness; and a thinker who has proved himself shallow at this dangerous spot—shallow in instinct!—may generally be regarded as suspicious, nay more, as betrayed, as discovered; he will probably prove too "short" for all fundamental questions of life, future as well as present, and will be unable to descend into *any* of the depths. On the other hand, a man who has depth of spirit as well as of desires, and has also the depth of benevolence which is capable of severity and harshness, and easily confounded with them, can only think of woman as *orientals* do: he must conceive of her as a possession, as confinable property, as a being predestined for service and accomplishing her mission therein—he must take his stand in this matter upon the immense rationality of Asia, upon the superiority of the instinct of Asia, as the Greeks did formerly; those best heirs and scholars of Asia—who, as is well known, with their *increasing* culture and amplitude of power, from Homer to the time of Pericles, became gradually *stricter* towards woman, in short, more Oriental. *how* necessary, *how* logical, even *how* humanely desirable this was, let us consider for ourselves!

239

The weaker sex has in no previous age been treated with so much respect by men as at present—this belongs to the tendency and fundamental taste of democracy, in the same way as disrespectfulness to old age—what wonder is it that abuse should be immediately made of this respect? They want more, they learn to make claims, the tribute of respect is at last felt to be well-nigh galling; rivalry for rights, indeed actual strife itself, would be preferred: in a word, woman is losing modesty. And let us immediately add that she is also losing taste. She is unlearning to *fear* man: but the woman who "unlearns to fear" sacrifices her most womanly instincts.

That woman should venture forward when the fear-inspiring quality in man—or more definitely, the *man* in man—is no longer either desired or fully developed, is reasonable enough and also intelligible enough; what is more difficult to understand is that precisely thereby—woman deteriorates. This is what is happening nowadays: let us not deceive ourselves about it!

Wherever the industrial spirit has triumphed over the military and aristocratic spirit, woman strives for the economic and legal independence of a clerk: "woman as clerkess" is inscribed on the portal of the modern society which is in course of formation. While she thus appropriates new rights, aspires to be "master," and inscribes "progress" of woman on her flags and banners, the very opposite realizes itself with terrible obviousness: *woman retrogrades.*

Since the French Revolution the influence of woman in Europe has *declined* in proportion as she has increased her rights and claims; and the "emancipation of woman," insofar as it is desired and demanded by women themselves (and not only by masculine shallow-pates), thus proves to be a remarkable symptom of the increased weakening and deadening of the most womanly instincts. There is *stupidity* in this movement, an almost masculine stupidity, of which a well-reared woman—who is always a sensible woman—might be heartily ashamed.

To lose the intuition as to the ground upon which she can most surely achieve victory; to neglect exercise in the use of her proper weapons; to let-herself-go before man, perhaps even "to the book," where formerly she kept herself in control and in refined, artful humility; to neutralize with her virtuous audacity man's faith in a *veiled*, fundamentally different ideal in woman, something eternally, necessarily feminine; to emphatically and loquaciously dissuade man from the idea that woman must be preserved, cared for, protected, and indulged, like some delicate, strangely wild, and often pleasant domestic animal; the clumsy and indignant collection of everything of the nature of servitude and bondage which the position of woman in the hitherto existing order of society has entailed and still entails (as though slavery were a counter-argument, and not rather a condition of every higher culture, of every elevation of culture):—what does all this betoken, if not a disintegration of womanly instincts, a defeminizing?

Certainly, there are enough of idiotic friends and corrupters of woman among the learned asses of the masculine sex, who advise woman to defeminize herself in this manner, and to imitate all the stupidities from which "man" in Europe, European "manliness," suffers,—who would like to lower woman to "general culture," indeed even to newspaper reading and meddling with politics. Here and there they wish even to make women into free spirits and literary workers: as though a woman without piety would not be something perfectly obnoxious or ludicrous to a profound and godless man;—almost everywhere her nerves are being ruined by the most morbid and dangerous kind of music (our latest German music), and she is daily being made more hysterical and more incapable of fulfilling her first and last function, that of bearing robust children. They wish to "cultivate" her in general still more, and intend, as they say, to make the "weaker sex" *strong* by culture: as if history did not teach in the most emphatic manner that the "cultivating" of mankind and his weakening—that is to say, the weakening, dissipating, and languishing of his *force of will*—have always kept pace with one another, and that the most powerful and influential women in the world (and lastly, the mother of Napoleon) had just to thank their force of will—and not their schoolmasters—for their power and ascendancy over men.

That which inspires respect in woman, and often enough fear also, is her *nature*, which is more "natural" than that of man, her genuine, carnivora-like, cunning flexibility, her tiger-claws beneath the glove, her *naïveté* in egoism, her untrainableness and innate wildness, the incomprehensibleness, extent, and deviation of her desires and virtues. That which, in spite of fear, excites one's sympathy for the dangerous and beautiful cat, "woman," is that she seems more afflicted, more vulnerable, more necessitous of love, and more condemned to disillusionment than any other creature. Fear and sympathy it is with these feelings that man has hitherto stood in the presence of woman, always with one foot already in tragedy, which rends while it delights.

What? And all that is now to be at an end? And the *disenchantment* of woman is in progress? The tediousness of woman is slowly evolving? Oh Europe! Europe! We know the horned animal which was always most attractive to thee, from which danger is ever again threatening thee! Thy old fable might once more become "history"—an immense stupidity might once again overmaster thee and carry thee away! And no God concealed beneath it—no! only an "idea," a "modern idea"!

Part Eight:
Peoples and Countries

240

I heard, once again for the first time, Richard Wagner's overture to the *Mastersinger*: it is a piece of magnificent, gorgeous, heavy, latter-day art, which has the pride to presuppose two centuries of music as still living, in order that it may be understood:—it is an honor to Germans that such a pride did not miscalculate! What flavors and forces, what seasons and climes do we not find mingled in it! It impresses us at one time as ancient, at another time as foreign, bitter, and too modern, it is as arbitrary as it is pompously traditional, it is not infrequently roguish, still oftener rough and coarse—it has fire and courage, and at the same time the loose, dun-colored skin of fruits which ripen too late. It flows broad and full: and suddenly there is a moment of inexplicable hesitation, like a gap that opens between cause and effect, an oppression that makes us dream, almost a nightmare; but already it broadens and widens anew, the old stream of delight— the most manifold delight,—of old and new happiness; including *especially* the joy of the artist in himself, which he refuses to conceal, his astonished, happy cognizance of his mastery of the expedients here employed, the new, newly acquired, imperfectly tested expedients of art which he apparently betrays to us.

All in all, however, no beauty, no South, nothing of the delicate southern clearness of the sky, nothing of grace, no dance, hardly a will to logic; a certain clumsiness even, which is also emphasized, as though the artist wished to say to us: "It is part of my intention"; a cumbersome drapery, something arbitrarily barbaric and ceremonious, a flurry of learned and venerable conceits and witticisms; something German in the best and worst sense of the word, something in the German style, manifold, formless, and inexhaustible; a certain German potency and super-plenitude of soul, which is not afraid to hide itself under the *raffinements* of decadence—which, perhaps, feels itself most at ease there; a real, genuine token of the German soul, which is at the same time young and aged, too ripe and yet still too rich in futurity. This kind of music expresses best what I think of the Germans: they belong to the day before yesterday and the day after tomorrow—*they have as yet no today.*

241

We "good Europeans," we also have hours when we allow ourselves a warm-hearted patriotism, a plunge and relapse into old loves and narrow views—I have just given an example of it—hours of national excitement, of patriotic anguish, and all other sorts of old-fashioned floods of sentiment. Duller spirits may perhaps only get done with what confines its operations in us to hours and plays itself out in hours—in a considerable time: some in half a year, others in half a lifetime, according to the speed and strength with which they digest and "change their material." Indeed, I could think of sluggish, hesitating races, which even in our rapidly moving Europe, would require half a century ere they could surmount such atavistic attacks of patriotism and soil-attachment, and return once more to reason, that is to say, to "good Europeanism."

And while digressing on this possibility, I happen to become an ear-witness of a conversation between two old patriots—they were evidently both hard of hearing and consequently spoke all the louder.

"*He* has as much, and knows as much, philosophy as a peasant or a corps-student," said the one—"he is still innocent. But what does that matter nowadays! It is the age of the masses: they lie on their belly before everything that is massive. And so also in *politicis*. A statesman who rears up for them a new Tower of Babel, some monstrosity of empire and power, they call 'great'—what does it matter that we more prudent and conservative ones do not meanwhile give up the old belief that it is only the great thought that gives greatness to an action or affair. Supposing a statesman were to bring his people into the position of being obliged henceforth to practice 'high politics,' for which they were by nature badly endowed and prepared, so that they would have to sacrifice their old and reliable virtues, out of love to a new and doubtful mediocrity;—supposing a statesman were to condemn his people generally to 'practice politics,' when they have hitherto had something better to do and think about, and when in the depths of their souls they have been unable to free themselves from a prudent loathing of the restlessness, emptiness, and noisy wranglings of the essentially politics-practicing nations;—supposing such a statesman were to stimulate the slumbering passions and avidities of his people, were to make a stigma out of their former diffidence and delight in aloofness, an offense out of their exoticism and hidden permanency, were to depreciate their most radical proclivities, subvert their consciences, make their minds narrow, and their tastes 'national'—what! a statesman who should do all this, which his people would have to do penance for throughout their whole future, if they had a future, such a statesman would be *great*, would he?"

"Undoubtedly!" replied the other old patriot vehemently, "otherwise he *could not* have done it! It was mad perhaps to wish such a thing! But perhaps everything great has been just as mad at its commencement!"

"Misuse of words!" cried his interlocutor, contradictorily—"strong! strong! Strong and mad! *Not* great!"

The old men had obviously become heated as they thus shouted their "truths" in each other's faces, but I, in my happiness and apartness, considered how soon a stronger one may become master of the strong, and also that there is a compensation for the intellectual superficializing of a nation—namely, in the deepening of another.

242

Whether we call it "civilization," or "humanizing," or "progress," which now distinguishes the European, whether we call it simply, without praise or blame, by the political formula the *democratic* movement in Europe—behind all the moral and political foregrounds pointed to by such formulas, an immense *physiological process* goes on, which is ever extending the process of the assimilation of Europeans, their increasing detachment from the conditions under which, climatically and hereditarily, united races originate, their increasing independence of every definite milieu, that for centuries would fain inscribe itself with equal demands on soul and body,—that is to say, the slow emergence of an essentially *super-national* and nomadic species of man, who possesses, physiologically speaking, a maximum of the art and power of adaptation as his typical distinction.

This process of the *evolving European*, which can be retarded in its *tempo* by great relapses, but will perhaps just gain and grow thereby in vehemence and depth—the still-raging storm and stress of "national sentiment" pertains to it, and also the anarchism which is appearing at present—this process will probably arrive at results on which its naive propagators and panegyrists, the apostles of "modern ideas," would least care to reckon. The same new conditions under which on an average a leveling and mediocrizing of man will take place—a useful, industrious, variously serviceable, and clever gregarious man—are in the highest degree suitable to give rise to exceptional men of the most dangerous and attractive qualities.

For, while the capacity for adaptation, which is every day trying changing conditions, and begins a new work with every generation, almost with every decade, makes the *powerfulness* of the type impossible; while the collective impression of such future Europeans will probably be that of numerous, talkative, weak-willed, and very handy workmen who *require* a master, a commander, as they require their daily bread; while, therefore, the democratizing of Europe will tend to the production of a type prepared for *slavery* in the most subtle sense of the term: the *strong* man will necessarily in individual and exceptional cases, become stronger and richer than he has perhaps ever been before—owing to the unprejudicedness of his schooling, owing to the immense variety of practice, art, and disguise. I meant to say that the democratizing of Europe is at the same time an involuntary arrangement for the rearing of *tyrants*—taking the word in all its meanings, even in its most spiritual sense.

243

I hear with pleasure that our sun is moving rapidly towards the constellation Hercules: and I hope that the men on this earth will do like the sun. And we foremost, we good Europeans!

244

There was a time when it was customary to call Germans "deep" by way of distinction; but now that the most successful type of new Germanism is covetous of quite other honors, and perhaps misses "smartness" in all that has depth, it is almost opportune and patriotic to doubt whether we did not formerly deceive ourselves with that commendation: in short, whether German depth is not at bottom something different and worse—and something from which, thank God, we are on the point of successfully ridding ourselves. Let us try, then, to relearn with regard to German depth; the only thing necessary for the purpose is a little vivisection of the German soul.

The German soul is above all manifold, varied in its source, aggregated and super-imposed, rather than actually built: this is owing to its origin. A German who would embolden himself to assert: "Two souls, alas, dwell in my breast," would make a bad guess at the truth, or, more correctly, he would come far short of the truth about the number of souls. As a people made up of the most extraordinary mixing and mingling of races, perhaps even with a preponderance of the pre-Aryan element as the "people of the center" in every sense of the term, the Germans are more intangible, more ample, more contradictory, more unknown, more incalculable, more surprising, and even more terrifying than other peoples are to themselves:—they escape *definition*, and are thereby alone the despair of the French.

It *is* characteristic of the Germans that the question: "What is German?" never dies out among them. Kotzebue certainly knew his Germans well enough: "We are known," they cried jubilantly to him—but Sand also thought he knew them. Jean Paul knew what he was doing when he declared himself incensed at Fichte's lying but patriotic flatteries and exaggerations,—but it is probable that Goethe thought differently about Germans from Jean Paul, even though he acknowledged him to be right with regard to Fichte. It is a question what Goethe really thought about the Germans?

But about many things around him he never spoke explicitly, and all his life he knew how to keep an astute silence—probably he had good reason for it. It is certain that it was not the "Wars of Independence" that made him look up more joyfully, any more than it was the French Revolution,—the event on account of which he *reconstructed* his *Faust*, and indeed the whole problem of "man," was the appearance of Napoleon. There are words of Goethe in which he condemns with impatient severity, as from a foreign land, that which Germans take a pride in, he once defined the famous German turn of mind as "Indulgence towards its own and others' weaknesses." Was he wrong? it is characteristic of Germans that one is seldom entirely wrong about them.

The German soul has passages and galleries in it, there are caves, hiding-places, and dungeons therein, its disorder has much of the charm of the mysterious, the German is well acquainted with the bypaths to chaos. And as everything loves its symbol, so the German loves the clouds and all that is obscure, evolving, crepuscular, damp, and shrouded, it seems to him that everything uncertain, undeveloped, self-displacing, and growing is "deep".

The German himself does not *exist*, he is *becoming*, he is "developing himself". "Development" is therefore the essentially German discovery and hit in the great domain of philosophical formulas,—a ruling idea, which, together with German beer and German music, is laboring to Germanize all Europe.

Foreigners are astonished and attracted by the riddles which the conflicting nature at the basis of the German soul propounds to them (riddles which Hegel systematized and Richard Wagner has in the end set to music). "Good-natured and spiteful"—such a juxtaposition, preposterous in the case of every other people, is unfortunately only too often justified in Germany one has only to live for a while among Swabians to know this! The clumsiness of the German scholar and his social distastefulness agree alarmingly well with his physical rope-dancing and nimble boldness, of which all the Gods have learnt to be afraid. If any one wishes to see the "German soul" demonstrated *ad oculos*, let him only look at German taste, at German arts and manners what boorish indifference to "taste"! How the noblest and the commonest stand there in juxtaposition! How disorderly and how rich is the whole constitution of this soul! The German *drags* at his soul, he drags at everything he experiences. He digests his events badly; he never gets "done" with them; and German depth is often only a difficult, hesitating "digestion." And just as all chronic invalids, all dyspeptics like what is convenient, so the German loves "frankness" and "honesty"; it is so *convenient* to be frank and honest!

This confidingness, this complaisance, this showing-the-cards of German *honesty*, is probably the most dangerous and most successful disguise which the German is up to nowadays: it is his proper Mephistophelean art; with this he can "still achieve much"! The German lets himself go, and thereby gazes with faithful, blue, empty German eyes—and other countries immediately confound him with his dressing-gown!

I meant to say that, let "German depth" be what it will—among ourselves alone we perhaps take the liberty to laugh at it—we shall do well to continue henceforth to honor its appearance and good name, and not barter away too cheaply our old reputation as a people of depth for Prussian "smartness," and Berlin wit and sand. It is wise for a people to pose, and *let* itself be regarded, as profound, clumsy, good-natured, honest, and foolish: it might even be— profound to do so! Finally, we should do honor to our name—we are not called the "*tiusche Volk*" (deceptive people) for nothing....

245

The "good old" time is past, it sang itself out in Mozart—how happy are *we* that his *rococo* still speaks to us, that his "good company," his tender enthusiasm, his childish delight in the Chinese and its flourishes, his courtesy of heart, his longing for the elegant, the amorous, the tripping, the tearful, and his belief in the South, can still appeal to *something left* in us! Ah, some time or other it will be over with it!—but who can doubt that it will be over still sooner with the intelligence and taste for Beethoven! For he was only the last echo of a break and transition in style, and *not*, like Mozart, the last echo of a great European taste which had existed for centuries.

Beethoven is the intermediate event between an old mellow soul that is constantly breaking down, and a future over-young soul that is always *coming*; there is spread over his music the twilight of eternal loss and eternal extravagant hope,—the same light in which Europe was bathed when it dreamed with Rousseau, when it danced round the Tree of Liberty of the Revolution, and finally almost fell down in adoration before Napoleon. But how rapidly does *this* very sentiment now pale, how difficult nowadays is even the *apprehension* of this sentiment, how strangely does the language of Rousseau, Schiller, Shelley, and Byron sound to our ear, in whom *collectively* the same fate of Europe was able to *speak*, which knew how to *sing* in Beethoven!

Whatever German music came afterwards, belongs to Romanticism, that is to say, to a movement which, historically considered, was still shorter, more fleeting, and more superficial than that great interlude, the transition of Europe from Rousseau to Napoleon, and to the rise of democracy. Weber—but what do *we* care nowadays for *Freischutz* and *Oberon*! Or Marschner's *Hans Heiling* and *Vampyre*! Or even Wagner's *Tannhauser*! That is extinct, although not yet forgotten music. This whole music of Romanticism, besides, was not noble enough, was not musical enough, to maintain its position anywhere but in the theatre and before the masses; from the beginning it was second-rate music, which was little thought of by genuine musicians.

It was different with Felix Mendelssohn, that halcyon master, who, on account of his lighter, purer, happier soul, quickly acquired admiration, and was equally quickly forgotten: as the beautiful *episode* of German music. But with regard to Robert Schumann, who took things seriously, and has been taken seriously from the first—he was the last that founded a school,—do we not now regard it as a satisfaction, a relief, a deliverance, that this very Romanticism of Schumann's has been surmounted?

Schumann, fleeing into the "Saxon Switzerland" of his soul, with a half Werther-like, half Jean-Paul-like nature (assuredly not like Beethoven! assuredly not like Byron!)—his *Manfred* music is a mistake and a misunderstanding to the extent of injustice; Schumann, with his taste, which was fundamentally a *petty* taste (that is to say, a dangerous propensity—doubly dangerous among Germans—for quiet lyricism and intoxication of the feelings), going constantly apart, timidly withdrawing and retiring, a noble weakling who reveled in nothing but anonymous joy and sorrow, from the beginning a sort of girl and *noli me tangere*—this Schumann was already merely a *German* event in music, and no longer a European event, as Beethoven had been, as in a still greater degree Mozart had been; with Schumann German music was threatened with its greatest danger, that of *losing the voice for the soul of Europe* and sinking into a merely national affair.

246

What a torture are books written in German to a reader who has a *third* ear! How indignantly he stands beside the slowly turning swamp of sounds without tune and rhythms without dance, which Germans call a "book"! And even the German who *reads* books! How lazily, how reluctantly, how badly he reads! How many Germans know, and consider it obligatory to know, that there is *art* in every good sentence—art which must be divined, if the sentence is to be understood! If there is a misunderstanding about its *tempo*, for instance, the sentence itself is misunderstood!

That one must not be doubtful about the rhythm-determining syllables, that one should feel the breaking of the too-rigid symmetry as intentional and as a charm, that one should lend a fine and patient ear to every *staccato* and every *rubato*, that one should divine the sense in the sequence of the vowels and diphthongs, and how delicately and richly they can be tinted and retinted in the order of their arrangement—who among book-reading Germans is complaisant enough to recognize such duties and requirements, and to listen to so much art and intention in language? After all, one just "has no ear for it"; and so the most marked contrasts of style are not heard, and the most delicate artistry is as it were *squandered* on the deaf.

These were my thoughts when I noticed how clumsily and unintuitively two masters in the art of prose-writing have been confounded: one, whose words drop down hesitatingly and coldly, as from the roof of a damp cave—he counts on their dull sound and echo; and another who manipulates his language like a flexible sword, and from his arm down into his toes feels the dangerous bliss of the quivering, over-sharp blade, which wishes to bite, hiss, and cut.

247

How little the German style has to do with harmony and with the ear, is shown by the fact that precisely our good musicians themselves write badly. The German does not read aloud, he does not read for the ear, but only with his eyes; he has put his ears away in the drawer for the time. In antiquity when a man read—which was seldom enough—he read something to himself, and in a loud voice; they were surprised when any one read silently, and sought secretly the reason of it. In a loud voice: that is to say, with all the swellings, inflections, and variations of key and changes of *tempo*, in which the ancient *public* world took delight.

The laws of the written style were then the same as those of the spoken style; and these laws depended partly on the surprising development and refined requirements of the ear and larynx; partly on the strength, endurance, and power of the ancient lungs. In the ancient sense, a period is above all a physiological whole, inasmuch as it is comprised in one breath. Such periods as occur in Demosthenes and Cicero, swelling twice and sinking twice, and all in one breath, were pleasures to the men of *antiquity*, who knew by their own schooling how to appreciate the virtue therein, the rareness and the difficulty in the deliverance of such a period;—*we* have really no right to the *big* period, we modern men, who are short of breath in every sense!

Those ancients, indeed, were all of them dilettanti in speaking, consequently connoisseurs, consequently critics—they thus brought their orators to the highest pitch; in the same manner as in the last century, when all Italian ladies and gentlemen knew how to sing, the virtuoso-ship of song (and with it also the art of melody) reached its elevation. In Germany, however (until quite recently when a kind of platform eloquence began shyly and awkwardly enough to flutter its young wings), there was properly speaking only one kind of public and *approximately* artistical discourse—that delivered from the pulpit.

The preacher was the only one in Germany who knew the weight of a syllable or a word, in what manner a sentence strikes, springs, rushes, flows, and comes to a close; he alone had a conscience in his ears, often enough a bad conscience: for reasons are not lacking why proficiency in oratory should be especially seldom attained by a German, or almost always too late. The masterpiece of German prose is therefore with good reason the masterpiece of its greatest preacher: the *Bible* has hitherto been the best German book. Compared with Luther's Bible, almost everything else is merely "literature"—something which has not grown in Germany, and therefore has not taken and does not take root in German hearts, as the Bible has done.

248

There are two kinds of geniuses: one which above all engenders and seeks to engender, and another which willingly lets itself be fructified and brings forth. And similarly, among the gifted nations, there are those on whom the woman's problem of pregnancy has devolved, and the secret task of forming, maturing, and perfecting—the Greeks, for instance, were a nation of this kind, and so are the French; and others which have to fructify and become the cause of new modes of life—like the Jews, the Romans, and, in all modesty be it asked: like the Germans?—nations tortured and enraptured by unknown fevers and irresistibly forced out of themselves, amorous and longing for foreign races (for such as "let themselves be fructified"), and withal imperious, like everything conscious of being full of generative force, and consequently empowered "by the grace of God." These two kinds of geniuses seek each other like man and woman; but they also misunderstand each other—like man and woman.

249

Every nation has its own "Tartuffery," and calls that its virtue.—One does not know—cannot know, the best that is in one.

250

What Europe owes to the Jews?—Many things, good and bad, and above all one thing of the nature both of the best and the worst: the grand style in morality, the fearfulness and majesty of infinite demands, of infinite significations, the whole Romanticism and sublimity of moral questionableness—and consequently just the most attractive, ensnaring, and exquisite element in those iridescences and allurements to life, in the aftersheen of which the sky of our European culture, its evening sky, now glows—perhaps glows out. For this, we artists among the spectators and philosophers, are—grateful to the Jews.

251

It must be taken into the bargain, if various clouds and disturbances—in short, slight attacks of stupidity—pass over the spirit of a people that suffers and *wants* to suffer from national nervous fever and political ambition: for instance, among present-day Germans there is alternately the anti-French folly, the anti-Semitic folly, the anti-Polish folly, the Christian-romantic folly, the Wagnerian folly, the Teutonic folly, the Prussian folly (just look at those poor historians, the Sybels and Treitschkes, and their closely bandaged heads), and whatever else these little obscurations of the German spirit and conscience may be called. May it be forgiven me that I, too, when on a short daring sojourn on very infected ground, did not remain wholly exempt from the disease, but like everyone else, began to entertain thoughts about matters which did not concern me—the first symptom of political infection. About the Jews, for instance, listen to the following:

I have never yet met a German who was favorably inclined to the Jews; and however decided the repudiation of actual anti-Semitism may be on the part of all prudent and political men, this prudence and policy is not perhaps directed against the nature of the sentiment itself, but only against its dangerous excess, and especially against the distasteful and infamous expression of this excess of sentiment;—on this point we must not deceive ourselves. That Germany has amply *sufficient* Jews, that the German stomach, the German blood, has difficulty (and will long have difficulty) in disposing only of this quantity of "Jew"—as the Italian, the Frenchman, and the Englishman have done by means of a stronger digestion:—that is the unmistakable declaration and language of a general instinct, to which one must listen and according to which one must act. "Let no more Jews come in! And shut the doors, especially towards the East (also towards Austria)!"—thus commands the instinct of a people whose nature is still feeble and uncertain, so that it could be easily wiped out, easily extinguished, by a stronger race. The Jews, however, are beyond all doubt the strongest, toughest, and purest race at present living in Europe, they know how to succeed even under the worst conditions (in fact better than under favorable ones), by means of virtues of some sort, which one would like nowadays to label as vices—owing above all to a resolute faith which does not need to be ashamed before "modern ideas", they alter only, *when* they do alter, in the same way that the Russian Empire makes its conquest—as an empire that has plenty of time and is not of yesterday—namely, according to the principle, "as slowly as possible"!

A thinker who has the future of Europe at heart, will, in all his perspectives concerning the future, calculate upon the Jews, as he will calculate upon the Russians, as above all the surest and likeliest factors in the great play and battle of forces. That which is at present called a "nation" in Europe, and is really rather a *res facta* than *nata* (indeed, sometimes confusingly similar to a *res ficta et picta*), is in every case something evolving, young, easily displaced, and not yet a race, much less such a race *aere perennus*, as the Jews are such "nations" should most carefully avoid all hot-headed rivalry and hostility! It is certain that the Jews, if they desired—or if they were driven to it, as the anti-Semites seem to wish—*could* now have the ascendancy, nay, literally the supremacy, over Europe, that they are *not* working and planning for that end is equally certain.

Meanwhile, they rather wish and desire, even somewhat importunely, to be insorbed and absorbed by Europe, they long to be finally settled, authorized, and respected somewhere, and wish to put an end to the nomadic life, to the "wandering Jew",—and one should certainly take account of this impulse and tendency, and *make advances* to it (it possibly betokens a mitigation of the Jewish instincts) for which purpose it would perhaps be useful and fair to banish the anti-Semitic bawlers out of the country. One should make advances with all prudence, and with selection, pretty much as the English nobility do. It stands to reason that the more powerful and strongly marked types of new Germanism could enter into relation with the Jews with the least hesitation; for instance, the nobleman officer from the Prussian border: it would be interesting in many ways to see whether the genius for money and patience (and especially some intellect and intellectuality—sadly lacking in the place referred to) could not in addition be annexed and trained to the hereditary art of commanding and obeying—for both of which the country in question has now a classic reputation. But here it is expedient to break off my festal discourse and my sprightly Teutonomania for I have already reached my *serious topic*, the "European problem," as I understand it, the rearing of a new ruling caste for Europe.

252

They are not a philosophical race—the English: Bacon represents an *attack* on the philosophical spirit generally, Hobbes, Hume, and Locke, an abasement, and a depreciation of the idea of a "philosopher" for more than a century. It was *against* Hume that Kant uprose and raised himself; it was Locke of whom Schelling *rightly* said, "*je méprise Locke*"; in the struggle against the English mechanical stultification of the world, Hegel and Schopenhauer (along with Goethe) were of one accord; the two hostile brother-geniuses in philosophy, who pushed in different directions towards the opposite poles of German thought, and thereby wronged each other as only brothers will do.

What is lacking in England, and has always been lacking, that half-actor and rhetorician knew well enough, the absurd muddle-head, Carlyle, who sought to conceal under passionate grimaces what he knew about himself: namely, what was *lacking* in Carlyle—real *power* of intellect, real *depth* of intellectual perception, in short, philosophy. It is characteristic of such an unphilosophical race to hold on firmly to Christianity—they *need* its discipline for "moralizing" and humanizing. The Englishman, more gloomy, sensual, headstrong, and brutal than the German—is for that very reason, as the baser of the two, also the most pious: he has all the *more need* of Christianity. To finer nostrils, this English Christianity itself has still a characteristic English taint of spleen and alcoholic excess, for which, owing to good reasons, it is used as an antidote—the finer poison to neutralize the coarser: a finer form of poisoning is in fact a step in advance with coarse-mannered people, a step towards spiritualization. The English coarseness and rustic demureness is still most satisfactorily disguised by Christian pantomime, and by praying and psalm-singing (or, more correctly, it is thereby explained and differently expressed); and for the herd of drunkards and rakes who formerly learned moral grunting under the influence of Methodism (and more recently as the "Salvation Army"), a penitential fit may really be the relatively highest manifestation of "humanity" to which they can be elevated: so much may reasonably be admitted. That, however, which offends even in the humanest Englishman is his lack of music, to speak figuratively (and also literally): he has neither rhythm nor dance in the movements of his soul and body; indeed, not even the desire for rhythm and dance, for "music." Listen to him speaking; look at the most beautiful Englishwoman *walking*—in no country on earth are there more beautiful doves and swans; finally, listen to them singing! But I ask too much...

253

There are truths which are best recognized by mediocre minds, because they are best adapted for them, there are truths which only possess charms and seductive power for mediocre spirits:—one is pushed to this probably unpleasant conclusion, now that the influence of respectable but mediocre Englishmen—I may mention Darwin, John Stuart Mill, and Herbert Spencer—begins to gain the ascendancy in the middle-class region of European taste. Indeed, who could doubt that it is a useful thing for *such* minds to have the ascendancy for a time? It would be an error to consider the highly developed and independently soaring minds as specially qualified for determining and collecting many little common facts, and deducing conclusions from them; as exceptions, they are rather from the first in no very favorable position towards those who are "the rules." After all, they have more to do than merely to perceive:—in effect, they have to *be* something new, they have to *signify* something new, they have to *represent* new values! The gulf between knowledge and capacity is perhaps greater, and also more mysterious, than one thinks: the capable man in the grand style, the creator, will possibly have to be an ignorant person;—while on the other hand, for scientific discoveries like those of Darwin, a certain narrowness, aridity, and industrious carefulness (in short, something English) may not be unfavorable for arriving at them.

Finally, let it not be forgotten that the English, with their profound mediocrity, brought about once before a general depression of European intelligence. What is called "modern ideas," or "the ideas of the eighteenth century," or "French ideas"—that, consequently, against which the *German* mind rose up with profound disgust—is of English origin, there is no doubt about it. The French were only the apes and actors of these ideas, their best soldiers, and likewise, alas! their first and profoundest *victims*; for owing to the diabolical Anglomania of "modern ideas," the âme française has in the end become so thin and emaciated, that at present one recalls its sixteenth and seventeenth centuries, its profound, passionate strength, its inventive excellency, almost with disbelief. One must, however, maintain this verdict of historical justice in a determined manner, and defend it against present prejudices and appearances: the European *noblesse*—of sentiment, taste, and manners, taking the word in every high sense—is the work and invention of *France*; the European ignobleness, the plebeianism of modern ideas—is *England's* work and invention.

254

Even at present France is still the seat of the most intellectual and refined culture of Europe, it is still the high school of taste; but one must know how to find this "France of taste." He who belongs to it keeps himself well concealed:—they may be a small number in whom it lives and is embodied, besides perhaps being men who do not stand upon the strongest legs, in part fatalists, hypochondriacs, invalids, in part persons over-indulged, over-refined, such as have the *ambition* to conceal themselves. They have all something in common: they keep their ears closed in presence of the delirious folly and noisy spouting of the democratic *bourgeois*. In fact, a besotted and brutalized France at present sprawls in the foreground—it recently celebrated a veritable orgy of bad taste, and at the same time of self-admiration, at the funeral of Victor Hugo. There is also something else common to them: a predilection to resist intellectual Germanizing—and a still greater inability to do so!

In this France of intellect, which is also a France of pessimism, Schopenhauer has perhaps become more at home, and more indigenous than he has ever been in Germany; not to speak of Heinrich Heine, who has long ago been re-incarnated in the more refined and fastidious lyrists of Paris; or of Hegel, who at present, in the form of Taine—the *first* of living historians—exercises an almost tyrannical influence. As regards Richard Wagner, however, the more French music learns to adapt itself to the actual needs of the âme *moderne*, the more will it "Wagnerize"; one can safely predict that beforehand,—it is already taking place sufficiently!

There are, however, three things which the French can still boast of with pride as their heritage and possession, and as indelible tokens of their ancient intellectual superiority in Europe, in spite of all voluntary or involuntary Germanizing and vulgarizing of taste. *Firstly,* the capacity for artistic emotion, for devotion to "form," for which the expression, *l'art pour l'art*, along with numerous others, has been invented:—such capacity has not been lacking in France for three centuries; and owing to its reverence for the "small number," it has again and again made a sort of chamber music of literature possible, which is sought for in vain elsewhere in Europe.

The *second* thing whereby the French can lay claim to a superiority over Europe is their ancient, many-sided, *moralistic* culture, owing to which one finds on an average, even in the petty *romanciers* of the newspapers and chance *boulevardiers de Paris*, a psychological sensitiveness and curiosity, of which, for example, one has no conception (to say nothing of the thing itself!) in Germany. The Germans lack a couple of centuries of the moralistic work requisite thereto, which, as we have said, France has not grudged: those who call the Germans "naive" on that account give them commendation for a defect. (As the opposite of the German inexperience and innocence *in voluptate psychologica*, which is not too remotely associated with the tediousness of German intercourse,—and as the most successful expression of genuine French curiosity and inventive talent in this domain of delicate thrills, Henri Beyle may be noted; that remarkable anticipatory and forerunning man, who, with a Napoleonic *tempo*, traversed *his* Europe, in fact, several centuries of the European soul, as a surveyor and discoverer thereof:—it has required two generations to *overtake* him one way or other, to divine long afterwards some of the riddles that perplexed and enraptured him—this strange Epicurean and man of interrogation, the last great psychologist of France).

There is yet a *third* claim to superiority: in the French character there is a successful half-way synthesis of the North and South, which makes them comprehend many things, and enjoins upon them other things, which an Englishman can never comprehend. Their temperament, turned alternately to and from the South, in which from time to time the Provencal and Ligurian blood froths over, preserves them from the dreadful, northern grey-in-grey, from sunless conceptual-spectrism and from poverty of blood—our *German* infirmity of taste, for the excessive prevalence of which at the present moment, blood and iron, that is to say "high politics," has with great resolution been prescribed (according to a dangerous healing art, which bids me wait and wait, but not yet hope).—There is also still in France a pre-understanding and ready welcome for those rarer and rarely gratified men, who are too comprehensive to find satisfaction in any kind of fatherlandism, and know how to love the South when in the North and the North when in the South—the born Midlanders, the "good Europeans."

For them *Bizet* has made music, this latest genius, who has seen a new beauty and seduction,—who has discovered a piece of the *south in music.*

255

I hold that many precautions should be taken against German music. Suppose a person loves the South as I love it—as a great school of recovery for the most spiritual and the most sensuous ills, as a boundless solar profusion and effulgence which o'erspreads a sovereign existence believing in itself—well, such a person will learn to be somewhat on his guard against German music, because, in injuring his taste anew, it will also injure his health anew.

Such a Southerner, a Southerner not by origin but by *belief,* if he should dream of the future of music, must also dream of it being freed from the influence of the North; and must have in his ears the prelude to a deeper, mightier, and perhaps more perverse and mysterious music, a super-German music, which does not fade, pale, and die away, as all German music does, at the sight of the blue, wanton sea and the Mediterranean clearness of sky—a super-European music, which holds its own even in presence of the brown sunsets of the desert, whose soul is akin to the palm-tree, and can be at home and can roam with big, beautiful, lonely beasts of prey...

I could imagine a music of which the rarest charm would be that it knew nothing more of good and evil; only that here and there perhaps some sailor's home-sickness, some golden shadows and tender weaknesses might sweep lightly over it; an art which, from the far distance, would see the colors of a sinking and almost incomprehensible *moral* world fleeing towards it, and would be hospitable enough and profound enough to receive such belated fugitives.

256

Owing to the morbid estrangement which the nationality-craze has induced and still induces among the nations of Europe, owing also to the short-sighted and hasty-handed politicians, who with the help of this craze, are at present in power, and do not suspect to what extent the disintegrating policy they pursue must necessarily be only an interlude policy—owing to all this and much else that is altogether unmentionable at present, the most unmistakable signs that *Europe wishes to be one*, are now overlooked, or arbitrarily and falsely misinterpreted.

With all the more profound and large-minded men of this century, the real general tendency of the mysterious labor of their souls was to prepare the way for that new *synthesis*, and tentatively to anticipate the European of the future; only in their simulations, or in their weaker moments, in old age perhaps, did they belong to the "fatherlands"—they only rested from themselves when they became "patriots." I think of such men as Napoleon, Goethe, Beethoven, Stendhal, Heinrich Heine, Schopenhauer: it must not be taken amiss if I also count Richard Wagner among them, about whom one must not let oneself be deceived by his own misunderstandings (geniuses like him have seldom the right to understand themselves), still less, of course, by the unseemly noise with which he is now resisted and opposed in France: the fact remains, nevertheless, that Richard Wagner and the *later French romanticism* of the forties, are most closely and intimately related to one another. They are akin, fundamentally akin, in all the heights and depths of their requirements; it is Europe, the *one* Europe, whose soul presses urgently and longingly, outwards and upwards, in their multifarious and boisterous art—whither? into a new light? towards a new sun? But who would attempt to express accurately what all these masters of new modes of speech could not express distinctly? It is certain that the same storm and stress tormented them, that they *sought* in the same manner, these last great seekers!

All of them steeped in literature to their eyes and ears—the first artists of universal literary culture—for the most part even themselves writers, poets, intermediaries and blenders of the arts and the senses (Wagner, as musician is reckoned among painters, as poet among musicians, as artist generally among actors); all of them fanatics for *expression* "at any cost"—I specially mention Delacroix, the nearest related to Wagner; all of them great discoverers in the realm of the sublime, also of the loathsome and dreadful, still greater discoverers in effect, in display, in the art of the show-shop; all of them talented far beyond their genius, out and out *virtuosi*, with mysterious accesses to all that seduces, allures, constrains, and upsets; born enemies of logic and of the straight line, hankering after the strange, the exotic, the monstrous, the crooked, and the self-contradictory; as men, Tantaluses of the will, plebeian parvenus, who knew themselves to be incapable of a noble *tempo* or of a *lento* in life and action—think of Balzac, for instance,—unrestrained workers, almost destroying themselves by work; antinomians and rebels in manners, ambitious and insatiable, without equilibrium and enjoyment; all of them finally shattering and sinking down at the Christian cross (and with right and reason, for who of them would have been sufficiently profound and sufficiently original for an *anti-Christian* philosophy?);—on the whole, a boldly daring, splendidly overbearing, high-flying, and aloft-up-dragging class of higher men, who had first to teach their century—and it is the century of the *masses*—the conception "higher man."...

Let the German friends of Richard Wagner advise together as to whether there is anything purely German in the Wagnerian art, or whether its distinction does not consist precisely in coming from *super-German* sources and impulses: in which connection it may not be underrated how indispensable Paris was to the development of his type, which the strength of his instincts made him long to visit at the most decisive time—and how the whole style of his proceedings, of his self-apostolate, could only perfect itself in sight of the French socialistic original.

On a more subtle comparison it will perhaps be found, to the honor of Richard Wagner's German nature, that he has acted in everything with more strength, daring, severity, and elevation than a nineteenth-century Frenchman could have done—owing to the circumstance that we Germans are as yet nearer to barbarism than the French;—perhaps even the most remarkable creation of Richard Wagner is not only at present, but for ever inaccessible, incomprehensible, and inimitable to the whole latter-day Latin race: the figure of Siegfried, that *very free* man, who is probably far too free, too hard, too cheerful, too healthy, too *anti-Catholic* for the taste of old and mellow civilized nations. He may even have been a sin against Romanticism, this anti-Latin Siegfried: well, Wagner atoned amply for this sin in his old sad days, when—anticipating a taste which has meanwhile passed into politics—he began, with the religious vehemence peculiar to him, to preach, at least, *the way to Rome*, if not to walk therein.

That these last words may not be misunderstood, I will call to my aid a few powerful rhymes, which will even betray to less delicate ears what I mean—what I mean *counter to* the "last Wagner" and his *Parsifal* music:—

> —Is this our mode?—
> From German heart came this vexed ululating?
> From German body, this self-lacerating?
> Is ours this priestly hand-dilation,
> This incense-fuming exaltation?
> Is ours this faltering, falling, shambling,
> This quite uncertain ding-dong-dangling?
> This sly nun-ogling, *Ave*-hour-bell ringing,
> This wholly false enraptured heaven-o'erspringing?
> —Is this our mode?—
> Think well!—ye still wait for admission—
> For what ye hear is *Rome—Rome's faith by intuition!*

Part Nine:
What Is Noble?

257

Every elevation of the type "man," has hitherto been the work of an aristocratic society and so it will always be—a society believing in a long scale of gradations of rank and differences of worth among human beings, and requiring slavery in some form or other. Without the *pathos of distance*, such as grows out of the incarnated difference of classes, out of the constant out-looking and down-looking of the ruling caste on subordinates and instruments, and out of their equally constant practice of obeying and commanding, of keeping down and keeping at a distance—that other more mysterious pathos could never have arisen, the longing for an ever new widening of distance within the soul itself, the formation of ever higher, rarer, further, more extended, more comprehensive states, in short, just the elevation of the type "man," the continued "self-surmounting of man," to use a moral formula in a supermoral sense.

To be sure, one must not resign oneself to any humanitarian illusions about the history of the origin of an aristocratic society (that is to say, of the preliminary condition for the elevation of the type "man"): the truth is hard. Let us acknowledge unprejudicedly how every higher civilization hitherto has *originated!* Men with a still natural nature, barbarians in every terrible sense of the word, men of prey, still in possession of unbroken strength of will and desire for power, threw themselves upon weaker, more moral, more peaceful races (perhaps trading or cattle-rearing communities), or upon old mellow civilizations in which the final vital force was flickering out in brilliant fireworks of wit and depravity. At the commencement, the noble caste was always the barbarian caste: their superiority did not consist first of all in their physical, but in their psychical power—they were more *complete* men (which at every point also implies the same as "more complete beasts").

258

Corruption—as the indication that anarchy threatens to break out among the instincts, and that the foundation of the emotions, called "life," is convulsed—is something radically different according to the organization in which it manifests itself. When, for instance, an aristocracy like that of France at the beginning of the Revolution, flung away its privileges with sublime disgust and sacrificed itself to an excess of its moral sentiments, it was corruption:—it was really only the closing act of the corruption which had existed for centuries, by virtue of which that aristocracy had abdicated step by step its lordly prerogatives and lowered itself to a *function* of royalty (in the end even to its decoration and parade-dress). The essential thing, however, in a good and healthy aristocracy is that it should not regard itself as a function either of the kingship or the commonwealth, but as the *significance* and highest justification thereof—that it should therefore accept with a good conscience the sacrifice of a legion of individuals, who, *for its sake*, must be suppressed and reduced to imperfect men, to slaves and instruments. Its fundamental belief must be precisely that society is *not* allowed to exist for its own sake, but only as a foundation and scaffolding, by means of which a select class of beings may be able to elevate themselves to their higher duties, and in general to a higher *existence*: like those sun-seeking climbing plants in Java—they are called Sipo Matador,—which encircle an oak so long and so often with their arms, until at last, high above it, but supported by it, they can unfold their tops in the open light, and exhibit their happiness.

259

To refrain mutually from injury, from violence, from exploitation, and put one's will on a par with that of others: this may result in a certain rough sense in good conduct among individuals when the necessary conditions are given (namely, the actual similarity of the individuals in amount of force and degree of worth, and their co-relation within one organization). As soon, however, as one wished to take this principle more generally, and if possible even as the *fundamental principle of society*, it would immediately disclose what it really is—namely, a Will to the *denial* of life, a principle of dissolution and decay.

Here one must think profoundly to the very basis and resist all sentimental weakness: life itself is *essentially* appropriation, injury, conquest of the strange and weak, suppression, severity, obtrusion of peculiar forms, incorporation, and at the least, putting it mildest, exploitation;—but why should one for ever use precisely these words on which for ages a disparaging purpose has been stamped?

Even the organization within which, as was previously supposed, the individuals treat each other as equal—it takes place in every healthy aristocracy—must itself, if it be a living and not a dying organization, do all that towards other bodies, which the individuals within it refrain from doing to each other it will have to be the incarnated Will to Power, it will endeavor to grow, to gain ground, attract to itself and acquire ascendancy—not owing to any morality or immorality, but because it *lives*, and because life *is* precisely Will to Power. On no point, however, is the ordinary consciousness of Europeans more unwilling to be corrected than on this matter, people now rave everywhere, even under the guise of science, about coming conditions of society in which "the exploiting character" is to be absent—that sounds to my ears as if they promised to invent a mode of life which should refrain from all organic functions. "Exploitation" does not belong to a depraved, or imperfect and primitive society it belongs to the nature of the living being as a primary organic function, it is a consequence of the intrinsic Will to Power, which is precisely the Will to Life.

Granting that as a theory this is a novelty—as a reality it is the *fundamental fact* of all history let us be so far honest towards ourselves!

260

In a tour through the many finer and coarser moralities which have hitherto prevailed or still prevail on the earth, I found certain traits recurring regularly together, and connected with one another, until finally two primary types revealed themselves to me, and a radical distinction was brought to light.

There is *master-morality* and *slave-morality*,—I would at once add, however, that in all higher and mixed civilizations, there are also attempts at the reconciliation of the two moralities, but one finds still oftener the confusion and mutual misunderstanding of them, indeed sometimes their close juxtaposition—even in the same man, within one soul. The distinctions of moral values have either originated in a ruling caste, pleasantly conscious of being different from the ruled—or among the ruled class, the slaves and dependents of all sorts.

In the first case, when it is the rulers who determine the conception "good," it is the exalted, proud disposition which is regarded as the distinguishing feature, and that which determines the order of rank. The noble type of man separates from himself the beings in whom the opposite of this exalted, proud disposition displays itself he despises them. Let it at once be noted that in this first kind of morality the antithesis "good" and "bad" means practically the same as "noble" and "despicable,"—the antithesis "good" and "*evil*" is of a different origin. The cowardly, the timid, the insignificant, and those thinking merely of narrow utility are despised; moreover, also, the distrustful, with their constrained glances, the self-abasing, the dog-like kind of men who let themselves be abused, the mendicant flatterers, and above all the liars:—it is a fundamental belief of all aristocrats that the common people are untruthful. "We truthful ones"—the nobility in ancient Greece called themselves.

It is obvious that everywhere the designations of moral value were at first applied to *men*; and were only derivatively and at a later period applied to *actions*; it is a gross mistake, therefore, when historians of morals start with questions like, "Why have sympathetic actions been praised?" The noble type of man regards *himself* as a determiner of values; he does not require to be approved of; he passes the judgment: "What is injurious to me is injurious in itself;" he knows that it is he himself only who confers honor on things; he is a *creator of values*. He honors whatever he recognizes in himself: such morality equals self-glorification. In the foreground there is the feeling of plenitude, of power, which seeks to overflow, the happiness of high tension, the consciousness of a wealth which would fain give and bestow:—the noble man also helps the unfortunate, but not—or scarcely—out of pity, but rather from an impulse generated by the super-abundance of power. The noble man honors in himself the powerful one, him also who has power over himself, who knows how to speak and how to keep silence, who takes pleasure in subjecting himself to severity and hardness, and has reverence for all that is severe and hard. "Wotan placed a hard heart in my breast," says an old Scandinavian Saga: it is thus rightly expressed from the soul of a proud Viking. Such a type of man is even proud of not being made for sympathy; the hero of the Saga therefore adds warningly: "He who has not a hard heart when young, will never have one." The noble and brave who think thus are the furthest removed from the morality which sees precisely in sympathy, or in acting for the good of others, or in *désintéressement*, the characteristic of the moral; faith in oneself, pride in oneself, a radical enmity and irony towards "selflessness," belong as definitely to noble morality, as do a careless scorn and precaution in presence of sympathy and the "warm heart."

It is the powerful who *know* how to honor, it is their art, their domain for invention. The profound reverence for age and for tradition—all law rests on this double reverence,—the belief and prejudice in favor of ancestors and unfavorable to newcomers, is typical in the morality of the powerful; and if, reversely, men of "modern ideas" believe almost instinctively in "progress" and the "future," and are more and more lacking in respect for old age, the ignoble origin of these "ideas" has complacently betrayed itself thereby.

A morality of the ruling class, however, is more especially foreign and irritating to present-day taste in the sternness of its principle that one has duties only to one's equals; that one may act towards beings of a lower rank, towards all that is foreign, just as seems good to one, or "as the heart desires," and in any case "beyond good and evil": it is here that sympathy and similar sentiments can have a place. The ability and obligation to exercise prolonged gratitude and prolonged revenge—both only within the circle of equals,—artfulness in retaliation, *raffinement* of the idea in friendship, a certain necessity to have enemies (as outlets for the emotions of envy, quarrelsomeness, arrogance—in fact, in order to be a good *friend*): all these are typical characteristics of the noble morality, which, as has been pointed out, is not the morality of "modern ideas," and is therefore at present difficult to realize, and also to unearth and disclose.

It is otherwise with the second type of morality, *slave-morality*. Supposing that the abused, the oppressed, the suffering, the unemancipated, the weary, and those uncertain of themselves should moralize, what will be the common element in their moral estimates? Probably a pessimistic suspicion with regard to the entire situation of man will find expression, perhaps a condemnation of man, together with his situation. The slave has an unfavorable eye for the virtues of the powerful; he has a skepticism and distrust, a *refinement* of distrust of everything "good" that is there honored—he would fain persuade himself that the very happiness there is not genuine. On the other hand, *those* qualities which serve to alleviate the existence of sufferers are brought into prominence and flooded with light; it is here that sympathy, the kind, helping hand, the warm heart, patience, diligence, humility, and friendliness attain to honor; for here these are the most useful qualities, and almost the only means of supporting the burden of existence. Slave-morality is essentially the morality of utility.

Here is the seat of the origin of the famous antithesis "good" and "evil":— power and dangerousness are assumed to reside in the evil, a certain dreadfulness, subtlety, and strength, which do not admit of being despised. According to slave-morality, therefore, the "evil" man arouses fear; according to master-morality, it is precisely the "good" man who arouses fear and seeks to arouse it, while the bad man is regarded as the despicable being.

The contrast attains its maximum when, in accordance with the logical consequences of slave-morality, a shade of depreciation—it may be slight and well-intentioned—at last attaches itself to the "good" man of this morality; because, according to the servile mode of thought, the good man must in any case be the *safe* man: he is good-natured, easily deceived, perhaps a little stupid, *un bonhomme*. Everywhere that slave-morality gains the ascendancy, language shows a tendency to approximate the significations of the words "good" and "stupid."

A last fundamental difference: the desire for *freedom*, the instinct for happiness and the refinements of the feeling of liberty belong as necessarily to slave-morals and morality, as artifice and enthusiasm in reverence and devotion are the regular symptoms of an aristocratic mode of thinking and estimating.

Hence we can understand without further detail why love *as a passion*—it is our European specialty—must absolutely be of noble origin; as is well known, its invention is due to the Provençal poet-cavaliers, those brilliant, ingenious men of the "*gai saber*," to whom Europe owes so much, and almost owes itself.

261

Vanity is one of the things which are perhaps most difficult for a noble man to understand: he will be tempted to deny it, where another kind of man thinks he sees it self-evidently. The problem for him is to represent to his mind beings who seek to arouse a good opinion of themselves which they themselves do not possess—and consequently also do not "deserve,"—and who yet *believe* in this good opinion afterwards. This seems to him on the one hand such bad taste and so self-disrespectful, and on the other hand so grotesquely unreasonable, that he would like to consider vanity an exception, and is doubtful about it in most cases when it is spoken of.

He will say, for instance: "I may be mistaken about my value, and on the other hand may nevertheless demand that my value should be acknowledged by others precisely as I rate it:—that, however, is not vanity (but self-conceit, or, in most cases, that which is called 'humility,' and also 'modesty')." Or he will even say: "For many reasons I can delight in the good opinion of others, perhaps because I love and honor them, and rejoice in all their joys, perhaps also because their good opinion endorses and strengthens my belief in my own good opinion, perhaps because the good opinion of others, even in cases where I do not share it, is useful to me, or gives promise of usefulness:—all this, however, is not vanity."

The man of noble character must first bring it home forcibly to his mind, especially with the aid of history, that, from time immemorial, in all social strata in any way dependent, the ordinary man *was* only that which he *passed for.*—not being at all accustomed to fix values, he did not assign even to himself any other value than that which his master assigned to him (it is the peculiar *right of masters* to create values).

It may be looked upon as the result of an extraordinary atavism, that the ordinary man, even at present, is still always *waiting* for an opinion about himself, and then instinctively submitting himself to it; yet by no means only to a "good" opinion, but also to a bad and unjust one (think, for instance, of the greater part of the self-appreciations and self-depreciations which believing women learn from their confessors, and which in general the believing Christian learns from his Church).

In fact, conformably to the slow rise of the democratic social order (and its cause, the blending of the blood of masters and slaves), the originally noble and rare impulse of the masters to assign a value to themselves and to "think well" of themselves, will now be more and more encouraged and extended; but it has at all times an older, ampler, and more radically ingrained propensity opposed to it—and in the phenomenon of "vanity" this older propensity overmasters the younger. The vain person rejoices over *every* good opinion which he hears about himself (quite apart from the point of view of its usefulness, and equally regardless of its truth or falsehood), just as he suffers from every bad opinion: for he subjects himself to both, he feels himself subjected to both, by that oldest instinct of subjection which breaks forth in him.

It is "the slave" in the vain man's blood, the remains of the slave's craftiness—and how much of the "slave" is still left in woman, for instance!—which seeks to *seduce* to good opinions of itself; it is the slave, too, who immediately afterwards falls prostrate himself before these opinions, as though he had not called them forth.

And to repeat it again: vanity is an atavism.

262

A *species* originates, and a type becomes established and strong in the long struggle with essentially constant *unfavorable* conditions. On the other hand, it is known by the experience of breeders that species which receive super-abundant nourishment, and in general a surplus of protection and care, immediately tend in the most marked way to develop variations, and are fertile in prodigies and monstrosities (also in monstrous vices).

Now look at an aristocratic commonwealth, say an ancient Greek *polis*, or Venice, as a voluntary or involuntary contrivance for the purpose of *rearing* human beings; there are there men beside one another, thrown upon their own resources, who want to make their species prevail, chiefly because they *must* prevail, or else run the terrible danger of being exterminated. The favor, the super-abundance, the protection are there lacking under which variations are fostered; the species needs itself as species, as something which, precisely by virtue of its hardness, its uniformity, and simplicity of structure, can in general prevail and make itself permanent in constant struggle with its neighbors, or with rebellious or rebellion-threatening vassals. The most varied experience teaches it what are the qualities to which it principally owes the fact that it still exists, in spite of all Gods and men, and has hitherto been victorious: these qualities it calls virtues, and these virtues alone it develops to maturity. It does so with severity, indeed it desires severity; every aristocratic morality is intolerant in the education of youth, in the control of women, in the marriage customs, in the relations of old and young, in the penal laws (which have an eye only for the degenerating): it counts intolerance itself among the virtues, under the name of "justice."

A type with few, but very marked features, a species of severe, warlike, wisely silent, reserved, and reticent men (and as such, with the most delicate sensibility for the charm and nuances of society) is thus established, unaffected by the vicissitudes of generations; the constant struggle with uniform *unfavorable* conditions is, as already remarked, the cause of a type becoming stable and hard.

Finally, however, a happy state of things results, the enormous tension is relaxed; there are perhaps no more enemies among the neighboring peoples, and the means of life, even of the enjoyment of life, are present in superabundance. With one stroke the bond and constraint of the old discipline severs: it is no longer regarded as necessary, as a condition of existence—if it would continue, it can only do so as a form of *luxury*, as an archaizing *taste*. Variations, whether they be deviations (into the higher, finer, and rarer), or deteriorations and monstrosities, appear suddenly on the scene in the greatest exuberance and splendor; the individual dares to be individual and detach himself.

At this turning-point of history there manifest themselves, side by side, and often mixed and entangled together, a magnificent, manifold, virgin-forest-like up-growth and up-striving, a kind of *tropical tempo* in the rivalry of growth, and an extraordinary decay and self-destruction, owing to the savagely opposing and seemingly exploding egoisms, which strive with one another "for sun and light," and can no longer assign any limit, restraint, or forbearance for themselves by means of the hitherto existing morality. It was this morality itself which piled up the strength so enormously, which bent the bow in so threatening a manner:—it is now "out of date," it is getting "out of date." The dangerous and disquieting point has been reached when the greater, more manifold, more comprehensive life *is lived beyond* the old morality; the "individual" stands out, and is obliged to have recourse to his own law-giving, his own arts and artifices for self-preservation, self-elevation, and self-deliverance.

Nothing but new "Whys," nothing but new "Hows," no common formulas any longer, misunderstanding and disregard in league with each other, decay, deterioration, and the loftiest desires frightfully entangled, the genius of the race overflowing from all the cornucopias of good and bad, a portentous simultaneousness of Spring and Autumn, full of new charms and mysteries peculiar to the fresh, still inexhausted, still unwearied corruption. Danger is again present, the mother of morality, great danger; this time shifted into the individual, into the neighbor and friend, into the street, into their own child, into their own heart, into all the most personal and secret recesses of their desires and volitions. What will the moral philosophers who appear at this time have to preach?

They discover, these sharp onlookers and loafers, that the end is quickly approaching, that everything around them decays and produces decay, that nothing will endure until the day after tomorrow, except one species of man, the incurably *mediocre*. The mediocre alone have a prospect of continuing and propagating themselves—they will be the men of the future, the sole survivors; "be like them! become mediocre!" is now the only morality which has still a significance, which still obtains a hearing.

But it is difficult to preach this morality of mediocrity! it can never avow what it is and what it desires! it has to talk of moderation and dignity and duty and brotherly love—it will have difficulty *in concealing its irony!*

263

There is an *instinct for rank*, which more than anything else is already the sign of a *high* rank; there is a *delight* in the *nuances* of reverence which leads one to infer noble origin and habits. The refinement, goodness, and loftiness of a soul are put to a perilous test when something passes by that is of the highest rank, but is not yet protected by the awe of authority from obtrusive touches and incivilities: something that goes its way like a living touchstone, undistinguished, undiscovered, and tentative, perhaps voluntarily veiled and disguised. He whose task and practice it is to investigate souls, will avail himself of many varieties of this very art to determine the ultimate value of a soul, the unalterable, innate order of rank to which it belongs: he will test it by its *instinct for reverence*.

Différence engendre haine: the vulgarity of many a nature spurts up suddenly like dirty water, when any holy vessel, any jewel from closed shrines, any book bearing the marks of great destiny, is brought before it; while on the other hand, there is an involuntary silence, a hesitation of the eye, a cessation of all gestures, by which it is indicated that a soul *feels* the nearness of what is worthiest of respect. The way in which, on the whole, the reverence for the *Bible* has hitherto been maintained in Europe, is perhaps the best example of discipline and refinement of manners which Europe owes to Christianity: books of such profoundness and supreme significance require for their protection an external tyranny of authority, in order to acquire the *period* of thousands of years which is necessary to exhaust and unriddle them.

Much has been achieved when the sentiment has been at last instilled into the masses (the shallow-pates and the boobies of every kind) that they are not allowed to touch everything, that there are holy experiences before which they must take off their shoes and keep away the unclean hand—it is almost their highest advance towards humanity. On the contrary, in the so-called cultured classes, the believers in "modern ideas," nothing is perhaps so repulsive as their lack of shame, the easy insolence of eye and hand with which they touch, taste, and finger everything; and it is possible that even yet there is more *relative* nobility of taste, and more tact for reverence among the people, among the lower classes of the people, especially among peasants, than among the newspaper-reading *demimonde* of intellect, the cultured class.

264

It cannot be effaced from a man's soul what his ancestors have preferably and most constantly done: whether they were perhaps diligent economizers attached to a desk and a cash-box, modest and citizen-like in their desires, modest also in their virtues; or whether they were accustomed to commanding from morning till night, fond of rude pleasures and probably of still ruder duties and responsibilities; or whether, finally, at one time or another, they have sacrificed old privileges of birth and possession, in order to live wholly for their faith—for their "God,"—as men of an inexorable and sensitive conscience, which blushes at every compromise. It is quite impossible for a man *not* to have the qualities and predilections of his parents and ancestors in his constitution, whatever appearances may suggest to the contrary. This is the problem of race.

Granted that one knows something of the parents, it is admissible to draw a conclusion about the child: any kind of offensive incontinence, any kind of sordid envy, or of clumsy self-vaunting—the three things which together have constituted the genuine plebeian type in all times—such must pass over to the child, as surely as bad blood; and with the help of the best education and culture one will only succeed in *deceiving* with regard to such heredity.

And what else does education and culture try to do nowadays! In our very democratic, or rather, very plebeian age, "education" and "culture" *must* be essentially the art of deceiving—deceiving with regard to origin, with regard to the inherited plebeianism in body and soul. An educator who nowadays preached truthfulness above everything else, and called out constantly to his pupils: "Be true! Be natural! Show yourselves as you are!"—even such a virtuous and sincere ass would learn in a short time to have recourse to the *furca* of Horace, *naturam expellere*: with what results? "Plebeianism" *usque recurret.*[6]

<h2 style="text-align:center">265</h2>

At the risk of displeasing innocent ears, I submit that egoism belongs to the essence of a noble soul, I mean the unalterable belief that to a being such as "we," other beings must naturally be in subjection, and have to sacrifice themselves. The noble soul accepts the fact of his egoism without question, and also without consciousness of harshness, constraint, or arbitrariness therein, but rather as something that may have its basis in the primary law of things:—if he sought a designation for it he would say: "It is justice itself." He acknowledges under certain circumstances, which made him hesitate at first, that there are other equally privileged ones; as soon as he has settled this question of rank, he moves among those equals and equally privileged ones with the same assurance, as regards modesty and delicate respect, which he enjoys in intercourse with himself—in accordance with an innate heavenly mechanism which all the stars understand. It is an *additional* instance of his egoism, this artfulness and self-limitation in intercourse with his equals—every star is a similar egoist; he honors *himself* in them, and in the rights which he concedes to them, he has no doubt that the exchange of honors and rights, as the *essence* of all intercourse, belongs also to the natural condition of things.

The noble soul gives as he takes, prompted by the passionate and sensitive instinct of requital, which is at the root of his nature. The notion of "favor" has*, inter pares,* neither significance nor good repute; there may be a sublime way of letting gifts as it were light upon one from above, and of drinking them thirstily like dew-drops; but for those arts and displays the noble soul has no aptitude.

---

6 Horace's *Epistles,* I. x. 24

His egoism hinders him here: in general, he looks "aloft" unwillingly—he looks either *forward*, horizontally and deliberately, or downwards—*he knows that he is on a height.*

266

"One can only truly esteem him who does not *look out for* himself."— Goethe to Rath Schlosser.

267

The Chinese have a proverb which mothers even teach their children: "*siao-sin*" ("*Make thy heart small*"). This is the essentially fundamental tendency in latter-day civilizations. I have no doubt that an ancient Greek, also, would first of all remark the self-dwarfing in us Europeans of today—in this respect alone we should immediately be "distasteful" to him.

268

What, after all, is ignobleness?

Words are vocal symbols for ideas; ideas, however, are more or less definite mental symbols for frequently returning and concurring sensations, for groups of sensations. It is not sufficient to use the same words in order to understand one another: we must also employ the same words for the same kind of internal experiences, we must in the end have experiences *in common.*

On this account the people of one nation understand one another better than those belonging to different nations, even when they use the same language; or rather, when people have lived long together under similar conditions (of climate, soil, danger, requirement, toil) there *originates* therefrom an entity that "understands itself"—namely, a nation. In all souls a like number of frequently recurring experiences have gained the upper hand over those occurring more rarely: about these matters people understand one another rapidly and always more rapidly—the history of language is the history of a process of abbreviation;

on the basis of this quick comprehension people always unite closer and closer.

The greater the danger, the greater is the need of agreeing quickly and readily about what is necessary; not to misunderstand one another in danger—that is what cannot at all be dispensed with in intercourse. Also in all loves and friendships one has the experience that nothing of the kind continues when the discovery has been made that in using the same words, one of the two parties has feelings, thoughts, intuitions, wishes, or fears different from those of the other. (The fear of the "eternal misunderstanding": that is the good genius which so often keeps persons of different sexes from too hasty attachments, to which sense and heart prompt them—and *not* some Schopenhauerian "genius of the species"!)

Whichever groups of sensations within a soul awaken most readily, begin to speak, and give the word of command—these decide as to the general order of rank of its values, and determine ultimately its list of desirable things. A man's estimates of value betray something of the *structure* of his soul, and wherein it sees its conditions of life, its intrinsic needs.

Supposing now that necessity has from all time drawn together only such men as could express similar requirements and similar experiences by similar symbols, it results on the whole that the easy *communicability* of need, which implies ultimately the undergoing only of average and *common* experiences, must have been the most potent of all the forces which have hitherto operated upon mankind. The more similar, the more ordinary people, have always had and are still having the advantage; the more select, more refined, more unique, and difficultly comprehensible, are liable to stand alone; they succumb to accidents in their isolation, and seldom propagate themselves. One must appeal to immense opposing forces, in order to thwart this natural, all-too-natural *progressus in simile*, the evolution of man to the similar, the ordinary, the average, the gregarious—to the *ignoble*—!

269

The more a psychologist—a born, an unavoidable psychologist and soul-diviner—turns his attention to the more select cases and individuals, the greater is his danger of being suffocated by sympathy: he *needs* sternness and cheerfulness more than any other man. For the corruption, the ruination of higher men, of the more unusually constituted souls, is in fact, the rule: it is dreadful to have such a rule always before one's eyes. The manifold torment of the psychologist who has discovered this ruination, who discovers once, and then discovers *almost* repeatedly throughout all history, this universal inner "desperateness" of higher men, this eternal "too late!" in every sense—may perhaps one day be the cause of his turning with bitterness against his own lot, and of his making an attempt at self-destruction—of his "going to ruin" himself.

One may perceive in almost every psychologist a tell-tale inclination for delightful intercourse with commonplace and well-ordered men; the fact is thereby disclosed that he always requires healing, that he needs a sort of flight and forgetfulness, away from what his insight and incisiveness—from what his "business"—has laid upon his conscience. The fear of his memory is peculiar to him. He is easily silenced by the judgment of others; he hears with unmoved countenance how people honor, admire, love, and glorify, where he has *perceived*—or he even conceals his silence by expressly assenting to some plausible opinion. Perhaps the paradox of his situation becomes so dreadful that, precisely where he has learnt *great sympathy*, together with great *contempt*, the multitude, the educated, and the visionaries, have on their part learnt great reverence—reverence for "great men" and marvelous animals, for the sake of whom one blesses and honors the fatherland, the earth, the dignity of mankind, and one's own self, to whom one points the young, and in view of whom one educates them.

And who knows but in all great instances hitherto just the same happened: that the multitude worshipped a God, and that the "God" was only a poor sacrificial animal! *success* has always been the greatest liar—and the "work" itself is a success; the great statesman, the conqueror, the discoverer, are disguised in their creations until they are unrecognizable; the "work" of the artist, of the philosopher, only invents him who has created it, is *reputed* to have created it; the "great men," as they are reverenced, are poor little fictions composed afterwards; in the world of historical values spurious coinage *prevails*.

Those great poets, for example, such as Byron, Musset, Poe, Leopardi, Kleist, Gogol (I do not venture to mention much greater names, but I have them in my mind), as they now appear, and were perhaps obliged to be: men of the moment, enthusiastic, sensuous, and childish, light-minded and impulsive in their trust and distrust; with souls in which usually some flaw has to be concealed; often taking revenge with their works for an internal defilement, often seeking forgetfulness in their soaring from a too true memory, often lost in the mud and almost in love with it, until they become like the Will-o'-the-Wisps around the swamps, and *pretend to be* stars—the people then call them idealists,—often struggling with protracted disgust, with an ever-reappearing phantom of disbelief, which makes them cold, and obliges them to languish for *gloria* and devour "faith as it is" out of the hands of intoxicated adulators:—what a *torment* these great artists are and the so-called higher men in general, to him who has once found them out!

It is thus conceivable that it is just from woman—who is clairvoyant in the world of suffering, and also unfortunately eager to help and save to an extent far beyond her powers—that *they* have learnt so readily those outbreaks of boundless devoted *sympathy*, which the multitude, above all the reverent multitude, do not understand, and overwhelm with prying and self-gratifying interpretations. This sympathizing invariably deceives itself as to its power; woman would like to believe that love can do *everything*—it is the *superstition* peculiar to her. Alas, he who knows the heart finds out how poor, helpless, pretentious, and blundering even the best and deepest love is—he finds that it rather *destroys* than saves!

It is possible that under the holy fable and travesty of the life of Jesus there is hidden one of the most painful cases of the martyrdom of *knowledge about love*: the martyrdom of the most innocent and most craving heart, that never had enough of any human love, that *demanded* love, that demanded inexorably and frantically to be loved and nothing else, with terrible outbursts against those who refused him their love; the story of a poor soul insatiated and insatiable in love, that had to invent hell to send thither those who *would not* love him—and that at last, enlightened about human love, had to invent a God who is entire love, entire *capacity* for love—who takes pity on human love, because it is so paltry, so ignorant! He who has such sentiments, he who has such *knowledge* about love—*seeks* for death!

But why should one deal with such painful matters? Provided, of course, that one is not obliged to do so.

270

The intellectual haughtiness and loathing of every man who has suffered deeply—it almost determines the order of rank *how* deeply men can suffer—the chilling certainty, with which he is thoroughly imbued and colored, that by virtue of his suffering he *knows more* than the shrewdest and wisest can ever know, that he has been familiar with, and "at home" in, many distant, dreadful worlds of which "*you* know nothing"!—this silent intellectual haughtiness of the sufferer, this pride of the elect of knowledge, of the "initiated," of the almost sacrificed, finds all forms of disguise necessary to protect itself from contact with officious and sympathizing hands, and in general from all that is not its equal in suffering. Profound suffering makes noble: it separates.

One of the most refined forms of disguise is Epicurism, along with a certain ostentatious boldness of taste, which takes suffering lightly, and puts itself on the defensive against all that is sorrowful and profound. They are "gay men" who make use of gaiety, because they are misunderstood on account of it— they *wish* to be misunderstood. There are "scientific minds" who make use of science, because it gives a gay appearance, and because scientificness leads to the conclusion that a person is superficial—they *wish* to mislead to a false conclusion. There are free insolent minds which would fain conceal and deny that they are broken, proud, incurable hearts (the cynicism of Hamlet—the case of Galiani); and occasionally folly itself is the mask of an unfortunate *over-assured* knowledge.

From which it follows that it is the part of a more refined humanity to have reverence "for the mask," and not to make use of psychology and curiosity in the wrong place.

271

That which separates two men most profoundly is a different sense and grade of purity. What does it matter about all their honesty and reciprocal usefulness, what does it matter about all their mutual good-will: the fact still remains—they "cannot smell each other!"

The highest instinct for purity places him who is affected with it in the most extraordinary and dangerous isolation, as a saint: for it is just holiness—the highest spiritualization of the instinct in question. Any kind of cognizance of an indescribable excess in the joy of the bath, any kind of ardor or thirst which perpetually impels the soul out of night into the morning, and out of gloom, out of "affliction" into clearness, brightness, depth, and refinement:—just as much as such a tendency *distinguishes*—it is a noble tendency—it also *separates*.

The pity of the saint is pity for the *filth* of the human, all-too-human. And there are grades and heights where pity itself is regarded by him as impurity, as filth.

272

Signs of nobility: never to think of lowering our duties to the rank of duties for everybody; to be unwilling to renounce or to share our responsibilities; to count our prerogatives, and the exercise of them, among our *duties*.

273

A man who strives after great things, looks upon every one whom he encounters on his way either as a means of advance, or a delay and hindrance—or as a temporary resting-place. His peculiar lofty *bounty* to his fellow-men is only possible when he attains his elevation and dominates. Impatience, and the consciousness of being always condemned to comedy up to that time—for even strife is a comedy, and conceals the end, as every means does—spoil all intercourse for him; this kind of man is acquainted with solitude, and what is most poisonous in it.

274

The problem of those who wait.—Happy chances are necessary, and many incalculable elements, in order that a higher man in whom the solution of a problem is dormant, may yet take action, or "break forth," as one might say—at the right moment. On an average it *does not* happen; and in all corners of the earth there are waiting ones sitting who hardly know to what extent they are waiting, and still less that they wait in vain. Occasionally, too, the waking call comes too late—the chance which gives "permission" to take action—when their best youth, and strength for action have been used up in sitting still; and how many a one, just as he "sprang up," has found with horror that his limbs are benumbed and his spirits are now too heavy! "It is too late," he has said to himself—and has become self-distrustful and henceforth forever useless.

In the domain of genius, may not the "Raphael without hands" (taking the expression in its widest sense) perhaps not be the exception, but the rule?

Perhaps genius is by no means so rare: but rather the five hundred *hands* which it requires in order to tyrannize over the *kairos*, "the right time"—in order to take chance by the forelock!

275

He who does not *wish* to see the height of a man, looks all the more sharply at what is low in him, and in the foreground—and thereby betrays himself.

276

In all kinds of injury and loss the lower and coarser soul is better off than the nobler soul: the dangers of the latter must be greater, the probability that it will come to grief and perish is in fact immense, considering the multiplicity of the conditions of its existence.

In a lizard a finger grows again which has been lost; not so in man.—

277

It is too bad! Always the old story! When a man has finished building his house, he finds that he has learnt unawares something which he *ought* absolutely to have known before he—began to build. The eternal, fatal "Too late!"

The melancholia of everything *completed!*—

278

Wanderer, who art thou? I see thee follow thy path without scorn, without love, with unfathomable eyes, wet and sad as a plummet which has returned to the light insatiated out of every depth—what did it seek down there?—with a bosom that never sighs, with lips that conceal their loathing, with a hand which only slowly grasps: who art thou? what hast thou done? Rest thee here: this place has hospitality for every one—refresh thyself! And whoever thou art, what is it that now pleases thee? What will serve to refresh thee? Only name it, whatever I have I offer thee!

"To refresh me? To refresh me? Oh, thou prying one, what sayest thou! But give me, I pray thee—"

What? what? Speak out!

"Another mask! A second mask!"

279

Men of profound sadness betray themselves when they are happy: they have a mode of seizing upon happiness as though they would choke and strangle it, out of jealousy—ah, they know only too well that it will flee from them!

280

"Bad! Bad! What? Does he not—go back?" Yes! But you misunderstand him when you complain about it. He goes back like everyone who is about to make a great spring.

281

—"Will people believe it of me? But I insist that they believe it of me: I have always thought very unsatisfactorily of myself and about myself, only in very rare cases, only compulsorily, always without delight in 'the subject,' ready to digress from 'myself,' and always without faith in the result, owing to an unconquerable distrust of the *possibility* of self-knowledge, which has led me so far as to feel a *contradictio in adjecto* even in the idea of 'direct knowledge' which theorists allow themselves:—this matter of fact is almost the most certain thing I know about myself. There must be a sort of repugnance in me to *believe* anything definite about myself.

Is there perhaps some enigma therein? Probably; but fortunately nothing for my own teeth.

Perhaps it betrays the species to which I belong?—but not to myself, as is sufficiently agreeable to me."

282

—"But what has happened to you?"

"I do not know," he said, hesitatingly; "perhaps the Harpies have flown over my table."

It sometimes happens nowadays that a gentle, sober, retiring man becomes suddenly mad, breaks the plates, upsets the table, shrieks, raves, and shocks everybody—and finally withdraws, ashamed, and raging at himself—whither? for what purpose? To famish apart? To suffocate with his memories?

To him who has the desires of a lofty and dainty soul, and only seldom finds his table laid and his food prepared, the danger will always be great—nowadays, however, it is extraordinarily so. Thrown into the midst of a noisy and plebeian age, with which he does not like to eat out of the same dish, he may readily perish of hunger and thirst—or, should he nevertheless finally "fall to," of sudden nausea.

We have probably all sat at tables to which we did not belong; and precisely the most spiritual of us, who are most difficult to nourish, know the dangerous *dyspepsia* which originates from a sudden insight and disillusionment about our food and our messmates—the *after-dinner nausea*.

283

If one wishes to praise at all, it is a delicate and at the same time a noble self-control, to praise only where one *does not* agree—otherwise in fact one would praise oneself, which is contrary to good taste:—a self-control, to be sure, which offers excellent opportunity and provocation to constant *misunderstanding.* To be able to allow oneself this veritable luxury of taste and morality, one must not live among intellectual imbeciles, but rather among men whose misunderstandings and mistakes amuse by their refinement—or one will have to pay dearly for it!

"He praises me, *therefore* he acknowledges me to be right"—this asinine method of inference spoils half of the life of us recluses, for it brings the asses into our neighborhood and friendship.

284

To live in a vast and proud tranquility; always beyond... To have, or not to have, one's emotions, one's For and Against, according to choice; to lower oneself to them for hours; to *seat* oneself on them as upon horses, and often as upon asses:—for one must know how to make use of their stupidity as well as of their fire. To conserve one's three hundred foregrounds; also one's black spectacles: for there are circumstances when nobody must look into our eyes, still less into our "motives." And to choose for company that roguish and cheerful vice, politeness. And to remain master of one's four virtues, courage, insight, sympathy, and solitude. For solitude is a virtue with us, as a sublime bent and bias to purity, which divines that in the contact of man and man—"in society"—it must be unavoidably impure. All society makes one somehow, somewhere, or sometime—"commonplace."

285

The greatest events and thoughts—the greatest thoughts, however, are the greatest events—are longest in being comprehended: the generations which are contemporary with them do not *experience* such events—they live past them.

Something happens there as in the realm of stars. The light of the furthest stars is longest in reaching man; and before it has arrived man *denies*—that there are stars there. "How many centuries does a mind require to be understood?"—that is also a standard, one also makes a gradation of rank and an etiquette therewith, such as is necessary for mind and for star.

286

"Here is the prospect free, the mind exalted."[7]

But there is a reverse kind of man, who is also upon a height, and has also a free prospect—but looks *downwards*.

287

—What is noble? What does the word "noble" still mean for us nowadays? How does the noble man betray himself, how is he recognized under this heavy overcast sky of the commencing plebeianism, by which everything is rendered opaque and leaden?

It is not his actions which establish his claim—actions are always ambiguous, always inscrutable; neither is it his "works." One finds nowadays among artists and scholars plenty of those who betray by their works that a profound longing for nobleness impels them; but this very *need* of nobleness is radically different from the needs of the noble soul itself, and is in fact the eloquent and dangerous sign of the lack thereof. It is not the works, but the *belief* which is here decisive and determines the order of rank—to employ once more an old religious formula with a new and deeper meaning—it is some fundamental certainty which a noble soul has about itself, something which is not to be sought, is not to be found, and perhaps, also, is not to be lost.

The noble soul has reverence for itself.—

---

7 Goethe's *Faust*, Part II, Act V. The words of Dr. Marianus.

288

There are men who are unavoidably intellectual, let them turn and twist themselves as they will, and hold their hands before their treacherous eyes—as though the hand were not a betrayer; it always comes out at last that they have something which they hide—namely, intellect. One of the subtlest means of deceiving, at least as long as possible, and of successfully representing oneself to be stupider than one really is—which in everyday life is often as desirable as an umbrella,—is called *enthusiasm*, including what belongs to it, for instance, virtue. For as Galiani said, who was obliged to know it: *vertu est enthousiasme.*

289

In the writings of a recluse one always hears something of the echo of the wilderness, something of the murmuring tones and timid vigilance of solitude; in his strongest words, even in his cry itself, there sounds a new and more dangerous kind of silence, of concealment. He who has sat day and night, from year's end to year's end, alone with his soul in familiar discord and discourse, he who has become a cave-bear, or a treasure-seeker, or a treasure-guardian and dragon in his cave—it may be a labyrinth, but can also be a gold-mine—his ideas themselves eventually acquire a twilight-color of their own, and an odor, as much of the depth as of the mold, something uncommunicative and repulsive, which blows chilly upon every passer-by.

The recluse does not believe that a philosopher—supposing that a philosopher has always in the first place been a recluse—ever expressed his actual and ultimate opinions in books: are not books written precisely to hide what is in us?—indeed, he will doubt whether a philosopher *can* have "ultimate and actual" opinions at all; whether behind every cave in him there is not, and must necessarily be, a still deeper cave: an ampler, stranger, richer world beyond the surface, an abyss behind every bottom, beneath every "foundation." Every philosophy is a foreground philosophy—this is a recluse's verdict: "There is something arbitrary in the fact that the *philosopher* came to a stand here, took a retrospect, and looked around; that he *here* laid his spade aside and did not dig any deeper—there is also something suspicious in it." Every philosophy also *conceals* a philosophy; every opinion is also a *lurking-place*, every word is also a *mask*.

290

Every deep thinker is more afraid of being understood than of being misunderstood. The latter perhaps wounds his vanity; but the former wounds his heart, his sympathy, which always says: "Ah, why would you also have as hard a time of it as I have?"

291

Man, a *complex*, mendacious, artful, and inscrutable animal, uncanny to the other animals by his artifice and sagacity, rather than by his strength, has invented the good conscience in order finally to enjoy his soul as something *simple*; and the whole of morality is a long, audacious falsification, by virtue of which generally enjoyment at the sight of the soul becomes possible. From this point of view there is perhaps much more in the conception of "art" than is generally believed.

292

A philosopher: that is a man who constantly experiences, sees, hears, suspects, hopes, and dreams extraordinary things; who is struck by his own thoughts as if they came from the outside, from above and below, as a species of events and lightning-flashes *peculiar to him*; who is perhaps himself a storm pregnant with new lightnings; a portentous man, around whom there is always rumbling and mumbling and gaping and something uncanny going on. A philosopher: alas, a being who often runs away from himself, is often afraid of himself—but whose curiosity always makes him "come to himself" again.

293

A man who says: "I like that, I take it for my own, and mean to guard and protect it from every one"; a man who can conduct a case, carry out a resolution, remain true to an opinion, keep hold of a woman, punish and overthrow insolence; a man who has his indignation and his sword, and to whom the weak, the suffering, the oppressed, and even the animals willingly submit and naturally belong; in short, a man who is a *master* by nature—when such a man has sympathy, well! *that* sympathy has value! But of what account is the sympathy of those who suffer! Or of those even who preach sympathy!

There is nowadays, throughout almost the whole of Europe, a sickly irritability and sensitiveness towards pain, and also a repulsive irrestrainableness in complaining, an effeminizing, which, with the aid of religion and philosophical nonsense, seeks to deck itself out as something superior—there is a regular cult of suffering. The *unmanliness* of that which is called "sympathy" by such groups of visionaries, is always, I believe, the first thing that strikes the eye.

One must resolutely and radically taboo this latest form of bad taste; and finally I wish people to put the good amulet, "*gai saber*" ("gay science," in ordinary language), on heart and neck, as a protection against it.

294

The Olympian vice.—Despite the philosopher who, as a genuine Englishman, tried to bring laughter into bad repute in all thinking minds— "Laughing is a bad infirmity of human nature, which every thinking mind will strive to overcome" (Hobbes),—I would even allow myself to rank philosophers according to the quality of their laughing—up to those who are capable of *golden* laughter. And supposing that Gods also philosophize, which I am strongly inclined to believe, owing to many reasons—I have no doubt that they also know how to laugh thereby in an overman-like and new fashion—and at the expense of all serious things! Gods are fond of ridicule: it seems that they cannot refrain from laughter even in holy matters.

295

The genius of the heart, as that great mysterious one possesses it, the tempter-god and born rat-catcher of consciences, whose voice can descend into the nether-world of every soul, who neither speaks a word nor casts a glance in which there may not be some motive or touch of allurement, to whose perfection it pertains that he knows how to appear,—not as he is, but in a guise which acts as an *additional* constraint on his followers to press ever closer to him, to follow him more cordially and thoroughly;—the genius of the heart, which imposes silence and attention on everything loud and self-conceited, which smooths rough souls and makes them taste a new longing—to lie placid as a mirror, that the deep heavens may be reflected in them;—the genius of the heart, which teaches the clumsy and too hasty hand to hesitate, and to grasp more delicately; which scents the hidden and forgotten treasure, the drop of goodness and sweet spirituality under thick dark ice, and is a divining-rod for every grain of gold, long buried and imprisoned in mud and sand; the genius of the heart, from contact with which everyone goes away richer; not favored or surprised, not as though gratified and oppressed by the good things of others; but richer in himself, newer than before, broken up, blown upon, and sounded by a thawing wind; more uncertain, perhaps, more delicate, more fragile, more bruised, but full of hopes which as yet lack names, full of a new will and current, full of a new ill-will and counter-current... but what am I doing, my friends?

Of whom am I talking to you? Have I forgotten myself so far that I have not even told you his name? Unless it be that you have already divined of your own accord who this questionable God and spirit is, that wishes to be *praised* in such a manner? For, as it happens to everyone who from childhood onward has always been on his legs, and in foreign lands, I have also encountered on my path many strange and dangerous spirits; above all, however, and again and again, the one of whom I have just spoken: in fact, no less a personage than the God *Dionysus*, the great equivocator and tempter, to whom, as you know, I once offered in all secrecy and reverence my first-fruits—the last, as it seems to me, who has offered a *sacrifice* to him, for I have found no one who could understand what I was then doing.

In the meantime, however, I have learned much, far too much, about the philosophy of this God, and, as I said, from mouth to mouth—I, the last disciple and initiate of the God Dionysus: and perhaps I might at last begin to give you, my friends, as far as I am allowed, a little taste of this philosophy? In a hushed voice, as is but seemly: for it has to do with much that is secret, new, strange, wonderful, and uncanny.

The very fact that Dionysus is a philosopher, and that therefore gods also philosophize, seems to me a novelty which is not unensnaring, and might perhaps arouse suspicion precisely among philosophers;—among you, my friends, there is less to be said against it, except that it comes too late and not at the right time; for, as it has been disclosed to me, you are loth nowadays to believe in God and gods. It may happen, too, that in the frankness of my story I must go further than is agreeable to the strict usages of your ears? Certainly the God in question went further, very much further, in such dialogues, and was always many paces ahead of me...

Indeed, if it were allowed, I should have to give him, according to human usage, fine ceremonious tides of luster and merit, I should have to extol his courage as investigator and discoverer, his fearless honesty, truthfulness, and love of wisdom. But such a God does not know what to do with all that respectable trumpery and pomp. "Keep that," he would say, "for thyself and those like thee, and whoever else require it! I—have no reason to cover my nakedness!"

One suspects that this kind of divinity and philosopher perhaps lacks shame?

He once said: "Under certain circumstances I love mankind"—and referred thereby to Ariadne, who was present; "in my opinion man is an agreeable, brave, inventive animal, that has not his equal upon earth, he makes his way even through all labyrinths. I like man, and often think how I can still further advance him, and make him stronger, more evil, and more profound."

"Stronger, more evil, and more profound?" I asked in horror. "Yes," he said again, "stronger, more evil, and more profound; also more beautiful"—and thereby the tempter-god smiled with his halcyon smile, as though he had just paid some charming compliment. One here sees at once that it is not only shame that this divinity lacks;—and in general there are good grounds for supposing that in some things the Gods could all of them come to us men for instruction. We men are—more human.—

296

Alas! what are you, after all, my written and painted thoughts! Not long ago you were so variegated, young and malicious, so full of thorns and secret spices, that you made me sneeze and laugh—and now? You have already doffed your novelty, and some of you, I fear, are ready to become truths, so immortal do they look, so pathetically honest, so tedious! And was it ever otherwise? What then do we write and paint, we mandarins with Chinese brush, we immortalizers of things which *lend* themselves to writing, what are we alone capable of painting? Alas, only that which is just about to fade and begins to lose its odor! Alas, only exhausted and departing storms and belated yellow sentiments! Alas, only birds strayed and fatigued by flight, which now let themselves be captured with the hand—with *our* hand! We immortalize what cannot live and fly much longer, things only which are exhausted and mellow! And it is only for your *afternoon*, you, my written and painted thoughts, for which alone I have colors, many colors, perhaps, many variegated softenings, and fifty yellows and browns and greens and reds;—but nobody will divine thereby how ye looked in your morning, you sudden sparks and marvels of my solitude, you, my old, beloved—*evil* thoughts!

From The Heights

Translated by L.A. Magnus

1

Midday of Life! Oh, season of delight!
            My summer's park!
Uneaseful joy to look, to lurk, to hark—
I peer for friends, am ready day and night,—
Where linger ye, my friends? The time is right!

2

Is not the glacier's grey today for you
            Rose-garlanded?
The brooklet seeks you, wind, cloud, with longing thread
And thrust themselves yet higher to the blue,
To spy for you from farthest eagle's view.

3

My table was spread out for you on high—
            Who dwelleth so
Star-near, so near the grisly pit below?—
My realm—what realm hath wider boundary?
My honey—who hath sipped its fragrancy?

4

Friends, ye are there! Woe me,—yet I am not
            He whom ye seek?
Ye stare and stop—better your wrath could speak!
I am not I? Hand, gait, face, changed?
And what I am, to you my friends, now am I not?

5

Am I an other? Strange am I to Me?
          Yet from Me sprung?
A wrestler, by himself too oft self-wrung?
Hindering too oft my own self's potency,
Wounded and hampered by self-victory?

6

I sought where-so the wind blows keenest. There
          I learned to dwell
Where no man dwells, on lonesome ice-lorn fell,
And unlearned Man and God and curse and prayer?
Became a ghost haunting the glaciers bare?

7

Ye, my old friends! Look! Ye turn pale, filled o'er
          With love and fear!
Go! Yet not in wrath. Ye could ne'er live here.
Here in the farthest realm of ice and scaur,
A huntsman must one be, like chamois soar.

8

An evil huntsman was I? See how taut
          My bow was bent!
Strongest was he by whom such bolt were sent—
Woe now! That arrow is with peril fraught,
Perilous as none.—Have yon safe home ye sought!

9

Ye go! Thou didst endure enough, oh, heart;—
      Strong was thy hope;
Unto new friends thy portals widely ope,
Let old ones be. Bid memory depart!
Wast thou young then, now—better young thou art!

10

What linked us once together, one hope's tie—
      (Who now doth con
Those lines, now fading, Love once wrote thereon?)—
Is like a parchment, which the hand is shy
To touch—like crackling leaves, all seared, all dry.

11

Oh! Friends no more! They are—what name for those?—
      Friends' phantom-flight
Knocking at my heart's window-pane at night,
Gazing on me, that speaks "We were" and goes,—
Oh, withered words, once fragrant as the rose!

12

Pinings of youth that might not understand!
      For which I pined,
Which I deemed changed with me, kin of my kind:
But they grew old, and thus were doomed and banned:
None but new kith are native of my land!

13

Midday of life! My second youth's delight!
     My summer's park!
Unrestful joy to long, to lurk, to hark!
I peer for friends!—am ready day and night,
For my new friends. Come! Come! The time is right!

14

This song is done,—the sweet sad cry of rue
     Sang out its end;
A wizard wrought it, he the timely friend,
The midday-friend,—no, do not ask me who;
At midday 'twas, when one became as two.

15

We keep our Feast of Feasts, sure of our bourne,
     Our aims self-same:
The Guest of Guests, friend Zarathustra, came!
The world now laughs, the grisly veil was torn,
And Light and Dark were one that wedding-morn.

THE GENEALOGY
OF MORALS

A Polemic

[1887]

by
Friedrich Nietzsche

Translated by Horace B. Samuel, M.A.

Editor's Note

In 1887, with the view of amplifying and completing certain new doctrines which he had merely sketched in *Beyond Good and Evil* (see especially Aphorism 260), Nietzsche published *The Genealogy of Morals*. This work is perhaps the least aphoristic, in form, of all Nietzsche's productions. For analytical power, more especially in those parts where Nietzsche examines the ascetic ideal, *The Genealogy of Morals* is unequalled by any other of his works; and, in the light which it throws upon the attitude of the ecclesiast to the man of resentment and misfortune, it is one of the most valuable contributions to sacerdotal psychology.

Preface

1

We are unknown, we knowers, ourselves to ourselves: this has its own good reason. We have never searched for ourselves—how should it then come to pass, that we should ever *find* ourselves? Rightly has it been said: "Where your treasure is, there will your heart be also." *Our* treasure is there, where stand the hives of our knowledge. It is to those hives that we are always striving; as born creatures of flight, and as the honey-gatherers of the spirit, we care really in our hearts only for one thing—to bring something "home to the hive!"

As far as the rest of life with its so-called "experiences" is concerned, which of us has even sufficient serious interest? or sufficient time? In our dealings with such points of life, we are, I fear, never properly to the point; to be precise, our heart is not there, and certainly not our ear. Rather like one who, delighting in a divine distraction, or sunken in the seas of his own soul, in whose ear the clock has just thundered with all its force its twelve strokes of noon, suddenly wakes up, and asks himself, "What has in point of fact just struck?" so do we at times rub afterwards, as it were, our puzzled ears, and ask in complete astonishment and complete embarrassment, "Through what have we in point of fact just lived?" further, "Who are we in point of fact?" and count, *after they have struck,* as I have explained, all the twelve throbbing beats of the clock of our experience, of our life, of our being—ah!—and count wrong in the endeavor. Of necessity we remain strangers to ourselves, we understand ourselves not, in ourselves we are bound to be mistaken, for of us holds good to all eternity the motto, "Each one is the farthest away from himself"—as far as ourselves are concerned we are not "knowers."

2

My thoughts concerning the *genealogy* of our moral prejudices—for they constitute the issue in this polemic—have their first, bald, and provisional expression in that collection of aphorisms entitled *Human, all-too-Human, a Book for Free Minds,* the writing of which was begun in Sorrento, during a winter which allowed me to gaze over the broad and dangerous territory through which my mind had up to that time wandered. This took place in the winter of 1876-77; the thoughts themselves are older.

They were in their substance already the same thoughts which I take up again in the following treatises:—we hope that they have derived benefit from the long interval, that they have grown riper, clearer, stronger, more complete. The fact, however, that I still cling to them even now, that in the meanwhile they have always held faster by each other, have, in fact, grown out of their original shape and into each other, all this strengthens in my mind the joyous confidence that they must have been originally neither separate disconnected capricious nor sporadic phenomena, but have sprung from a common root, from a fundamental "*fiat*" of knowledge, whose empire reached to the soul's depth, and that ever grew more definite in its voice, and more definite in its demands. That is the only state of affairs that is proper in the case of a philosopher.

We have no right to be "*disconnected*"; we must neither err "disconnectedly" nor strike the truth "disconnectedly." Rather with the necessity with which a tree bears its fruit, so do our thoughts, our values, our Yes's and No's and If's and Whether's, grow connected and interrelated, mutual witnesses of *one will, one health, one kingdom, one sun*—as to whether they are to *your* taste, these fruits of ours?

But what matters that to the trees? What matters that to us, us the philosophers?

3

Owing to a scrupulosity peculiar to myself, which I confess reluctantly,—it concerns indeed *morality*,—a scrupulosity, which manifests itself in my life at such an early period, with so much spontaneity, with so chronic a persistence and so keen an opposition to environment, epoch, precedent, and ancestry that I should have been almost entitled to style it my "à priori"—my curiosity and my suspicion felt themselves betimes bound to halt at the question, of what in point of actual fact was the *origin* of our "Good" and of our "Evil." Indeed, at the boyish age of thirteen the problem of the origin of Evil already haunted me: at an age "when games and God divide one's heart," I devoted to that problem my first childish attempt at the literary game, my first philosophic essay—and as regards my infantile solution of the problem, well, I gave quite properly the honor to God, and made him the *father* of evil. Did my own "â *priori*" demand that precise solution from me? that new, immoral, or at least "amoral" "â priori" and that "categorical imperative" which was its voice (but oh! how hostile to the Kantian article, and how pregnant with problems!), to which since then I have given more and more attention, and indeed what is more than attention. Fortunately I soon learned to separate theological from moral prejudices, and I gave up looking for a *supernatural* origin of evil. A certain amount of historical and philological education, to say nothing of an innate faculty of psychological discrimination *par excellence* succeeded in transforming almost immediately my original problem into the following one:—Under what conditions did Man invent for himself those judgments of values, "Good" and "Evil"? And what intrinsic value do they possess in themselves? Have they up to the present hindered or advanced human well-being? Are they a symptom of the distress, impoverishment, and degeneration of Human Life? Or, conversely, is it in them that is manifested the fullness, the strength, and the will of Life, its courage, its self-confidence, its future? On this point I found and hazarded in my mind the most diverse answers, I established distinctions in periods, peoples, and castes, I became a specialist in my problem, and from my answers grew new questions, new investigations, new conjectures, new probabilities; until at last I had a land of my own and a soil of my own, a whole secret world growing and flowering, like hidden gardens of whose existence no one could have an inkling—oh, how happy are we, we finders of knowledge, provided that we know how to keep silent sufficiently long.

4

My first impulse to publish some of my hypotheses concerning the origin of morality I owe to a clear, well-written, and even precocious little book, in which a perverse and vicious kind of moral philosophy (your real English kind) was definitely presented to me for the first time; and this attracted me—with that magnetic attraction, inherent in that which is diametrically opposed and antithetical to one's own ideas. The title of the book was *The Origin of the*

Moral Emotions; its author, Dr. Paul Rée; the year of its appearance, 1877. I may almost say that I have never read anything in which every single dogma and conclusion has called forth from me so emphatic a negation as did that book; albeit a negation tainted by either pique or intolerance. I referred accordingly both in season and out of season in the previous works, at which I was then working, to the arguments of that book, not to refute them—for what have I got to do with mere refutations but substituting, as is natural to a positive mind, for an improbable theory one which is more probable, and occasionally no doubt, for one philosophic error, another. In that early period I gave, as I have said, the first public expression to those theories of origin to which these essays are devoted, but with a clumsiness which I was the last to conceal from myself, for I was as yet cramped, being still without a special language for these special subjects, still frequently liable to relapse and to vacillation. To go into details, compare what I say in *Human, all-too-Human*, part i., about the parallel early history of Good and Evil, Aph. 45 (namely, their origin from the castes of the aristocrats and the slaves); similarly, Aph. 136 et seq., concerning the birth and value of ascetic morality; similarly, Aphs. 96, 99, vol. ii., Aph. 89, concerning the Morality of Custom, that far older and more original kind of morality which is *toto cœlo* different from the altruistic ethics (in which Dr. Rée, like all the English moral philosophers, sees the ethical "Thing-in-itself"); finally, Aph. 92. Similarly, Aph. 26 in *Human, all-too-Human*, part ii., and Aph. 112, the *Dawn of Day*, concerning the origin of Justice as a balance between persons of approximately equal power (equilibrium as the hypothesis of all contract, consequently of all law); similarly, concerning the origin of Punishment, *Human, all-too-Human*, part ii., Aphs. 22, 23, in regard to which the deterrent object is neither essential nor original (as Dr. Rée thinks:—rather is it that this object is only imported, under certain definite conditions, and always as something extra and additional).

5

In reality I had set my heart at that time on something much more important than the nature of the theories of myself or others concerning the origin of morality (or, more precisely, the real function from my view of these theories was to point an end to which they were one among many means). The issue for me was the value of morality, and on that subject I had to place myself in a state of abstraction, in which I was almost alone with my great teacher Schopenhauer, to whom that book, with all its passion and inherent contradiction (for that book also was a polemic), turned for present help as though he were still alive. The issue was, strangely enough, the value of the "un-egoistic" instincts, the instincts of pity, self-denial, and self-sacrifice which Schopenhauer had so persistently painted in golden colors, deified and etherealized, that eventually they appeared to him, as it were, high and dry, as "intrinsic values in themselves," on the strength of which he uttered both to Life and to himself his own negation. But against *these very* instincts there voiced itself in my soul a more and more fundamental mistrust, a skepticism that dug ever deeper and deeper: and in this very instinct I saw the *great* danger of mankind, its most sublime temptation and seduction— seduction to what? to nothingness?—in these very instincts I saw the beginning of the end, stability, the exhaustion that gazes backwards, the will turning *against* Life, the last illness announcing itself with its own mincing melancholy: I realized that the morality of pity which spread wider and wider, and whose grip infected even philosophers with its disease, was the most sinister symptom of our modern European civilization; I realized that it was the route along which that civilization slid on its way to—a new Buddhism?—a European Buddhism?—*Nihilism?* This exaggerated estimation in which modern philosophers have held pity, is quite a new phenomenon: up to that time philosophers were absolutely unanimous as to the worthlessness of pity. I need only mention Plato, Spinoza, La Rochefoucauld, and Kant—four minds as mutually different as is possible, but united on one point; their contempt of pity.

6

This problem of the value of pity and of the pity-morality (I am an opponent of the modern infamous emasculation of our emotions) seems at the first blush a mere isolated problem, a note of interrogation for itself; he, however, who once halts at this problem, and learns how to put questions, will experience what I experienced:—a new and immense vista unfolds itself before him, a sense of potentiality seizes him like a vertigo, every species of doubt, mistrust, and fear springs up, the belief in morality, nay, in all morality, totters,—finally a new demand voices itself. Let us speak out this *new demand*: we need a *critique* of moral values, *the value of these values* is for the first time to be called into question—and for this purpose a knowledge is necessary of the conditions and circumstances out of which these values grew, and under which they experienced their evolution and their distortion (morality as a result, as a symptom, as a mask, as Tartuffism, as disease, as a misunderstanding; but also morality as a cause, as a remedy, as a stimulant, as a fetter, as a drug), especially as such a knowledge has neither existed up to the present time nor is even now generally desired. The value of these "values" was taken for granted as an indisputable fact, which was beyond all question. No one has, up to the present, exhibited the faintest doubt or hesitation in judging the "good man" to be of a higher value than the "evil man," of a higher value with regard specifically to human progress, utility, and prosperity generally, not forgetting the future. What? Suppose the converse were the truth! What? Suppose there lurked in the "good man" a symptom of retrogression, such as a danger, a temptation, a poison, a *narcotic*, by means of which the present *battened on the future*! More comfortable and less risky perhaps than its opposite, but also pettier, meaner! So that morality would really be saddled with the guilt, if the *maximum potentiality of the power and splendor* of the human species were never to be attained? So that really morality would be the danger of dangers?

7

Enough, that after this vista had disclosed itself to me, I myself had reason to search for learned, bold, and industrious colleagues (I am doing it even to this very day). It means traversing with new clamorous questions, and at the same time with new eyes, the immense, distant, and completely unexplored land of morality—of a morality which has actually existed and been actually lived! and is this not practically equivalent to first *discovering* that land? If, in this context, I thought, amongst others, of the aforesaid Dr. Rée, I did so because I had no doubt that from the very nature of his questions he would be compelled to have recourse to a truer method, in order to obtain his answers. Have I deceived myself on that score? I wished at all events to give a better direction of vision to an eye of such keenness, and such impartiality. I wished to direct him to the real *history of morality*, and to warn him, while there was yet time, against a world of English theories that culminated in *the blue vacuum of heaven*. Other colors, of course, rise immediately to one's mind as being a hundred times more potent than blue for a genealogy of morals:—for instance, grey, by which I mean authentic facts capable of definite proof and having actually existed, or, to put it shortly, the whole of that long hieroglyphic script (which is so hard to decipher) about the past history of human morals. This script was unknown to Dr. Rée; but he had read Darwin:—and so in his philosophy the Darwinian beast and that pink of modernity, the demure weakling and dilettante, who "bites no longer," shake hands politely in a fashion that is at least instructive, the latter exhibiting a certain facial expression of refined and good-humored indolence, tinged with a touch of pessimism and exhaustion; as if it really did not pay to take all these things—I mean moral problems—so seriously. I, on the other hand, think that there are no subjects which pay better for being taken seriously; part of this payment is, that perhaps eventually they admit of being taken gaily. This gaiety indeed, or, to use my own language, this joyful wisdom, is a payment; a payment for a protracted, brave, laborious, and burrowing seriousness, which, it goes without saying, is the attribute of but a few. But on that day on which we say from the fullness of our hearts, "Forward! our old morality too is fit material for Comedy," we shall have discovered a new plot, and a new possibility for the Dionysian drama entitled *The Soul's Fate*—and he will speedily utilize it, one can wager safely, he, the great ancient eternal dramatist of the comedy of our existence.

8

If this writing be obscure to any individual, and jar on his ears, I do not think that it is necessarily I who am to blame. It is clear enough, on the hypothesis which I presuppose, namely, that the reader has first read my previous writings and has not grudged them a certain amount of trouble: it is not, indeed, a simple matter to get really at their essence. Take, for instance, my *Zarathustra*; I allow no one to pass muster as knowing that book, unless every single word therein has at some time wrought in him a profound wound, and at some time exercised on him a profound enchantment: then and not till then can he enjoy the privilege of participating reverently in the halcyon element, from which that work is born, in its sunny brilliance, its distance, its spaciousness, its certainty. In other cases the aphoristic form produces difficulty, but this is only because this form is treated *too casually*. An aphorism properly coined and cast into its final mold is far from being "deciphered" as soon as it has been read; on the contrary, it is then that it first requires *to be expounded*—of course for that purpose an art of exposition is necessary. The third essay in this book provides an example of what is offered, of what in such cases I call exposition: an aphorism is prefixed to that essay, the essay itself is its commentary. Certainly one *quality* which nowadays has been best forgotten—and that is why it will take some time yet for my writings to become readable—is essential in order to practice reading as an art—a quality for the exercise of which it is necessary to be a cow, and under no circumstances a modern man!— rumination.

Sils-Maria, Upper Engadine
July 1887.

First Essay:
"Good and Evil," "Good and Bad"

1

Those English psychologists, who up to the present are the only philosophers who are to be thanked for any endeavor to get as far as a history of the origin of morality—these men, I say, offer us in their own personalities no paltry problem;—they even have, if I am to be quite frank about it, in their capacity of living riddles, an advantage over their books—*they themselves are interesting!* These English psychologists—what do they really mean? We always find them voluntarily or involuntarily at the same task of pushing to the front the *partie honteuse* of our inner world, and looking for the efficient, governing, and decisive principle in that precise quarter where the intellectual self-respect of the race would be the most reluctant to find it (for example, in the *vis inertiæ* of habit, or in forgetfulness, or in a blind and fortuitous mechanism and association of ideas, or in some factor that is purely passive, reflex, molecular, or fundamentally stupid)—what is the real motive power which always impels these psychologists in precisely *this* direction? Is it an instinct for human disparagement somewhat sinister, vulgar, and malignant, or perhaps incomprehensible even to itself? or perhaps a touch of pessimistic jealousy, the mistrust of disillusioned idealists who have become gloomy, poisoned, and bitter? or a petty subconscious enmity and rancor against Christianity (and Plato), that has conceivably never crossed the threshold of consciousness? or just a vicious taste for those elements of life which are bizarre, painfully paradoxical, mystical, and illogical? or, as a final alternative, a dash of each of these motives—a little vulgarity, a little gloominess, a little anti-Christianity, a little craving for the necessary piquancy?

But I am told that it is simply a case of old frigid and tedious frogs crawling and hopping around men and inside men, as if they were as thoroughly at home there, as they would be in a *swamp*.

I am opposed to this statement, nay, I do not believe it; and if, in the impossibility of knowledge, one is permitted to wish, so do I wish from my heart that just the converse metaphor should apply, and that these analysts with their psychological microscopes should be, at bottom, brave, proud, and magnanimous animals who know how to bridle both their hearts and their smarts, and have specifically trained themselves to sacrifice what is desirable to what is true, any truth in fact, even the simple, bitter, ugly, repulsive, unchristian, and immoral truths—for there are truths of that description.

2

All honor, then, to the noble spirits who would fain dominate these historians of morality. But it is certainly a pity that they lack the *historical sense* itself, that they themselves are quite deserted by all the beneficent spirits of history. The whole train of their thought runs, as was always the way of old-fashioned philosophers, on thoroughly unhistorical lines: there is no doubt on this point. The crass ineptitude of their genealogy of morals is immediately apparent when the question arises of ascertaining the origin of the idea and judgment of "good." "Man had originally," so speaks their decree, "praised and called 'good' altruistic acts from the standpoint of those on whom they were conferred, that is, those to whom they were *useful*; subsequently the origin of this praise was *forgotten*, and altruistic acts, simply because, as a sheer matter of habit, they were praised as good, came also to be felt as good—as though they contained in themselves some intrinsic goodness." The thing is obvious:— this initial derivation contains already all the typical and idiosyncratic traits of the English psychologists—we have "utility," "forgetting," "habit," and finally "error," the whole assemblage forming the basis of a system of values, on which the higher man has up to the present prided himself as though it were a kind of privilege of man in general. This pride *must* be brought low, this system of values *must* lose its values: is that attained?

Now the first argument that comes ready to my hand is that the real homestead of the concept "good" is sought and located in the wrong place: the judgment "good" did not originate among those to whom goodness was shown. Much rather has it been the good themselves, that is, the aristocratic, the powerful, the high-stationed, the high-minded, who have felt that they themselves were good, and that their actions were good, that is to say of the first order, in contradistinction to all the low, the low-minded, the vulgar, and the plebeian. It was out of this pathos of distance that they first arrogated the right to create values for their own profit, and to coin the names of such values: what had they to do with utility? The standpoint of utility is as alien and as inapplicable as it could possibly be, when we have to deal with so volcanic an effervescence of supreme values, creating and demarcating as they do a hierarchy within themselves: it is at this juncture that one arrives at an appreciation of the contrast to that tepid temperature, which is the presupposition on which every combination of worldly wisdom and every calculation of practical expediency is always based—and not for one occasional, not for one exceptional instance, but chronically. The pathos of nobility and distance, as I have said, the chronic and despotic *esprit de corps* and fundamental instinct of a higher dominant race coming into association with a meaner race, an "under race," this is the origin of the antithesis of good and bad.

(The masters' right of giving names goes so far that it is permissible to look upon language itself as the expression of the power of the masters: they say "this *is* that, and that," they seal finally every object and every event with a sound, and thereby at the same time take possession of it.) It is because of this origin that the word "good" is far from having any necessary connection with altruistic acts, in accordance with the superstitious belief of these moral philosophers. On the contrary, it is on the occasion of the *decay* of aristocratic values, that the antitheses between "egoistic" and "altruistic" presses more and more heavily on the human conscience—it is, to use my own language, the *herd instinct* which finds in this antithesis an expression in many ways. And even then it takes a considerable time for this instinct to become sufficiently dominant, for the valuation to be inextricably dependent on this antithesis (as is the case in contemporary Europe); for to-day that prejudice is predominant, which, acting even now with all the intensity of an obsession and brain disease, holds that "moral," "altruistic," and "*désintéressé*" are concepts of equal value.

3

In the second place, quite apart from the fact that this hypothesis as to the genesis of the value "good" cannot be historically upheld, it suffers from an inherent psychological contradiction. The utility of altruistic conduct has presumably been the origin of its being praised, and this origin has become *forgotten.*—But in what conceivable way is this forgetting *possible*? Has perchance the utility of such conduct ceased at some given moment? The contrary is the case. This utility has rather been experienced every day at all times, and is consequently a feature that obtains a new and regular emphasis with every fresh day; it follows that, so far from vanishing from the consciousness, so far indeed from being forgotten, it must necessarily become impressed on the consciousness with ever-increasing distinctness. How much more logical is that contrary theory (it is not the truer for that) which is represented, for instance, by Herbert Spencer, who places the concept "good" as essentially similar to the concept "useful," "purposive," so that in the judgments "good" and "bad" mankind is simply summarizing and investing with a sanction its *unforgotten* and *unforgettable* experiences concerning the "useful-purposive" and the "mischievous-non-purposive." According to this theory, "good" is the attribute of that which has previously shown itself useful; and so is able to claim to be considered "valuable in the highest degree," "valuable in itself." This method of explanation is also, as I have said, wrong, but at any rate the explanation itself is coherent, and psychologically tenable.

4

The guide-post which first put me on the right track was this question— what is the true etymological significance of the various symbols for the idea "good" which have been coined in the various languages? I then found that they all led back to *the same evolution of the same idea*—that everywhere "aristocrat," "noble" (in the social sense), is the root idea, out of which have necessarily developed "good" in the sense of "with aristocratic soul," "noble," in the sense of "with a soul of high caliber," "with a privileged soul"—a development which invariably runs parallel with that other evolution by which "vulgar," "plebeian," "low," are made to change finally into "bad." The most eloquent proof of this last contention is the German word "*schlecht*" itself: this word is identical with "*schlicht*"—(compare "*schlechtweg*" and "*schlechterdings*")—which, originally and as yet without any sinister innuendo, simply denoted the plebeian man in contrast to the aristocratic man. It is at the sufficiently late period of the Thirty Years' War that this sense becomes changed to the sense now current. From the standpoint of the Genealogy of Morals this discovery seems to be substantial: the lateness of it is to be attributed to the retarding influence exercised in the modern world by democratic prejudice in the sphere of all questions of origin. This extends, as will shortly be shown, even to the province of natural science and physiology, which, *prima facie* is the most objective. The extent of the mischief which is caused by this prejudice (once it is free of all trammels except those of its own malice), particularly to Ethics and History, is shown by the notorious case of Buckle: it was in Buckle that that *plebeianism* of the modern spirit, which is of English origin, broke out once again from its malignant soil with all the violence of a slimy volcano, and with that salted, rampant, and vulgar eloquence with which up to the present time all volcanoes have spoken.

5

With regard to our problem, which can justly be called an intimate problem, and which elects to appeal to only a limited number of ears: it is of no small interest to ascertain that in those words and roots which denote "good" we catch glimpses of that arch-trait, on the strength of which the aristocrats feel themselves to be beings of a higher order than their fellows. Indeed, they call themselves in perhaps the most frequent instances simply after their superiority in power (*e.g.* "the powerful," "the lords," "the commanders"), or after the most obvious sign of their superiority, as for example "the rich," "the possessors" (that is the meaning of *arya;* and the Iranian and Slav languages correspond). But they also call themselves after some *characteristic idiosyncrasy,* and this is the case which now concerns us. They name themselves, for instance, "the truthful": this is first done by the Greek nobility whose mouthpiece is found in Theognis, the Megarian poet. The word ἐσθλός, which is coined for the purpose, signifies etymologically "one who *is,*" who has reality, who is real, who is true; and then with a subjective twist, the "true," as the "truthful": at this stage in the evolution of the idea, it becomes the motto and party cry of the nobility, and quite completes the transition to the meaning "noble," so as to place outside the pale the lying, vulgar man, as Theognis conceives and portrays him—till finally the word after the decay of the nobility is left to delineate psychological *noblesse,* and becomes as it were ripe and mellow. In the word κακός as in δειλός (the plebeian in contrast to the ἀγαθός) the cowardice is emphasized. This affords perhaps an inkling on what lines the etymological origin of the very ambiguous ἀγαθός is to be investigated. In the Latin *malus* (which I place side by side with μέλας) the vulgar man can be distinguished as the dark-colored, and above all as the black-haired ("*hic niger est*"), as the pre-Aryan inhabitants of the Italian soil, whose complexion formed the clearest feature of distinction from the dominant blondes, namely, the Aryan conquering race:—at any rate Gaelic has afforded me the exact analogue—*Fin* (for instance, in the name Fin-Gal), the distinctive word of the nobility, finally—good, noble, clean, but originally the blonde-haired man in contrast to the dark black-haired aboriginals. The Celts, if I may make a parenthetic statement, were throughout a blonde race; and it is wrong to connect, as Virchow still connects, those traces of an essentially dark-haired population which are to be seen on the more elaborate ethnographical maps of Germany with any Celtic ancestry or with any admixture of Celtic blood: in this context it is rather the *pre-Aryan* population of Germany which surges up to these districts. (The same is true substantially of the whole of Europe: in point of fact, the subject race has finally again obtained the upper hand, in complexion and the shortness of the skull, and perhaps in the intellectual and social qualities. Who can guarantee that modern democracy, still more modern anarchy, and indeed that tendency to the "Commune," the most primitive form of society, which is now common to all the Socialists in Europe, does not in its real essence signify a monstrous reversion—and that the conquering and *master* race—the Aryan race, is not also becoming inferior physiologically?) I believe that I can explain the Latin *bonus* as the "warrior": my hypothesis is that I am right in deriving *bonus* from an older *duonus* (compare *bellum* = *duellum* = *duen-lum*, in which the word *duonus* appears to me to be contained). Bonus accordingly as the man of discord, of variance, "entzweiung" (*duo*), as the warrior: one sees what in ancient Rome "the good" meant for a man. Must not our actual German word *gut* mean "*the godlike*, the man of godlike race"? and be identical with the national name (originally the nobles' name) of the *Goths*?

The grounds for this supposition do not appertain to this work.

6

Above all, there is no exception (though there are opportunities for exceptions) to this rule, that the idea of political superiority always resolves itself into the idea of psychological superiority, in those cases where the highest caste is at the same time the *priestly* caste, and in accordance with its general characteristics confers on itself the privilege of a title which alludes specifically to its priestly function. It is in these cases, for instance, that "clean" and "unclean" confront each other for the first time as badges of class distinction; here again there develops a "good" and a "bad," in a sense which has ceased to be merely social. Moreover, care should be taken not to take these ideas of "clean" and "unclean" too seriously, too broadly, or too symbolically: all the ideas of ancient man have, on the contrary, got to be understood in their initial stages, in a sense which is, to an almost inconceivable extent, crude, coarse, physical, and narrow, and above all essentially unsymbolical. The "clean man" is originally only a man who washes himself, who abstains from certain foods which are conducive to skin diseases, who does not sleep with the unclean women of the lower classes, who has a horror of blood—not more, not much more! On the other hand, the very nature of a priestly aristocracy shows the reasons why just at such an early juncture there should ensue a really dangerous sharpening and intensification of opposed values: it is, in fact, through these opposed values that gulfs are cleft in the social plane, which a veritable Achilles of free thought would shudder to cross. There is from the outset a certain *diseased taint* in such sacerdotal aristocracies, and in the habits which prevail in such societies—habits which, *averse* as they are to action, constitute a compound of introspection and explosive emotionalism, as a result of which there appears that introspective morbidity and neurasthenia, which adheres almost inevitably to all priests at all times: with regard, however, to the remedy which they themselves have invented for this disease—the philosopher has no option but to state, that it has proved itself in its effects a hundred times more dangerous than the disease, from which it should have been the deliverer. Humanity itself is still diseased from the effects of the naïvetés of this priestly cure. Take, for instance, certain kinds of diet (abstention from flesh), fasts, sexual continence, flight into the wilderness (a kind of Weir-Mitchell isolation, though of course without that system of excessive feeding and fattening which is the most efficient antidote to all the hysteria of the ascetic ideal); consider too the whole metaphysic of the priests, with its war on the senses, its enervation, its hair-splitting; consider its self-hypnotism on the fakir and Brahman principles (it uses Brahman as a glass disc and obsession), and that climax which we can understand only too well of an unusual satiety with its panacea of *nothingness* (or God:—the demand for a *unio mystica* with God is the demand of the Buddhist for nothingness, Nirvana—and nothing else!). In sacerdotal societies *every* element is on a more dangerous scale, not merely cures and remedies, but also pride, revenge, cunning, exaltation, love, ambition, virtue, morbidity:—further, it can fairly be stated that it is on the soil of this *essentially dangerous* form of human society, the sacerdotal form, that man really becomes for the first time an *interesting animal*, that it is in this form that the soul of man has in a higher sense attained *depths* and become *evil*—and those are the two fundamental forms of the superiority which up to the present man has exhibited over every other animal.

7

The reader will have already surmised with what ease the priestly mode of valuation can branch off from the knightly aristocratic mode, and then develop into the very antithesis of the latter: special impetus is given to this opposition, by every occasion when the castes of the priests and warriors confront each other with mutual jealousy and cannot agree over the prize. The knightly-aristocratic "values" are based on a careful cult of the physical, on a flowering, rich, and even effervescing healthiness, that goes considerably beyond what is necessary for maintaining life, on war, adventure, the chase, the dance, the tourney— on everything, in fact, which is contained in strong, free, and joyous action. The priestly-aristocratic mode of valuation is—we have seen—based on other hypotheses: it is bad enough for this class when it is a question of war! Yet the priests are, as is notorious, *the worst enemies*—why? Because they are the weakest. Their weakness causes their hate to expand into a monstrous and sinister shape, a shape which is most crafty and most poisonous. The really great haters in the history of the world have always been priests, who are also the cleverest haters—in comparison with the cleverness of priestly revenge, every other piece of cleverness is practically negligible. Human history would be too fatuous for anything were it not for the cleverness imported into it by the weak—take at once the most important instance. All the world's efforts against the "aristocrats," the "mighty," the "masters," the "holders of power," are negligible by comparison with what has been accomplished against those classes by *the Jews*—the Jews, that priestly nation which eventually realized that the one method of effecting satisfaction on its enemies and tyrants was by means of a radical transvaluation of values, which was at the same time an act of the *cleverest revenge*. Yet the method was only appropriate to a nation of priests, to a nation of the most jealously nursed priestly revengefulness. It was the Jews who, in opposition to the aristocratic equation (good = aristocratic = beautiful = happy = loved by the gods), dared with a terrifying logic to suggest the contrary equation, and indeed to maintain with the teeth of the most profound hatred (the hatred of weakness) this contrary equation, namely, "the wretched are alone the good; the poor, the weak, the lowly, are alone the good; the suffering, the needy, the sick, the loathsome, are the only ones who are pious, the only ones who are blessed, for them alone is salvation—but you, on the other hand, you aristocrats, you men of power, you are to all eternity the evil, the horrible, the covetous, the insatiate, the godless; eternally also shall you be the unblessed, the cursed, the damned!" We know who it was who reaped the heritage of this Jewish transvaluation. In the context of the monstrous and inordinately fateful initiative which the Jews have exhibited in connection with this most fundamental of all declarations of war, I remember the passage which came to my pen on another occasion (*Beyond Good and Evil*, Aph. 195)—that it was, in fact, with the Jews that the *revolt of the slaves* begins in the sphere *of morals*; that revolt which has behind it a history of two millennia, and which at the present day has only moved out of our sight, because it—has achieved victory.

8

But you understand this not? You have no eyes for a force which has taken two thousand years to achieve victory?—There is nothing wonderful in this: all *lengthy* processes are hard to see and to realize. But *this* is what took place: from the trunk of that tree of revenge and hate, Jewish hate,—that most profound and sublime hate, which creates ideals and changes old values to new creations, the like of which has never been on earth,—there grew a phenomenon which was equally incomparable, *a new love*, the most profound and sublime of all kinds of love;—and from what other trunk could it have grown? But beware of supposing that this love has soared on its upward growth, as in any way a real negation of that thirst for revenge, as an antithesis to the Jewish hate! No, the contrary is the truth! This love grew out of that hate, as its crown, as its triumphant crown, circling wider and wider amid the clarity and fullness of the sun, and pursuing in the very kingdom of light and height its goal of hatred, its victory, its spoil, its strategy, with the same intensity with which the roots of that tree of hate sank into everything which was deep and evil with increasing stability and increasing desire. This Jesus of Nazareth, the incarnate gospel of love, this "Redeemer" bringing salvation and victory to the poor, the sick, the sinful—was he not really temptation in its most sinister and irresistible form, temptation to take the tortuous path to those very *Jewish* values and those very Jewish ideals? Has not Israel really obtained the final goal of its sublime revenge, by the tortuous paths of this "Redeemer," for all that he might pose as Israel's adversary and Israel's destroyer? Is it not due to the black magic of a really *great* policy of revenge, of a far-seeing, burrowing revenge, both acting and calculating with slowness, that Israel himself must repudiate before all the world the actual instrument of his own revenge and nail it to the cross, so that all the world—that is, all the enemies of Israel—could nibble without suspicion at this very bait? Could, moreover, any human mind with all its elaborate ingenuity invent a bait that was more truly *dangerous*? Anything that was even equivalent in the power of its seductive, intoxicating, defiling, and corrupting influence to that symbol of the holy cross, to that awful paradox of a "god on the cross," to that mystery of the unthinkable, supreme, and utter horror of the self-crucifixion of a god for the *salvation of man*? It is at least certain that *sub hoc signo* Israel, with its revenge and transvaluation of all values, has up to the present always triumphed again over all other ideals, over all more aristocratic ideals.

9

"But why do you talk of nobler ideals? Let us submit to the facts; that the people have triumphed—or the slaves, or the populace, or the herd, or whatever name you care to give them—if this has happened through the Jews, so be it! In that case no nation ever had a greater mission in the world's history. The 'masters' have been done away with; the morality of the vulgar man has triumphed. This triumph may also be called a blood-poisoning (it has mutually fused the races)—I do not dispute it; but there is no doubt but that this intoxication has succeeded. The 'redemption' of the human race (that is, from the masters) is progressing swimmingly; everything is obviously becoming Judaized, or Christianized, or vulgarized (what is there in the words?). It seems impossible to stop the course of this poisoning through the whole body politic of mankind—but its *tempo* and pace may from the present time be slower, more delicate, quieter, more discreet—there is time enough. In view of this context has the Church nowadays any necessary purpose? has it, in fact, a right to live? Or could man get on without it? *Quæritur.* It seems that it fetters and retards this tendency, instead of accelerating it. Well, even that might be its utility. The Church certainly is a crude and boorish institution, that is repugnant to an intelligence with any pretense at delicacy, to a really modern taste. Should it not at any rate learn to be somewhat more subtle? It alienates nowadays, more than it allures. Which of us would, forsooth, be a freethinker if there were no Church? It is the Church which repels us, not its poison—apart from the Church we like the poison." This is the epilogue of a freethinker to my discourse, of an honorable animal (as he has given abundant proof), and a democrat to boot; he had up to that time listened to me, and could not endure my silence, but for me, indeed, with regard to this topic there is much on which to be silent.

10

The revolt of the slaves in morals begins in the very principle of *resentment* becoming creative and giving birth to values—a resentment experienced by creatures who, deprived as they are of the proper outlet of action, are forced to find their compensation in an imaginary revenge. While every aristocratic morality springs from a triumphant affirmation of its own demands, the slave morality says "no" from the very outset to what is "outside itself," "different from itself," and "not itself": and this "no" is its creative deed. This volte-face of the valuing standpoint—this *inevitable* gravitation to the objective instead of back to the subjective—is typical of "resentment": the slave-morality requires as the condition of its existence an external and objective world, to employ physiological terminology, it requires objective stimuli to be capable of action at all—its action is fundamentally a reaction. The contrary is the case when we come to the aristocrat's system of values: it acts and grows spontaneously, it merely seeks its antithesis in order to pronounce a more grateful and exultant "yes" to its own self;—its negative conception, "low," "vulgar," "bad," is merely a pale late-born foil in comparison with its positive and fundamental conception (saturated as it is with life and passion), of "we aristocrats, we good ones, we beautiful ones, we happy ones."

When the aristocratic morality goes astray and commits sacrilege on reality, this is limited to that particular sphere with which it is *not* sufficiently acquainted—a sphere, in fact, from the real knowledge of which it disdainfully defends itself. It misjudges, in some cases, the sphere which it despises, the sphere of the common vulgar man and the low people: on the other hand, due weight should be given to the consideration that in any case the mood of contempt, of disdain, of superciliousness, even on the supposition that it *falsely* portrays the object of its contempt, will always be far removed from that degree of falsity which will always characterize the attacks—in effigy, of course—of the vindictive hatred and revengefulness of the weak in onslaughts on their enemies. In point of fact, there is in contempt too strong an admixture of nonchalance, of casualness, of boredom, of impatience, even of personal exultation, for it to be capable of distorting its victim into a real caricature or a real monstrosity. Attention again should be paid to the almost benevolent *nuances* which, for instance, the Greek nobility imports into all the words by which it distinguishes the common people from itself; note how continuously a kind of pity, care, and consideration imparts its honeyed *flavor*, until at last almost all the words which are applied to the vulgar man survive finally as expressions for "unhappy," "worthy of pity" (compare δειλο, δείλαιος, πονηρός, μοχθηρός]; the latter two names really denoting the vulgar man as labor-slave and beast of burden)—and how, conversely, "bad," "low," "unhappy" have never ceased to ring in the Greek ear with a tone in which "unhappy" is the predominant note: this is a heritage of the old noble aristocratic morality, which remains true to itself even in contempt (let philologists remember the sense in which MIused to be employed). The "well-born" simply *felt* themselves the "happy"; they did not have to manufacture their happiness artificially through looking at their enemies, or in cases to talk and *lie themselves* into happiness (as is the custom with all resentful men); and similarly, complete men as they were, exuberant with strength, and consequently *necessarily* energetic, they were too wise to dissociate happiness from action—activity becomes in their minds necessarily counted as happiness (that is the etymology of εὖ πράττειν)—all in sharp contrast to the "happiness" of the weak and the oppressed, with their festering venom and malignity, among whom happiness appears essentially as a narcotic, a deadening, a quietude, a peace, a "Sabbath," an enervation of the mind and relaxation of the limbs,—in short, a purely *passive* phenomenon. While the aristocratic man lived in confidence and openness with himself (*gennaios*, "noble-born," emphasizes the nuance "sincere," and perhaps also "naïf"), the resentful man, on the other hand, is neither sincere nor naïf, nor honest and candid with himself. His soul *squints*; his mind loves hidden crannies, tortuous paths and back-doors, everything secret appeals to him as *his* world, *his* safety, *his* balm; he is past master in silence, in not forgetting, in waiting, in provisional self-depreciation and self-abasement. A race of such *resentful* men will of necessity eventually prove more *prudent* than any aristocratic race, it will honor prudence on quite a distinct scale, as, in fact, a paramount condition of existence, while prudence among aristocratic men is apt to be tinged with a delicate flavor of luxury and refinement; so among them it plays nothing like so integral a part as that complete certainty of function of the governing *unconscious* instincts, or as indeed a certain lack of prudence, such as a vehement and valiant charge, whether against danger or the enemy, or as those ecstatic bursts of rage, love, reverence, gratitude, by which at all times noble souls have recognized each other. When the resentment of the aristocratic man manifests itself, it fulfils and exhausts itself in an immediate reaction, and consequently instills no *venom*: on the other hand, it never manifests itself at all in countless instances, when in the case of the feeble and weak it would be inevitable. An inability to take seriously for any length of time their enemies, their disasters, their *misdeeds*—that is the sign of the full strong natures who possess a superfluity of molding plastic force, that heals completely and produces forgetfulness: a good example of this in the modern world is Mirabeau, who had no memory for any insults and meannesses which were practiced on him, and who was only incapable of forgiving because he forgot. Such a man indeed shakes off with a shrug many a worm which would have buried itself in another; it is only in characters like these that we see the possibility (supposing, of course, that there is such a possibility in the world) of the real "*love* of one's enemies." What respect for his enemies is found, forsooth, in an aristocratic man—and such a reverence is already a bridge to love! He insists on having his enemy to himself as his distinction. He tolerates no other enemy but a man in whose character there is nothing to despise and much to honor! On the other hand, imagine the "enemy" as the resentful man conceives him—and it is here exactly that we see his work, his creativeness; he has conceived "the evil enemy," the "evil one," and indeed that is the root idea from which he now evolves as a contrasting and corresponding figure a "good one," himself—his very self!

11

The method of this man is quite contrary to that of the aristocratic man, who conceives the root idea "good" spontaneously and straight away, that is to say, out of himself, and from that material then creates for himself a concept of "bad"! This "bad" of aristocratic origin and that "evil" out of the cauldron of unsatisfied hatred—the former an imitation, an "extra," an additional nuance; the latter, on the other hand, the original, the beginning, the essential act in the conception of a slave-morality—these two words "bad" and "evil," how great a difference do they mark, in spite of the fact that they have an identical contrary in the idea "good." But the idea "good" is not the same: much rather let the question be asked, "Who is really evil according to the meaning of the morality of resentment?" In all sternness let it be answered thus:—*just* the good man of the other morality, just the aristocrat, the powerful one, the one who rules, but who is distorted by the venomous eye of resentfulness, into a new color, a new signification, a new appearance. This particular point we would be the last to deny: the man who learnt to know those "good" ones only as enemies, learnt at the same time not to know them only as "*evil enemies*" and the same men who *inter pares* were kept so rigorously in bounds through convention, respect, custom, and gratitude, though much more through mutual vigilance and jealousy *inter pares*, these men who in their relations with each other find so many new ways of manifesting consideration, self-control, delicacy, loyalty, pride, and friendship, these men are in reference to what is outside their circle (where the foreign element, a *foreign* country, begins), not much better than beasts of prey, which have been let loose. They enjoy there freedom from all social control, they feel that in the wilderness they can give vent with impunity to that tension which is produced by enclosure and imprisonment in the peace of society, they *revert* to the innocence of the beast-of-prey conscience, like jubilant monsters, who perhaps come from a ghastly bout of murder, arson, rape, and torture, with bravado and a moral equanimity, as though merely some wild student's prank had been played, perfectly convinced that the poets have now an ample theme to sing and celebrate. It is impossible not to recognize at the core of all these aristocratic races the beast of prey; the magnificent *blonde brute*, avidly rampant for spoil and victory; this hidden core needed an outlet from time to time, the beast must get loose again, must return into the wilderness—the Roman, Arabic, German, and Japanese nobility, the Homeric heroes, the Scandinavian Vikings, are all alike in this need. It is the aristocratic races who have left the idea "Barbarian" on all the tracks in which they have marched; nay, a consciousness of this very barbarianism, and even a pride in it, manifests itself even in their highest civilization (for example, when Pericles says to his Athenians in that celebrated funeral oration, "Our audacity has forced a way over every land and sea, rearing everywhere imperishable memorials of itself for *good* and for *evil*"). This audacity of aristocratic races, mad, absurd, and spasmodic as may be its expression; the incalculable and fantastic nature of their enterprises, Pericles sets in special relief and glory the ραθυμία of the Athenians, their nonchalance and contempt for safety, body, life, and comfort, their awful joy and intense delight in all destruction, in all the ecstasies of victory and cruelty,—all these features become crystallized, for those who suffered thereby in the picture of the "barbarian," of the "evil enemy," perhaps of the "Goth" and of the "Vandal." The profound, icy mistrust which the German provokes, as soon as he arrives at power,—even at the present time,—is always still an aftermath of that inextinguishable horror with which for whole centuries Europe has regarded the wrath of the blonde Teuton beast (although between the old Germans and ourselves there exists scarcely a psychological, let alone a physical, relationship). I have once called attention to the embarrassment of Hesiod, when he conceived the series of social ages, and endeavored to express them in gold, silver, and bronze. He could only dispose of the contradiction, with which he was confronted, by the Homeric world, an age magnificent indeed, but at the same time so awful and so violent, by making two ages out of one, which he henceforth placed one behind each other—first, the age of the heroes and demigods, as that world had remained in the memories of the aristocratic families, who found therein their own ancestors; secondly, the bronze age, as that corresponding age appeared to the descendants of the oppressed, spoiled, ill-treated, exiled, enslaved; namely, as an age of bronze, as I have said, hard, cold, terrible, without feelings and without conscience, crushing everything, and bespattering everything with blood. Granted the truth of the theory now believed to be true, that the very *essence of all civilization* is to *train* out of man, the beast of prey, a tame and civilized animal, a domesticated animal, it follows indubitably that we must regard as the real *tools of civilization* all those instincts of reaction and resentment, by the help of which the aristocratic races, together with their ideals, were finally degraded and overpowered; though that has not yet come to be synonymous with saying that the bearers of those tools also *represented* the civilization. It is rather the contrary that is not only probable—nay, it is *palpable* to-day; these bearers of vindictive instincts that have to be bottled up, these descendants of all European and non-European slavery, especially of the pre-Aryan population—these people, I say, represent the *decline* of humanity! These "tools of civilization" are a disgrace to humanity, and constitute in reality more of an argument against civilization, more of a reason why civilization should be suspected. One may be perfectly justified in being always afraid of the blonde beast that lies at the core of all aristocratic races, and in being on one's guard: but who would not a hundred times prefer to be afraid, when one at the same time admires, than to be immune from fear, at the cost of being perpetually obsessed with the loathsome spectacle of the distorted, the dwarfed, the stunted, the envenomed? And is that not our fate? What produces to-day our repulsion towards "man"?—for we *suffer* from "man," there is no doubt about it. It is not fear; it is rather that we have nothing more to fear from men; it is that the worm "man" is in the foreground and pullulates; it is that the "tame man," the wretched mediocre and unedifying creature, has learnt to consider himself a goal and a pinnacle, an inner meaning, an historic principle, a "higher man"; yes, it is that he has a certain right so to consider himself, in so far as he feels that in contrast to that excess of deformity, disease, exhaustion, and effeteness whose odor is beginning to pollute present-day Europe, he at any rate has achieved a relative success, he at any rate still says "yes" to life.

12

I cannot refrain at this juncture from uttering a sigh and one last hope. What is it precisely which I find intolerable? That which I alone cannot get rid of, which makes me choke and faint? Bad air! bad air! That something misbegotten comes near me; that I must inhale the odor of the entrails of a misbegotten soul!—That excepted, what can one not endure in the way of need, privation, bad weather, sickness, toil, solitude? In point of fact, one manages to get over everything, born as one is to a burrowing and battling existence; one always returns once again to the light, one always lives again one's golden hour of victory—and then one stands as one was born, unbreakable, tense, ready for something more difficult, for something more distant, like a bow stretched but the tauter by every strain. But from time to time do ye grant me—assuming that "beyond good and evil" there are goddesses who can grant—one glimpse, grant me but one glimpse only, of something perfect, fully realized, happy, mighty, triumphant, of something that still gives cause for fear! A glimpse of a man that justifies the existence of man, a glimpse of an incarnate human happiness that realizes and redeems, for the sake of which one may hold fast to *the belief in man*! For the position is this: in the dwarfing and levelling of the European man lurks *our* greatest peril, for it is this outlook which fatigues—we see to-day nothing which wishes to be greater, we surmise that the process is always still backwards, still backwards towards something more attenuated, more inoffensive, more cunning, more comfortable, more mediocre, more indifferent, more Chinese, more Christian—man, there is no doubt about it, grows always "better" —the destiny of Europe lies even in this—that in losing the fear of man, we have also lost the hope in man, yea, the will to be man. The sight of man now fatigues.—What is present-day Nihilism if it is not *that*?—We are tired of *man*.

13

But let us come back to it; the problem of another origin of the *good*—of the good, as the resentful man has thought it out—demands its solution. It is not surprising that the lambs should bear a grudge against the great birds of prey, but that is no reason for blaming the great birds of prey for taking the little lambs. And when the lambs say among themselves, "These birds of prey are evil, and he who is as far removed from being a bird of prey, who is rather its opposite, a lamb,—is he not good?" then there is nothing to cavil at in the setting up of this ideal, though it may also be that the birds of prey will regard it a little sneeringly, and perchance say to themselves, "*We* bear no grudge against them, these good lambs, we even like them: nothing is tastier than a tender lamb." To require of strength that it should not express itself as strength, that it should not be a wish to overpower, a wish to overthrow, a wish to become master, a thirst for enemies and antagonisms and triumphs, is just as absurd as to require of weakness that it should express itself as strength. A quantum of force is just such a quantum of movement, will, action—rather it is nothing else than just those very phenomena of moving, willing, acting, and can only appear otherwise in the misleading errors of language (and the fundamental fallacies of reason which have become petrified therein), which understands, and understands wrongly, all working as conditioned by a worker, by a "subject." And just exactly as the people separate the lightning from its flash, and interpret the latter as a thing done, as the working of a subject which is called lightning, so also does the popular morality separate strength from the expression of strength, as though behind the strong man there existed some indifferent neutral *substratum*, which enjoyed a *caprice and option* as to whether or not it should express strength. But there is no such *substratum*, there is no "being" behind doing, working, becoming; "the doer" is a mere appanage to the action. The action is everything. In point of fact, the people duplicate the doing, when they make the lightning lighten, that is a "doing-doing": they make the same phenomenon first a cause, and then, secondly, the effect of that cause. The scientists fail to improve matters when they say, "Force moves, force causes," and so on. Our whole science is still, in spite of all its coldness, of all its freedom from passion, a dupe of the tricks of language, and has never succeeded in getting rid of that superstitious changeling "the subject" (the atom, to give another instance, is such a changeling, just as the Kantian "Thing-in-itself"). What wonder, if the suppressed and stealthily simmering passions of revenge and hatred exploit for their own advantage this belief, and indeed hold no belief with a more steadfast enthusiasm than this—"that the strong has the *option* of being weak, and the bird of prey of being a lamb." Thereby do they win for themselves the right of attributing to the birds of prey the *responsibility* for being birds of prey: when the oppressed, down-trodden, and overpowered say to themselves with the vindictive guile of weakness, "Let us be otherwise than the evil, namely, good! and good is every one who does not oppress, who hurts no one, who does not attack, who does not pay back, who hands over revenge to God, who holds himself, as we do, in hiding; who goes out of the way of evil, and demands, in short, little from life; like ourselves the patient, the meek, the just,"—yet all this, in its cold and unprejudiced interpretation, means nothing more than "once for all, the weak are weak; it is good to do *nothing for which we are not strong enough*"; but this dismal state of affairs, this prudence of the lowest order, which even insects possess (which in a great danger are fain to sham death so as to avoid doing "too much"), has, thanks to the counterfeiting and self-deception of weakness, come to masquerade in the pomp of an ascetic, mute, and expectant virtue, just as though the *very* weakness of the weak—that is, forsooth, its *being*, its working, its whole unique inevitable inseparable reality—were a voluntary result, something wished, chosen, a deed, an act of *merit*. This kind of man finds the belief in a neutral, free-choosing "subject" *necessary* from an instinct of self-preservation, of self-assertion, in which every lie is fain to sanctify itself. The subject (or, to use popular language, the *soul*) has perhaps proved itself the best dogma in the world simply because it rendered possible to the horde of mortal, weak, and oppressed individuals of every kind, that most sublime specimen of self-deception, the interpretation of weakness as freedom, of being this, or being that, as *merit*.

14

Will any one look a little into—right into—the mystery of how *ideals are manufactured* in this world? Who has the courage to do it? Come!

Here we have a vista opened into these grimy workshops. Wait just a moment, dear Mr. Inquisitive and Foolhardy; your eye must first grow accustomed to this false changing light—Yes! Enough! Now speak! What is happening below down yonder? Speak out that what you see, man of the most dangerous curiosity—for now *I* am the listener.

"I see nothing, I hear the more. It is a cautious, spiteful, gentle whispering and muttering together in all the corners and crannies. It seems to me that they are lying; a sugary softness adheres to every sound. Weakness is turned to *merit*, there is no doubt about it—it is just as you say."

Further!

"And the impotence which requites not, is turned to 'goodness,' craven baseness to meekness, submission to those whom one hates, to obedience (namely, obedience to one of whom they say that he ordered this submission—they call him God). The inoffensive character of the weak, the very cowardice in which he is rich, his standing at the door, his forced necessity of waiting, gain here fine names, such as 'patience,' which is also called 'virtue'; not being able to avenge one's self, is called not wishing to avenge one's self, perhaps even forgiveness (for *they* know not what they do—we alone know what *they* do). They also talk of the 'love of their enemies' and sweat thereby."

Further!

"They are miserable, there is no doubt about it, all these whisperers and counterfeiters in the corners, although they try to get warm by crouching close to each other, but they tell me that their misery is a favor and distinction given to them by God, just as one beats the dogs one likes best; that perhaps this misery is also a preparation, a probation, a training; that perhaps it is still more something which will one day be compensated and paid back with a tremendous interest in gold, nay in happiness. This they call 'Blessedness.'"

Further!

"They are now giving me to understand, that not only are they better men than the mighty, the lords of the earth, whose spittle they have got to lick (not out of fear, not at all out of fear! But because God ordains that one should honor all authority)—not only are they better men, but that they also have a 'better time,' at any rate, will one day have a 'better time.' But enough! Enough! I can endure it no longer. Bad air! Bad air! These workshops *where ideals are manufactured*—verily they reek with the crassest lies."

Nay. Just one minute! You are saying nothing about the masterpieces of these virtuosos of black magic, who can produce whiteness, milk, and innocence out of any black you like: have you not noticed what a pitch of refinement is attained by their *chef d'œuvre*, their most audacious, subtle, ingenious, and lying artist-trick? Take care! These cellar-beasts, full of revenge and hate—what do they make, forsooth, out of their revenge and hate? Do you hear these words? Would you suspect, if you trusted only their words, that you are among men of resentment and nothing else?

"I understand, I prick my ears up again (ah! ah! ah! and I hold my nose). Now do I hear for the first time that which they have said so often: 'We good, *we are the righteous*'—what they demand they call not revenge but 'the triumph of *righteousness*'; what they hate is not their enemy, no, they hate 'unrighteousness,' 'godlessness'; what they believe in and hope is not the hope of revenge, the intoxication of sweet revenge (—"sweeter than honey," did Homer call it?), but the victory of God, of the *righteous God* over the 'godless'; what is left for them to love in this world is not *their* brothers in hate, but their 'brothers in love,' as they say, all the good and righteous on the earth."

And how do they name that which serves them as a solace against all the troubles of life—their phantasmagoria of their anticipated future blessedness?

"How? Do I hear right? They call it 'the last judgment,' the advent of their kingdom, 'the kingdom of God'—but *in the meanwhile* they live 'in faith,' 'in love,' 'in hope.'"

Enough! Enough!

15

In the faith in what? In the love for what? In the hope of what? These weaklings!—they also, forsooth, wish to be the strong some time; there is no doubt about it, some time *their* kingdom also must come—"the kingdom of God" is their name for it, as has been mentioned: they are so meek in everything! Yet in order to experience *that* kingdom it is necessary to live long, to live beyond death,—yes, *eternal* life is necessary so that one can make up for ever for that earthly life "in faith," "in love," "in hope." Make up for what? Make up by what? Dante, as it seems to me, made a crass mistake when with awe-inspiring ingenuity he placed that inscription over the gate of his hell, "Me too made eternal love": at any rate the following inscription would have a much better right to stand over the gate of the Christian Paradise and its "eternal blessedness"—"Me too made eternal hate"—granted of course that a truth may rightly stand over the gate to a lie! For what is the blessedness of that Paradise? Possibly we could quickly surmise it; but it is better that it should be explicitly attested by an authority who in such matters is not to be disparaged, Thomas of Aquinas, the great teacher and saint. "*Beati in regno celesti*" says he, as gently as a lamb, "*videbunt pœnas damnatorum, ut beatitudo illis magis complaceat.*" Or if we wish to hear a stronger tone, a word from the mouth of a triumphant father of the Church, who warned his disciples against the cruel ecstasies of the public spectacles—But why? Faith offers us much more,—says he, *de Spectac.*, c. 29 ss.,—something much stronger; thanks to the redemption, joys of quite another kind stand at our disposal; instead of athletes we have our martyrs; we wish for blood, well, we have the blood of Christ—but what then awaits us on the day of his return, of his triumph. And then does he proceed, does this enraptured visionary: "*at enim supersunt alia spectacula, ille ultimas et perpetuus judicii dies, ille nationibus insperatus, ille derisus, cum tanta sæculi vetustas et tot ejus nativitates uno igne haurientur. Quæ tunc spectaculi latitudo! Quid admirer! quid rideam! Ubigaudeam! Ubi exultem, spectans tot et tantos reges, qui in cœlum recepti nuntiabantur, cum ipso Jove et ipsis suis testibus in imis tenebris congemescentes! Item præsides*" (the provincial governors) "*persecutores dominici nominis sævioribus quam ipsi flammis sævierunt insultantibus contra Christianos liquescentes! Quos præterea sapientes illos philosophos coram discipulis suis una conflagrantibus erubescentes, quibus nihil ad deum pertinere suadebant, quibus animas aut nullas aut non in pristina corpora redituras affirmabant! Etiam poetas non ad Rhadamanti nec ad Minois, sed ad inopinati Christi tribunal palpitantes! Tunc magis tragœdi audiendi, magis scilicet vocales*" (with louder tones and more violent shrieks) "*in sua propria calamitate; tunc histriones cognoscendi, solutiores multo per ignem; tunc spectandus auriga in flammea rota totus rubens, tunc xystici contemplandi non in gymnasiis, sed in igne jaculati, nisi quod ne tunc quidem illos velim vivos, ut qui malim ad eos potius conspectum insatiabilem conferre, qui in dominum scevierunt. Hic est ille, dicam fabri aut quæstuariæ filius*" (as is shown by the whole of the following, and in particular by this well-known description of the mother of Jesus from the Talmud, Tertullian is henceforth referring to the Jews), "*sabbati destructor, Samarites et dæmonium habens. Hic est quem a Juda redemistis, hic est ille arundine et colaphis diverberatus, sputamentis de decoratus, felle et acete potatus.*

Hic est, quem clam discentes subripuerunt, ut resurrexisse dicatur vel hortulanus detraxit, ne lactucæ suæ frequentia commeantium laderentur. Ut talia species, ut talibus exultes, quis tibi prætor aut consul aut sacerdos de sua liberalitate prastabit? Et tamen hæc jam habemus quodammodo per fidem spiritu imaginante repræsentata. Ceterum qualia illa sunt, quæ nec oculus vidit nec auris audivit nec in cor hominis ascenderunt?' (I Cor. ii. 9.) "*Credo circo et utraque cavea*" (first and fourth row, or, according to others, the comic and the tragic stage) "*et omni studio gratiora.*" *Per fidem*: so stands it written.

16

Let us come to a conclusion. The two *opposing values*, "good and bad," "good and evil," have fought a dreadful, thousand-year fight in the world, and though indubitably the second value has been for a long time in the preponderance, there are not wanting places where the fortune of the fight is still undecisive. It can almost be said that in the meanwhile the fight reaches a higher and higher level, and that in the meanwhile it has become more and more intense, and always more and more psychological; so that nowadays there is perhaps no more decisive mark of the *higher nature*, of the more psychological nature, than to be in that sense self-contradictory, and to be actually still a battleground for those two opposites. The symbol of this fight, written in a writing which has remained worthy of perusal throughout the course of history up to the present time, is called "Rome against Judæa, Judæa against Rome." Hitherto there has been no greater event than *that* fight, the putting of *that* question, *that* deadly antagonism. Rome found in the Jew the incarnation of the unnatural, as though it were its diametrically opposed monstrosity, and in Rome the Jew was held to be *convicted of hatred* of the whole human race: and rightly so, in so far as it is right to link the well-being and the future of the human race to the unconditional mastery of the aristocratic values, of the Roman values. What, conversely, did the Jews feel against Rome? One can surmise it from a thousand symptoms, but it is sufficient to carry one's mind back to the Johannian Apocalypse, that most obscene of all the written outbursts, which has revenge on its conscience. (One should also appraise at its full value the profound logic of the Christian instinct, when over this very book of hate it wrote the name of the Disciple of Love, that self-same disciple to whom it attributed that impassioned and ecstatic Gospel—therein lurks a portion of truth, however much literary forging may have been necessary for this purpose.) The Romans were the strong and aristocratic; a nation stronger and more aristocratic has never existed in the world, has never even been dreamed of; every relic of them, every inscription enraptures, granted that one can divine *what* it is that writes the inscription. The Jews, conversely, were that priestly nation of resentment par excellence, possessed by a unique genius for popular morals: just compare with the Jews the nations with analogous gifts, such as the Chinese or the Germans, so as to realize afterwards what is first rate, and what is fifth rate.

Which of them has been provisionally victorious, Rome or Judæa? but there is not a shadow of doubt; just consider to whom in Rome itself nowadays you bow down, as though before the quintessence of all the highest values—and not only in Rome, but almost over half the world, everywhere where man has been tamed or is about to be tamed—to *three Jews*, as we know, and *one Jewess* (to Jesus of Nazareth, to Peter the fisher, to Paul the tent-maker, and to the mother of the aforesaid Jesus, named Mary). This is very remarkable: Rome is undoubtedly defeated. At any rate there took place in the Renaissance a brilliantly sinister revival of the classical ideal, of the aristocratic valuation of all things: Rome herself, like a man waking up from a trance, stirred beneath the burden of the new Judaized Rome that had been built over her, which presented the appearance of an œcumenical synagogue and was called the "Church": but immediately Judæa triumphed again, thanks to that fundamentally popular (German and English) movement of revenge, which is called the Reformation, and taking also into account its inevitable corollary, the restoration of the Church—the restoration also of the ancient graveyard peace of classical Rome. Judæa proved yet once more victorious over the classical ideal in the French Revolution, and in a sense which was even more crucial and even more profound: the last political aristocracy that existed in Europe, that of the *French* seventeenth and eighteenth centuries, broke into pieces beneath the instincts of a resentful populace—never had the world heard a greater jubilation, a more uproarious enthusiasm: indeed, there took place in the midst of it the most monstrous and unexpected phenomenon; the ancient ideal *itself* swept before the eyes and conscience of humanity with all its life and with unheard-of splendor, and in opposition to resentment's lying war-cry of *the prerogative of the most*, in opposition to the will to lowliness, abasement, and equalization, the will to a retrogression and twilight of humanity, there rang out once again, stronger, simpler, more penetrating than ever, the terrible and enchanting counter-war cry of *the prerogative of the few*! Like a final signpost to other ways, there appeared Napoleon, the most unique and violent anachronism that ever existed, and in him the incarnate problem *of the aristocratic ideal in itself*—consider well what a problem it is:—Napoleon, that synthesis of Monster and Superman.

17

Was it therewith over? Was that greatest of all antitheses of ideals thereby relegated *ad acta* for all time? Or only postponed, postponed for a long time? May there not take place at some time or other a much more awful, much more carefully prepared flaring up of the old conflagration? Further! Should not one wish *that* consummation with all one's strength?—will it one's self? demand it one's self? He who at this juncture begins, like my readers, to reflect, to think further, will have difficulty in coming quickly to a conclusion,—ground enough for me to come myself to a conclusion, taking it for granted that for some time past what I mean has been sufficiently clear, what I exactly *mean* by that dangerous motto which is inscribed on the body of my last book: *Beyond Good and Evil*—at any rate that is not the same as "Beyond Good and Bad."

Note.—I avail myself of the opportunity offered by this treatise to express, openly and formally, a wish which up to the present has only been expressed in occasional conversations with scholars, namely, that some Faculty of philosophy should, by means of a series of prize essays, gain the glory of having promoted the further study of the *history of morals*—perhaps this book may serve to give forcible impetus in such a direction. With regard to a possibility of this character, the following question deserves consideration. It merits quite as much the attention of philologists and historians as of actual professional philosophers.

"*What indication of the history of the evolution of the moral ideas is afforded by philology, and especially by etymological investigation?*"

On the other hand, it is of course equally necessary to induce physiologists and doctors to be interested in these problems (*of the value of the valuations* which have prevailed up to the present): in this connection the professional philosophers may be trusted to act as the spokesmen and intermediaries in these particular instances, after, of course, they have quite succeeded in transforming the relationship between philosophy and physiology and medicine, which is originally one of coldness and suspicion, into the most friendly and fruitful reciprocity. In point of fact, all tables of values, all the "thou shalts" known to history and ethnology, need primarily a *physiological*, at any rate in preference to a psychological, elucidation and interpretation; all equally require a critique from medical science. The question, "What is the *value* of this or that table of 'values' and morality?" will be asked from the most varied standpoints. For instance, the question of "valuable *for what*" can never be analyzed with sufficient nicety. That, for instance, which would evidently have value with regard to promoting in a race the greatest possible powers of endurance (or with regard to increasing its adaptability to a specific climate, or with regard to the preservation of the greatest number) would have nothing like the same value, if it were a question of evolving a stronger species. In gauging values, the good of the majority and the good of the minority are opposed standpoints: we leave it to the naïveté of English biologists to regard the former standpoint as *intrinsically* superior. *All the sciences have now to pave the way for the future task of the philosopher; this task being understood to mean, that he must solve the problem of value, that he has to fix the hierarchy of values.*

Second Essay:
"Guilt," "Bad Conscience," and Related Matters

1

The breeding of an animal that *can promise*—is not this just that very paradox of a task which nature has set itself in regard to man? Is not this the very problem of man? The fact that this problem has been to a great extent solved, must appear all the more phenomenal to one who can estimate at its full value that force of *forgetfulness* which works in opposition to it. Forgetfulness is no mere *vis inertiæ*, as the superficial believe, rather is it a power of obstruction, active and, in the strictest sense of the word, positive—a power responsible for the fact that what we have lived, experienced, taken into ourselves, no more enters into consciousness during the process of digestion (it might be called psychic absorption) than all the whole manifold process by which our physical nutrition, the so-called "incorporation," is carried on. The temporary shutting of the doors and windows of consciousness, the relief from the clamant alarums and excursions, with which our subconscious world of servant organs works in mutual co-operation and antagonism; a little quietude, a little *tabula rasa* of the consciousness, so as to make room again for the new, and above all for the more noble functions and functionaries, room for government, foresight, predetermination (for our organism is on an oligarchic model)—this is the utility, as I have said, of the active forgetfulness, which is a very sentinel and nurse of psychic order, repose, etiquette; and this shows at once why it is that there can exist no happiness, no gladness, no hope, no pride, no real *present*, without forgetfulness. The man in whom this preventative apparatus is damaged and discarded, is to be compared to a dyspeptic, and it is something more than a comparison—he can "get rid of" nothing. But this very animal who finds it necessary to be forgetful, in whom, in fact, forgetfulness represents a force and a form of *robust* health, has reared for himself an opposition-power, a memory, with whose help forgetfulness is, in certain instances, kept in check—in the cases, namely, where promises have to be made;—so that it is by no means a mere passive inability to get rid of a once indented impression, not merely the indigestion occasioned by a once pledged word, which one cannot dispose of, but an *active* refusal to get rid of it, a continuing and a wish to continue what has once been willed, an actual *memory of the will*; so that between the original "I will," "I shall do," and the actual discharge of the will, its act, we can easily interpose a world of new strange phenomena, circumstances, veritable volitions, without the snapping of this long chain of the will. But what is the underlying hypothesis of all this? How thoroughly, in order to be able to regulate the future in this way, must man have first learnt to distinguish between necessitated and accidental phenomena, to think causally, to see the distant as present and to anticipate it, to fix with certainty what is the end, and what is the means to that end; above all, to reckon, to have power to calculate—how thoroughly must man have first become *calculable, disciplined, necessitated* even for himself and his own conception of himself, that, like a man entering into a promise, he could guarantee himself *as a future*.

2

This is simply the long history of the origin of *responsibility*. That task of breeding an animal which can make promises, includes, as we have already grasped, as its condition and preliminary, the more immediate task of first *making* man to a certain extent, necessitated, uniform, like among his like, regular, and consequently calculable. The immense work of what I have called, "morality of custom"[1] (cp. *Dawn of Day*, Aphs. 9, 14, and 16), the actual work of man on himself during the longest period of the human race, his whole prehistoric work, finds its meaning, its great justification (in spite of all its innate hardness, despotism, stupidity, and idiocy) in this fact: man, with the help of the morality of customs and of social strait-waistcoats, was *made* genuinely calculable. If, however, we place ourselves at the end of this colossal process, at the point where the tree finally matures its fruits, when society and its morality of custom finally bring to light that to which it was only the means, then do we find as the ripest fruit on its tree the *sovereign individual*, that resembles only himself, that has got loose from the morality of custom, the autonomous "super-moral" individual (for "autonomous" and "moral" are mutually-exclusive terms),—in

---

1 The German is: "*Sittlichkeit der Sitte.*"—H.B.S

short, the man of the personal, long, and independent will, *competent to promise*, and we find in him a proud consciousness (vibrating in every fiber), of *what* has been at last achieved and become vivified in him, a genuine consciousness of power and freedom, a feeling of human perfection in general. And this man who has grown to freedom, who is really *competent* to promise, this lord of the *free* will, this sovereign—how is it possible for him not to know how great is his superiority over everything incapable of binding itself by promises, or of being its own security, how great is the trust, the awe, the reverence that he awakes—he "deserves" all three—not to know that with this mastery over himself he is necessarily also given the mastery over circumstances, over nature, over all creatures with shorter wills, less reliable characters? The "free" man, the owner of a long unbreakable will, finds in this possession his *standard of value*: looking out from himself upon the others, he honors or he despises, and just as necessarily as he honors his peers, the strong and the reliable (those who can bind themselves by promises),—that is, every one who promises like a sovereign, with difficulty, rarely and slowly, who is sparing with his trusts but confers *honor* by the very fact of trusting, who gives his word as something that can be relied on, because he knows himself strong enough to keep it even in the teeth of disasters, even in the "teeth of fate,"—so with equal necessity will he have the heel of his foot ready for the lean and empty jackasses, who promise when they have no business to do so, and his rod of chastisement ready for the liar, who already breaks his word at the very minute when it is on his lips. The proud knowledge of the extraordinary privilege of *responsibility*, the consciousness of this rare freedom, of this power over himself and over fate, has sunk right down to his innermost depths, and has become an instinct, a dominating instinct—what name will he give to it, to this dominating instinct, if he needs to have a word for it? But there is no doubt about it—the sovereign man calls it his *conscience*.

3

His conscience?—One apprehends at once that the idea "conscience," which is here seen in its supreme manifestation, supreme in fact to almost the point of strangeness, should already have behind it a long history and evolution. The ability to guarantee one's self with all due pride, and also at the same time to *say yes* to one's self—that is, as has been said, a ripe fruit, but also a *late* fruit:—How long must needs this fruit hang sour and bitter on the tree! And for an even longer period there was not a glimpse of such a fruit to be had—no one had taken it on himself to promise it, although everything on the tree was quite ready for it, and everything was maturing for that very consummation. "How is a memory to be made for the man-animal? How is an impression to be so deeply fixed upon this ephemeral understanding, half dense, and half silly, upon this incarnate forgetfulness, that it will be permanently present?" As one may imagine, this primeval problem was not solved by exactly gentle answers and gentle means; perhaps there is nothing more awful and more sinister in the early history of man than his *system of mnemonics.* "Something is burnt in so as to remain in his memory: only that which never stops *hurting* remains in his memory." This is an axiom of the oldest (unfortunately also the longest) psychology in the world. It might even be said that wherever solemnity, seriousness, mystery, and gloomy colors are now found in the life of the men and of nations of the world, there is some *survival* of that horror which was once the universal concomitant of all promises, pledges, and obligations. The past, the past with all its length, depth, and hardness, wafts to us its breath, and bubbles up in us again, when we become "serious." When man thinks it necessary to make for himself a memory, he never accomplishes it without blood, tortures, and sacrifice; the most dreadful sacrifices and forfeitures (among them the sacrifice of the first-born), the most loathsome mutilation (for instance, castration), the most cruel rituals of all the religious cults (for all religions are really at bottom systems of cruelty)—all these things originate from that instinct which found in pain its most potent mnemonic. In a certain sense the whole of asceticism is to be ascribed to this: certain ideas have got to be made inextinguishable, omnipresent, "fixed," with the object of hypnotizing the whole nervous and intellectual system through these "fixed ideas"—and the ascetic methods and modes of life are the means of freeing those ideas from the competition of all other ideas so as to make them "unforgettable." The worse memory man had, the ghastlier the signs presented by his customs; the severity of the penal laws affords in particular a gauge of the extent of man's difficulty in conquering forgetfulness, and in keeping a few primal postulates of social intercourse ever present to the minds of those who were the slaves of every momentary emotion and every momentary desire. We Germans do certainly not regard ourselves as an especially cruel and hard-hearted nation, still less as an especially casual and happy-go-lucky one; but one has only to look at our old penal ordinances in order to realize what a lot of trouble it takes in the world to evolve a "nation of thinkers" (I mean: *the* European nation which exhibits at this very day the maximum of reliability, seriousness, bad taste, and positiveness, which has on the strength of these qualities a right to train every kind of European mandarin). These Germans employed terrible means to make for themselves a memory, to enable them to master their rooted plebeian instincts and the brutal crudity of those instincts: think of the old German punishments, for instance, stoning (as far back as the legend, the millstone falls on the head of the guilty man), breaking on the wheel (the most original invention and speciality of the German genius in the sphere of punishment), dart-throwing, tearing, or trampling by horses ("quartering"), boiling the criminal in oil or wine (still prevalent in the fourteenth and fifteenth centuries), the highly popular flaying ("slicing into strips"), cutting the flesh out of the breast; think also of the evil-doer being besmeared with honey, and then exposed to the flies in a blazing sun. It was by the help of such images and precedents that man eventually kept in his memory five or six "I will nots" with regard to which he had already given his *promise*, so as to be able to enjoy the advantages of society—and verily with the help of this kind of memory man eventually attained "reason"! Alas! reason, seriousness, mastery over the emotions, all these gloomy, dismal things which are called reflection, all these privileges and pageantries of humanity: how dear is the price that they have exacted! How much blood and cruelty is the foundation of all "good things"!

4

But how is it that that other melancholy object, the consciousness of sin, the whole "bad conscience," came into the world? And it is here that we turn back to our genealogists of morals. For the second time I say—or have I not said it yet?—that they are worth nothing. Just their own five-spans-long limited modern experience; no knowledge of the past, and no wish to know it; still less a historic instinct, a power of "second sight" (which is what is really required in this case)—and despite this to go in for the history of morals. It stands to reason that this must needs produce results which are removed from the truth by something more than a respectful distance.

Have these current genealogists of morals ever allowed themselves to have even the vaguest notion, for instance, that the cardinal moral idea of "ought"[2] originates from the very material idea of "owe"? Or that punishment developed as a retaliation absolutely independently of any preliminary hypothesis of the freedom or determination of the will?—And this to such an extent, that a high degree of civilization was always first necessary for the animal man to begin to make those much more primitive distinctions of "intentional," "negligent," "accidental," "responsible," and their contraries, and apply them in the assessing of punishment. That idea—"the wrong-doer deserves punishment *because* he might have acted otherwise," in spite of the fact that it is nowadays so cheap, obvious, natural, and inevitable, and that it has had to serve as an illustration of the way in which the sentiment of justice appeared on earth, is in point of fact an exceedingly late, and even refined form of human judgment and inference; the placing of this idea back at the beginning of the world is simply a clumsy violation of the principles of primitive psychology. Throughout the longest period of human history punishment was *never* based on the responsibility of the evil-doer for his action, and was consequently not based on the hypothesis that only the guilty should be punished;—on the contrary, punishment was inflicted in those days for the same reason that parents punish their children even nowadays, out of anger at an injury that they have suffered, an anger which vents itself mechanically on the author of the injury—but this anger is kept in bounds and modified through the idea that every injury has somewhere or other its *equivalent* price, and can really be paid off, even though it be by means of pain to the author. Whence is it that this ancient deep-rooted and now perhaps ineradicable idea has drawn its strength, this idea of an equivalency between injury and pain? I have already revealed its origin, in the contractual relationship between *creditor* and *ower*, that is as old as the existence of legal rights at all, and in its turn points back to the primary forms of purchase, sale, barter, and trade.

2 The German word "*schuld*" means both debt and guilt. Cp. the English "owe" and "ought," by which I occasionally render the double meaning.—H.B.S.

5

The realization of these contractual relations excites, of course (as would be already expected from our previous observations), a great deal of suspicion and opposition towards the primitive society which made or sanctioned them. In this society promises will be made; in this society the object is to provide the promiser with a memory; in this society, so may we suspect, there will be full scope for hardness, cruelty, and pain: the "ower," in order to induce credit in his promise of repayment, in order to give a guarantee of the earnestness and sanctity of his promise, in order to drill into his own conscience the duty, the solemn duty, of repayment, will, by virtue of a contract with his creditor to meet the contingency of his not paying, pledge something that he still possesses, something that he still has in his power, for instance, his life or his wife, or his freedom or his body (or under certain religious conditions even his salvation, his soul's welfare, even his peace in the grave; so in Egypt, where the corpse of the ower found even in the grave no rest from the creditor—of course, from the Egyptian standpoint, this peace was a matter of particular importance). But especially has the creditor the power of inflicting on the body of the ower all kinds of pain and torture—the power, for instance, of cutting off from it an amount that appeared proportionate to the greatness of the debt;—this point of view resulted in the universal prevalence at an early date of precise schemes of valuation, frequently horrible in the minuteness and meticulosity of their application, *legally* sanctioned schemes of valuation for individual limbs and parts of the body. I consider it as already a progress, as a proof of a freer, less petty, and more Roman conception of law, when the Roman Code of the Twelve Tables decreed that it was immaterial how much or how little the creditors in such a contingency cut off, "*si plus minusve secuerunt, ne fraude esto.*" Let us make the logic of the whole of this equalization process clear; it is strange enough. The equivalence consists in this: instead of an advantage directly compensatory of his injury (that is, instead of an equalization in money, lands, or some kind of chattel), the creditor is granted by way of repayment and compensation a certain *sensation of satisfaction*—the satisfaction of being able to vent, without any trouble, his power on one who is powerless, the delight "*de faire le mal pour le plaisir de le faire,*" the joy in sheer violence: and this joy will be relished in proportion to the lowness and humbleness of the creditor in the social scale, and is quite apt to have the effect of the most delicious dainty, and even seem the foretaste of a higher social position. Thanks to the punishment of the "ower," the creditor participates in the rights of the masters. At last he too, for once in a way, attains the edifying consciousness of being able to despise and ill-treat a creature—as an "inferior"—or at any rate of *seeing* him being despised and ill-treated, in case the actual power of punishment, the administration of punishment, has already become transferred to the "authorities." The compensation consequently consists in a claim on cruelty and a right to draw thereon.

6

It is then in *this* sphere of the law of contract that we find the cradle of the whole moral world of the ideas of "guilt," "conscience," "duty," the "sacredness of duty,"—their commencement, like the commencement of all great things in the world, is thoroughly and continuously saturated with blood. And should we not add that this world has never really lost a certain savor of blood and torture (not even in old Kant; the categorical imperative reeks of cruelty). It was in this sphere likewise that there first became formed that sinister and perhaps now indissoluble association of the ideas of "guilt" and "suffering." To put the question yet again, why can suffering be a compensation for "owing"?—Because the *infliction* of suffering produces the highest degree of happiness, because the injured party will get in exchange for his loss (including his vexation at his loss) an extraordinary counter-pleasure: the *infliction* of suffering—a real *feast*, something that, as I have said, was all the more appreciated the greater the paradox created by the rank and social status of the creditor. These observations are purely conjectural; for, apart from the painful nature of the task, it is hard to plumb such profound depths: the clumsy introduction of the idea of "revenge" as a connecting-link simply hides and obscures the view instead of rendering it clearer (revenge itself simply leads back again to the identical problem—"How can the infliction of suffering be a satisfaction?"). In my opinion it is repugnant to the delicacy, and still more to the hypocrisy of tame domestic animals (that is, modern men; that is, ourselves), to realize with all their energy the extent to which *cruelty* constituted the great joy and delight of ancient man, was an ingredient which seasoned nearly all his pleasures, and conversely the extent of the naïveté and innocence with which he manifested his need for cruelty, when he actually made as a matter of principle "disinterested malice" (or, to use Spinoza's expression, the *sympathia malevolens*) into a *normal* characteristic of man—as consequently something to which the conscience says a hearty yes. The more profound observer has perhaps already had sufficient opportunity for noticing this most ancient and radical joy and delight of mankind; in *Beyond Good and Evil*, Aph. 188 (and even earlier, in *The Dawn of Day*, Aphs. 18, 77, 113), I have cautiously indicated the continually growing spiritualization and "deification" of cruelty, which pervades the whole history of the higher civilization (and in the larger sense even constitutes it). At any rate the time is not so long past when it was impossible to conceive of royal weddings and national festivals on a grand scale, without executions, tortures, or perhaps an *auto-da-fé*, or similarly to conceive of an aristocratic household, without a creature to serve as a butt for the cruel and malicious baiting of the inmates. (The reader will perhaps remember Don Quixote at the court of the Duchess: we read nowadays the whole of *Don Quixote* with a bitter taste in the mouth, almost with a sensation of torture, a fact which would appear very strange and very incomprehensible to the author and his contemporaries—they read it with the best conscience in the world as the gayest of books; they almost died with laughing at it.) The sight of suffering does one good, the infliction of suffering does one more good—this is a hard maxim, but none the less a fundamental maxim, old, powerful, and "human, all-too-human"; one, moreover, to which perhaps even the apes as well would subscribe: for it is said that in inventing bizarre cruelties they are giving abundant proof of their future humanity, to which, as it were, they are playing the prelude. Without cruelty, no feast: so teaches the oldest and longest history of man—and in punishment too is there so much of the festive.

7

Entertaining, as I do, these thoughts, I am, let me say in parenthesis, fundamentally opposed to helping our pessimists to new water for the discordant and groaning mills of their disgust with life; on the contrary, it should be shown specifically that, at the time when mankind was not yet ashamed of its cruelty, life in the world was brighter than it is nowadays when there are pessimists. The darkening of the heavens over man has always increased in proportion to the growth of man's shame *before man*. The tired pessimistic outlook, the mistrust of the riddle of life, the icy negation of disgusted ennui, all those are not the signs of the *most evil* age of the human race: much rather do they come first to the light of day, as the swamp-flowers, which they are, when the swamp to which they belong, comes into existence—I mean the diseased refinement and moralization, thanks to which the "animal man" has at last learnt to be ashamed of all his instincts. On the road to angelhood (not to use in this context a harder word) man has developed that dyspeptic stomach and coated tongue, which have made not only the joy and innocence of the animal repulsive to him, but also life itself:—so that sometimes he stands with stopped nostrils before his own self, and, like Pope Innocent the Third, makes a black list of his own horrors ("unclean generation, loathsome nutrition when in the maternal body, badness of the matter out of which man develops, awful stench, secretion of saliva, urine, and excrement"). Nowadays, when suffering is always trotted out as the first argument *against* existence, as its most sinister query, it is well to remember the times when men judged on converse principles because they could not dispense with the *infliction* of suffering, and saw therein a magic of the first order, a veritable bait of seduction to life.

Perhaps in those days (this is to solace the weaklings) pain did not hurt so much as it does nowadays: any physician who has treated negroes (granted that these are taken as representative of the prehistoric man) suffering from severe internal inflammations which would bring a European, even though he had the soundest constitution, almost to despair, would be in a position to come to this conclusion. Pain has *not* the same effect with negroes. (The curve of human sensibilities to pain seems indeed to sink in an extraordinary and almost sudden fashion, as soon as one has passed the upper ten thousand or ten millions of over-civilized humanity, and I personally have no doubt that, by comparison with one painful night passed by one single hysterical chit of a cultured woman, the suffering of all the animals taken together who have been put to the question of the knife, so as to give scientific answers, are simply negligible.) We may perhaps be allowed to admit the possibility of the craving for cruelty not necessarily having become really extinct: it only requires, in view of the fact that pain hurts more nowadays, a certain sublimation and subtilization, it must especially be translated to the imaginative and psychic plane, and be adorned with such smug euphemisms, that even the most fastidious and hypocritical conscience could never grow suspicious of their real nature ("Tragic pity" is one of these euphemisms: another is "*les nostalgies de la croix*"). What really raises one's indignation against suffering is not suffering intrinsically, but the senselessness of suffering; such a *senselessness*, however, existed neither in Christianity, which interpreted suffering into a whole mysterious salvation-apparatus, nor in the beliefs of the naive ancient man, who only knew how to find a meaning in suffering from the standpoint of the spectator, or the inflictor of the suffering. In order to get the secret, undiscovered, and unwitnessed suffering out of the world it was almost compulsory to invent gods and a hierarchy of intermediate beings, in short, something which wanders even among secret places, sees even in the dark, and makes a point of never missing an interesting and painful spectacle. It was with the help of such inventions that life got to learn the *tour de force*, which has become part of its stock-in-trade, the *tour de force* of self-justification, of the justification of evil; nowadays this would perhaps require other auxiliary devices (for instance, life as a riddle, life as a problem of knowledge). "Every evil is justified in the sight of which a god finds edification," so rang the logic of primitive sentiment—and, indeed, was it only of primitive? The gods conceived as friends of spectacles of cruelty—oh how far does this primeval conception extend even nowadays into our European civilization! One would perhaps like in this context to consult Luther and Calvin. It is at any rate certain that even the Greeks knew no more piquant seasoning for the happiness of their gods than the joys of cruelty. What, do you think, was the mood with which Homer makes his gods look down upon the fates of men? What final meaning have at bottom the Trojan War and similar tragic horrors? It is impossible to entertain any doubt on the point: they were intended as festival games for the gods, and, in so far as the poet is of a more godlike breed than other men, as festival games also for the poets. It was in just this spirit and no other, that at a later date the moral philosophers of Greece conceived the eyes of God as still looking down on the moral struggle, the heroism, and the self-torture of the virtuous; the Heracles of duty was on a stage, and was conscious of the fact; virtue without witnesses was something quite unthinkable for this nation of actors. Must not that philosophic invention, so audacious and so fatal, which was then absolutely new to Europe, the invention of "free will," of the absolute spontaneity of man in good and evil, simply have been made for the specific purpose of justifying the idea, that the interest of the gods in humanity and human virtue was *inexhaustible*?

There would never on the stage of this free-will world be a dearth of really new, really novel and exciting situations, plots, catastrophes. A world thought out on completely deterministic lines would be easily guessed by the gods, and would consequently soon bore them—sufficient reason for these *friends of the gods*, the philosophers, not to ascribe to their gods such a deterministic world. The whole of ancient humanity is full of delicate consideration for the spectator, being as it is a world of thorough publicity and theatricality, which could not conceive of happiness without spectacles and festivals.—And, as has already been said, even in great punishment there is so much which is festive.

8

The feeling of "ought," of personal obligation (to take up again the train of our inquiry), has had, as we saw, its origin in the oldest and most original personal relationship that there is, the relationship between buyer and seller, creditor and ower: here it was that individual confronted individual, and that individual *matched himself against* individual. There has not yet been found a grade of civilization so low, as not to manifest some trace of this relationship. Making prices, assessing values, thinking out equivalents, exchanging—all this preoccupied the primal thoughts of man to such an extent that in a certain sense it constituted *thinking* itself: it was here that was trained the oldest form of sagacity, it was here in this sphere that we can perhaps trace the first commencement of man's pride, of his feeling of superiority over other animals. Perhaps our word "Mensch" (*manas*) still expresses just something of *this* self-pride: man denoted himself as the being who measures values, who values and measures, as the "assessing" animal *par excellence*. Sale and purchase, together with their psychological concomitants, are older than the origins of any form of social organization and union: it is rather from the most rudimentary form of individual right that the budding consciousness of exchange, commerce, debt, right, obligation, compensation was first transferred to the rudest and most elementary of the social complexes (in their relation to similar complexes), the habit of comparing force with force, together with that of measuring, of calculating. His eye was now focused to this perspective; and with that ponderous consistency characteristic of ancient thought, which, though set in motion with difficulty, yet proceeds inflexibly along the line on which it has started, man soon arrived at the great generalization, "everything has its price, *all* can be paid for," the oldest and most naïve moral canon of *justice*, the beginning of all "kindness," of all "equity," of all "goodwill," of all "objectivity" in the world. Justice in this initial phase is the goodwill among people of about equal power to come to terms with each other, to come to an understanding again by means of a settlement, and with regard to the less powerful, to *compel* them to agree among themselves to a settlement.

9

Measured always by the standard of antiquity (this antiquity, moreover, is present or again possible at all periods), the community stands to its members in that important and radical relationship of creditor to his "owers." Man lives in a community, man enjoys the advantages of a community (and what advantages! we occasionally underestimate them nowadays), man lives protected, spared, in peace and trust, secure from certain injuries and enmities, to which the man outside the community, the "peaceless" man, is exposed,—a German understands the original meaning of "Elend" (êlend),—secure because he has entered into pledges and obligations to the community in respect of these very injuries and enmities. What happens *when this is not the case?* The community, the defrauded creditor, will get itself paid, as well as it can, one can reckon on that. In this case the question of the direct damage done by the offender is quite subsidiary: quite apart from this the criminal[3] is above all a breaker, a breaker of word and covenant *to the whole*, as regards all the advantages and amenities of the communal life in which up to that time he had participated. The criminal is an "ower" who not only fails to repay the advances and advantages that have been given to him, but even sets out to attack his creditor: consequently he is in the future not only, as is fair, deprived of all these advantages and amenities—he is in addition reminded of the *importance* of those advantages. The wrath of the injured creditor, of the community, puts him back in the wild and outlawed

---

3 German: "*Verbrecher.*"—H.B.S

status from which he was previously protected: the community repudiates him—and now every kind of enmity can vent itself on him. Punishment is in this stage of civilization simply the copy, the mimic, of the normal treatment of the hated, disdained, and conquered enemy, who is not only deprived of every right and protection but of every mercy; so we have the martial law and triumphant festival of the *væ victis!* in all its mercilessness and cruelty. This shows why war itself (counting the sacrificial cult of war) has produced all the forms under which punishment has manifested itself in history.

10

As it grows more powerful, the community tends to take the offenses of the individual less seriously, because they are now regarded as being much less revolutionary and dangerous to the corporate existence: the evil-doer is no more outlawed and put outside the pale, the common wrath can no longer vent itself upon him with its old license,—on the contrary, from this very time it is against this wrath, and particularly against the wrath of those directly injured, that the evil-doer is carefully shielded and protected by the community. As, in fact, the penal law develops, the following characteristics become more and more clearly marked: compromise with the wrath of those directly affected by the misdeed; a consequent endeavor to localize the matter and to prevent a further, or indeed a general spread of the disturbance; attempts to find equivalents and to settle the whole matter (*compositio*); above all, the will, which manifests itself with increasing definiteness, to treat every offense as in a certain degree capable of *being paid off*, and consequently, at any rate up to a certain point, to *isolate* the offender from his act. As the power and the self-consciousness of a community increases, so proportionately does the penal law become mitigated; conversely every weakening and jeopardizing of the community revives the harshest forms of that law. The creditor has always grown more humane proportionately as he has grown more rich; finally the amount of injury he can endure without really suffering becomes the criterion of his wealth. It is possible to conceive of a society blessed with so great a *consciousness of its own power* as to indulge in the most aristocratic luxury of letting its wrong-doers go *scot-free.*—"What do my parasites matter to me?" might society say. "Let them live and flourish! I am strong enough for it."—The justice which began with the maxim, "Everything can be paid off, everything must be paid off," ends with connivance at the escape of those who cannot pay to escape—it ends, like every good thing on earth, by *destroying itself.*—The self-destruction of Justice! we know the pretty name it calls itself—*Grace!* it remains, as is obvious, the privilege of the strongest, better still, their super-law.

11

A deprecatory word here against the attempts, that have lately been made, to find the origin of justice on quite another basis—namely, on that of *resentment.* Let me whisper a word in the ear of the psychologists, if they would fain study revenge itself at close quarters: this plant blooms its prettiest at present among Anarchists and anti-Semites, a hidden flower, as it has ever been, like the violet, though, forsooth, with another perfume. And as like must necessarily emanate from like, it will not be a matter for surprise that it is just in such circles that we see the birth of endeavors (it is their old birthplace—compare above, First Essay, paragraph 14), to sanctify *revenge* under the name of *justice* (as though Justice were at bottom merely a *development* of the consciousness of injury), and thus with the rehabilitation of revenge to reinstate generally and collectively all the *reactive* emotions. I object to this last point least of all. It even seems *meritorious* when regarded from the standpoint of the whole problem of biology (from which standpoint the value of these emotions has up to the present been underestimated). And that to which I alone call attention, is the circumstance that it is the spirit of revenge itself, from which develops this new nuance of scientific equity (for the benefit of hate, envy, mistrust, jealousy, suspicion, rancor, revenge). This scientific "equity" stops immediately and makes way for the accents of deadly enmity and prejudice, so soon as another group of emotions comes on the scene, which in my opinion are of a much higher biological value than these reactions, and consequently have a paramount claim to the valuation and appreciation of science: I mean the really *active* emotions, such as personal and material ambition, and so forth. (E. Dühring, *Value of Life; Course of Philosophy*, and *passim.*) So much against this tendency in general: but as for the particular maxim of Dühring's, that the home of Justice is to be found in the sphere of the reactive feelings, our love of truth compels us drastically to invert his own proposition and to oppose to him this other maxim: the *last* sphere conquered by the spirit of justice is the sphere of the feeling of reaction! When it really comes about that the just man remains just even as regards his injurer (and not merely cold, moderate, reserved, indifferent: being just is always a *positive* state); when, in spite of the strong provocation of personal insult, contempt, and calumny, the lofty and clear objectivity of the just and judging eye (whose glance is as profound as it is gentle) is untroubled, why then we have a piece of perfection, a past master of the world—something, in fact, which it would not be wise to expect, and which should not at any rate be too easily *believed.* Speaking generally, there is no doubt but that even the justest individual only requires a little dose of hostility, malice, or innuendo to drive the blood into his brain and the fairness *from* it. The active man, the attacking, aggressive man is always a hundred degrees nearer to justice than the man who merely reacts; he certainly has no need to adopt the tactics, necessary in the case of the reacting man, of making false and biased valuations of his object. It is, in point of fact, for this reason that the aggressive man has at all times enjoyed the stronger, bolder, more aristocratic, and also *freer* outlook, the *better* conscience. On the other hand, we already surmise who it really is that has on his conscience the invention of the "bad conscience,"—the resentful man! Finally, let man look at himself in history. In what sphere up to the present has the whole administration of law, the actual need of law, found its earthly home? Perchance in the sphere of the reacting man? Not for a minute: rather in that of the active, strong, spontaneous, aggressive man? I deliberately defy the above-mentioned agitator (who himself makes this self-confession, "the creed of revenge has run through all my works and endeavors like the red thread of Justice"), and say, that judged historically law in the world represents the very war *against* the reactive feelings, the very war waged on those feelings by the powers of activity and aggression, which devote some of their strength to damming and keeping within bounds this effervescence of hysterical reactivity, and to forcing it to some compromise. Everywhere where justice is practiced and justice is maintained, it is to be observed that the stronger power, when confronted with the weaker powers which are inferior to it (whether they be groups, or individuals), searches for weapons to put an end to the senseless fury of resentment, while it carries on its object, partly by taking the victim of resentment out of the clutches of revenge, partly by substituting for revenge a campaign of its own against the enemies of peace and order, partly by finding, suggesting, and occasionally enforcing settlements, partly by standardizing certain equivalents for injuries, to which equivalents the element of resentment is henceforth finally referred. The most drastic measure, however, taken and effectuated by the supreme power, to combat the preponderance of the feelings of spite and vindictiveness—it takes this measure as soon as it is at all strong enough to do so—is the foundation of *law*, the imperative declaration of what in its eyes is to be regarded as just and lawful, and what unjust and unlawful: and while, after the foundation of law, the supreme power treats the aggressive and arbitrary acts of individuals, or of whole groups, as a violation of law, and a revolt against itself, it distracts the feelings of its subjects from the immediate injury inflicted by such a violation, and thus eventually attains the very opposite result to that always desired by revenge, which sees and recognizes nothing but the standpoint of the injured party. From henceforth the eye becomes trained to a more and more *impersonal* valuation of the deed, even the eye of the injured party himself (though this is in the final stage of all, as has been previously remarked)—on this principle "right" and "wrong" first manifest themselves after the foundation of law (and not, as Dühring maintains, only after the act of violation). To talk of intrinsic right and intrinsic wrong is absolutely nonsensical; intrinsically, an injury, an oppression, an exploitation, an annihilation can be nothing wrong, inasmuch as life is *essentially* (that is, in its cardinal functions) something which functions by injuring, oppressing, exploiting, and annihilating, and is absolutely inconceivable without such a character. It is necessary to make an even more serious confession:—viewed from the most advanced biological standpoint, conditions of legality can be only *exceptional conditions*, in that they are partial restrictions of the real life-will, which makes for power, and in that they are subordinated to the life-will's general end as particular means, that is, as means to create *larger* units of strength. A legal organization, conceived of as sovereign and universal, not as a weapon in a fight of complexes of power, but as a weapon *against* fighting, generally something after the style of Dühring's communistic model of treating every will as equal with every other will, would be a principle *hostile to life*, a destroyer and dissolver of man, an outrage on the future of man, a symptom of fatigue, a secret cut to Nothingness.—

12

A word more on the origin and end of punishment—two problems which are or ought to be kept distinct, but which unfortunately are usually lumped into one. And what tactics have our moral genealogists employed up to the present in these cases? Their inveterate naïveté. They find out some "end" in the punishment, for instance, revenge and deterrence, and then in all their innocence set this end at the beginning, as the *causa fiendi* of the punishment, and—they have done the trick. But the patching up of a history of the origin of law is the last use to which the "End in Law"[4] ought to be put. Perhaps there is no more pregnant principle for any kind of history than the following, which, difficult though it is to master, *should* none the less be *mastered* in every detail.—The origin of the existence of a thing and its final utility, its practical application and incorporation in a system of ends, are *toto cælo* opposed to each other—everything, anything, which exists and which prevails anywhere, will always be put to new purposes by a force superior to itself, will be commandeered afresh, will be turned and transformed to new uses; all "happening" in the organic world consists of *overpowering* and dominating, and again all overpowering and domination is a new interpretation and adjustment, which must necessarily obscure or absolutely extinguish the subsisting "meaning" and "end." The most perfect comprehension of the utility of any physiological organ (or also of a legal institution, social custom, political habit, form in art or in religious worship) does not for a minute imply any simultaneous comprehension of its origin: this may seem uncomfortable and unpalatable to the older men,—for it has been the immemorial belief that understanding the final cause or the utility of a thing, a form, an institution, means also understanding the reason for its origin: to give an example of this logic, the eye was made to see, the hand was made to grasp. So even punishment was conceived as invented with a view to punishing. But all ends and all utilities are only *signs* that a Will to Power has mastered a less powerful force, has impressed thereon out of its own self the meaning of a function; and the whole history of a "Thing," an organ, a custom, can on the same principle be regarded as a continuous "sign-chain" of perpetually new interpretations and adjustments, whose causes, so far from needing to have even

---

4 An allusion to *Der Zweck im Recht*, by the great German jurist, Professor Ihering.

a mutual connection, sometimes follow and alternate with each other absolutely haphazard. Similarly, the evolution of a "thing," of a custom, is anything but its *progressus* to an end, still less a logical and direct *progressus* attained with the minimum expenditure of energy and cost: it is rather the succession of processes of subjugation, more or less profound, more or less mutually independent, which operate on the thing itself; it is, further, the resistance which in each case invariably displayed this subjugation, the Protean wriggles by way of defense and reaction, and, further, the results of successful counter-efforts. The form is fluid, but the meaning is even more so—even inside every individual organism the case is the same: with every genuine growth of the whole, the "function" of the individual organs becomes shifted,—in certain cases a partial perishing of these organs, a diminution of their numbers (for instance, through annihilation of the connecting members), can be a symptom of growing strength and perfection. What I mean is this: even partial *loss of utility*, decay, and degeneration, loss of function and purpose, in a word, death, appertain to the conditions of the genuine *progressus*; which always appears in the shape of a will and way to *greater* power, and is always realized at the expense of innumerable smaller powers. The magnitude of a "progress" is gauged by the greatness of the sacrifice that it requires: humanity as a mass sacrificed to the prosperity of the one *stronger* species of Man—that *would be* a progress. I emphasize all the more this cardinal characteristic of the historic method, for the reason that in its essence it runs counter to predominant instincts and prevailing taste, which much prefer to put up with absolute casualness, even with the mechanical senselessness of all phenomena, than with the theory of a power-will, in exhaustive play throughout all phenomena. The democratic idiosyncrasy against everything which rules and wishes to rule, the modern *misarchism* (to coin a bad word for a bad thing), has gradually but so thoroughly transformed itself into the guise of intellectualism, the most abstract intellectualism, that even nowadays it penetrates and *has the right* to penetrate step by step into the most exact and apparently the most objective sciences: this tendency has, in fact, in my view already dominated the whole of physiology and biology, and to their detriment, as is obvious, in so far as it has spirited away a radical idea, the idea of true *activity*. The tyranny of this idiosyncrasy, however, results in the theory of "adaptation" being pushed forward into the van of the argument, exploited; adaptation—that means to say, a second-class activity, a mere capacity for "reacting"; in fact, life itself has been defined (by Herbert Spencer) as an increasingly effective internal adaptation to external circumstances. This definition, however, fails to realize the real essence of life, its will to power. It fails to appreciate the paramount superiority enjoyed by those plastic forces of spontaneity, aggression, and encroachment with their new interpretations and tendencies, to the operation of which adaptation is only a natural corollary: consequently the sovereign office of the highest functionaries in the organism itself (among which the life-will appears as an active and formative principle) is repudiated. One remembers Huxley's reproach to Spencer of his "administrative Nihilism": but it is a case of something much *more* than "administration."

13

To return to our subject, namely *punishment*, we must make consequently a double distinction: first, the relatively permanent *element*, the custom, the act, the "drama," a certain rigid sequence of methods of procedure; on the other hand, the fluid element, the meaning, the end, the expectation which is attached to the operation of such procedure. At this point we immediately assume, *per analogiam* (in accordance with the theory of the historic method, which we have elaborated above), that the procedure itself is something older and earlier than its utilization in punishment, that this utilization was *introduced* and interpreted into the procedure (which had existed for a long time, but whose employment had another meaning), in short, that the case is *different* from that hitherto supposed by our *naïf* genealogists of morals and of law, who thought that the procedure was *invented* for the purpose of punishment, in the same way that the hand had been previously thought to have been invented for the purpose of grasping. With regard to the other element in *punishment*, its fluid element, its meaning, the idea of punishment in a very late stage of civilization (for instance, contemporary Europe) is not content with manifesting merely one meaning, but manifests a whole synthesis "of meanings." The past general history of punishment, the history of its employment for the most diverse ends, crystallizes eventually into a kind of unity, which is difficult to analyze into its parts, and which, it is necessary to emphasize, absolutely defies definition. (It is nowadays impossible to say definitely *the precise reason* for punishment: all ideas, in which a whole process is promiscuously comprehended, elude definition; it is only that which has no history, which can be defined.) At an earlier stage, on the contrary, that synthesis of meanings appears much less rigid and much more elastic; we can realize how in each individual case the elements of the synthesis change their value and their position, so that now one element and now another stands out and predominates over the others, nay, in certain cases one element (perhaps the end of deterrence) seems to eliminate all the rest. At any rate, so as to give some idea of the uncertain, supplementary, and accidental nature of the meaning of punishment and of the manner in which one identical procedure can be employed and adapted for the most diametrically opposed objects, I will at this point give a scheme that has suggested itself to me, a scheme itself based on comparatively small and accidental material.—Punishment, as rendering the criminal harmless and incapable of further injury.—Punishment, as compensation for the injury sustained by the injured party, in any form whatsoever (including the form of sentimental compensation).—Punishment, as an isolation of that which disturbs the equilibrium, so as to prevent the further spreading of the disturbance.— Punishment as a means of inspiring fear of those who determine and execute the punishment.—Punishment as a kind of compensation for advantages which the wrong-doer has up to that time enjoyed (for example, when he is utilized as a slave in the mines).—Punishment, as the elimination of an element of decay (sometimes of a whole branch, as according to the Chinese laws, consequently as a means to the purification of the race, or the preservation of a social type).— Punishment as a festival, as the violent oppression and humiliation of an enemy that has at last been subdued.—Punishment as a mnemonic, whether for him who suffers the punishment—the so-called "correction," or for the witnesses of its administration. Punishment, as the payment of a fee stipulated for by the power which protects the evil-doer from the excesses of revenge.—Punishment, as a compromise with the natural phenomenon of revenge, in so far as revenge is still maintained and claimed as a privilege by the stronger races.—Punishment as a declaration and measure of war against an enemy of peace, of law, of order, of authority, who is fought by society with the weapons which war provides, as a spirit dangerous to the community, as a breaker of the contract on which the community is based, as a rebel, a traitor, and a breaker of the peace.

14

This list is certainly not complete; it is obvious that punishment is overloaded with utilities of all kinds. This makes it all the more permissible to eliminate one supposed utility, which passes, at any rate in the popular mind, for its most essential utility, and which is just what even now provides the strongest support for that faith in punishment which is nowadays for many reasons tottering. Punishment is supposed to have the value of exciting in the guilty the consciousness of guilt; in punishment is sought the proper *instrumentum* of that psychic reaction which becomes known as a "bad conscience," "remorse." But this theory is even, from the point of view of the present, a violation of reality and psychology: and how much more so is the case when we have to deal with the longest period of man's history, his primitive history! Genuine remorse is certainly extremely rare among wrong-doers and the victims of punishment; prisons and houses of correction are not *the* soil on which this worm of remorse pullulates for choice—this is the unanimous opinion of all conscientious observers, who in many cases arrive at such a judgment with enough reluctance and against their own personal wishes. Speaking generally, punishment hardens and numbs, it produces concentration, it sharpens the consciousness of alienation, it strengthens the power of resistance. When it happens that it breaks the man's energy and brings about a piteous prostration and abjectness, such a result is certainly even less salutary than the average effect of punishment, which is characterized by a harsh and sinister doggedness. The thought of those *prehistoric* millennia brings us to the unhesitating conclusion, that it was simply through punishment that the evolution of the consciousness of guilt was most forcibly retarded—at any rate in the victims of the punishing power. In particular, let us not underestimate the extent to which, by the very sight of the judicial and executive procedure, the wrong-doer is himself prevented from feeling that his deed, the character of his act, is *intrinsically* reprehensible: for he sees clearly the same kind of acts practiced in the service of justice, and then called good, and practiced with a good conscience; acts such as espionage, trickery, bribery, trapping, the whole intriguing and insidious art of the policeman and the informer—the whole system, in fact, manifested in the different kinds of punishment (a system not excused by passion, but based on principle), of robbing, oppressing, insulting, imprisoning, racking, murdering.—All this he sees treated by his judges, not as acts meriting censure and condemnation *in themselves*, but only in a particular context and application. It was not on this soil that grew the "bad conscience," that most sinister and interesting plant of our earthly vegetation—in point of fact, throughout a most lengthy period, no suggestion of having to do with a "guilty man" manifested itself in the consciousness of the man who judged and punished. One had merely to deal with an author of an injury, an irresponsible piece of fate. And the man himself, on whom the punishment subsequently fell like a piece of fate, was occasioned no more of an "inner pain" than would be occasioned by the sudden approach of some uncalculated event, some terrible natural catastrophe, a rushing, crushing avalanche against which there is no resistance.

15

This truth came insidiously enough to the consciousness of Spinoza (to the disgust of his commentators, who (like Kuno Fischer, for instance) give themselves no end of *trouble* to misunderstand him on this point), when one afternoon (as he sat raking up who knows what memory) he indulged in the question of what was really left for him personally of the celebrated *Morsus conscientiæ*—Spinoza, who had relegated "good and evil" to the sphere of human imagination, and indignantly defended the honor of his "free" God against those blasphemers who affirmed that God did everything *sub ratione boni* ("but this was tantamount to subordinating God to fate, and would really be the greatest of all absurdities"). For Spinoza the world had returned again to that innocence in which it lay before the discovery of the bad conscience: what, then, had happened to the *morsus conscientiæ*? "The antithesis of *gaudium*," said he at last to himself,—"A sadness accompanied by the recollection of a past event which has turned out contrary to all expectation" (*Eth.* III., Propos. XVIII. Schol. i. ii.). Evil-doers have throughout thousands of years felt when overtaken by punishment *exactly like Spinoza*, on the subject of their "offense": "here is something which went wrong contrary to my anticipation," not "I ought not to have done this."—They submitted themselves to punishment, just as one submits one's self to a disease, to a misfortune, or to death, with that stubborn and resigned fatalism which gives the Russians, for instance, even nowadays, the advantage over us Westerners, in the handling of life. If at that period there was a critique of action, the criterion was prudence: the real *effect* of punishment is unquestionably chiefly to be found in a sharpening of the sense of prudence, in a lengthening of the memory, in a will to adopt more of a policy of caution, suspicion, and secrecy; in the recognition that there are many things which are unquestionably beyond one's capacity; in a kind of improvement in self-criticism. The broad effects which can be obtained by punishment in man and beast, are the increase of fear, the sharpening of the sense of cunning, the mastery of the desires: so it is that punishment *tames* man, but does not make him "better"—it would be more correct even to go so far as to assert the contrary ("Injury makes a man cunning," says a popular proverb: so far as it makes him cunning, it makes him also bad. Fortunately, it often enough makes him stupid).

16

At this juncture I cannot avoid trying to give a tentative and provisional expression to my own hypothesis concerning the origin of the bad conscience: it is difficult to make it fully appreciated, and it requires continuous meditation, attention, and digestion. I regard the bad conscience as the serious illness which man was bound to contract under the stress of the most radical change which he has ever experienced—that change, when he found himself finally imprisoned within the pale of society and of peace.

Just like the plight of the water-animals, when they were compelled either to become land-animals or to perish, so was the plight of these half-animals, perfectly adapted as they were to the savage life of war, prowling, and adventure—suddenly all their instincts were rendered worthless and "switched off." Henceforward they had to walk on their feet—"carry themselves," whereas heretofore they had been carried by the water: a terrible heaviness oppressed them. They found themselves clumsy in obeying the simplest directions, confronted with this new and unknown world they had no longer their old guides—the regulative instincts that had led them unconsciously to safety—they were reduced, were those unhappy creatures, to thinking, inferring, calculating, putting together causes and results, reduced to that poorest and most erratic organ of theirs, their "consciousness." I do not believe there was ever in the world such a feeling of misery, such a leaden discomfort—further, those old instincts had not immediately ceased their demands! Only it was difficult and rarely possible to gratify them: speaking broadly, they were compelled to satisfy themselves by new and, as it were, hole-and-corner methods. All instincts which do not find a vent without, *turn inwards*—this is what I mean by the growing "internalization" of man: consequently we have the first growth in man, of what subsequently was called his soul. The whole inner world, originally as thin as if it had been stretched between two layers of skin, burst apart and expanded proportionately, and obtained depth, breadth, and height, when man's external outlet became *obstructed*. These terrible bulwarks, with which the social organization protected itself against the old instincts of freedom (punishments belong pre-eminently to these bulwarks), brought it about that all those instincts of wild, free, prowling man became turned backwards against man himself. Enmity, cruelty, the delight in persecution, in surprises, change, destruction—the turning all these instincts against their own possessors: this is the origin of the "bad conscience." It was man, who, lacking external enemies and obstacles, and imprisoned as he was in the oppressive narrowness and monotony of custom, in his own impatience lacerated, persecuted, gnawed, frightened, and ill-treated himself; it was this animal in the hands of the tamer, which beat itself against the bars of its cage; it was this being who, pining and yearning for that desert home of which it had been deprived, was compelled to create out of its own self, an adventure, a torture-chamber, a hazardous and perilous desert—it was this fool, this homesick and desperate prisoner—who invented the "bad conscience." But thereby he introduced that most grave and sinister illness, from which mankind has not yet recovered, the suffering of man from the disease called man, as the result of a violent breaking from his animal past, the result, as it were, of a spasmodic plunge into a new environment and new conditions of existence, the result of a declaration of war against the old instincts, which up to that time had been the staple of his power, his joy, his formidableness. Let us immediately add that this fact of an animal ego turning against itself, taking part against itself, produced in the world so novel, profound, unheard-of, problematic, inconsistent, and *pregnant* a phenomenon, that the aspect of the world was radically altered thereby. In sooth, only divine spectators could have appreciated the drama that then began, and whose end baffles conjecture as yet—a drama too subtle, too wonderful, too paradoxical to warrant its undergoing a nonsensical and unheeded performance on some random grotesque planet! Henceforth man is to be counted as one of the most unexpected and sensational lucky shots in the game of the "big baby" of Heraclitus, whether he be called Zeus or Chance—he awakens on his behalf the interest, excitement, hope, almost the confidence, of his being the harbinger and forerunner of something, of man being no end, but only a stage, an interlude, a bridge, a great promise.

17

It is primarily involved in this hypothesis of the origin of the bad conscience, that that alteration was no gradual and no voluntary alteration, and that it did not manifest itself as an organic adaptation to new conditions, but as a break, a jump, a necessity, an inevitable fate, against which there was no resistance and never a spark of resentment. And secondarily, that the fitting of a hitherto unchecked and amorphous population into a fixed form, starting as it had done in an act of violence, could only be accomplished by acts of violence and nothing else—that the oldest "State" appeared consequently as a ghastly tyranny, a grinding ruthless piece of machinery, which went on working, till this raw material of a semi-animal populace was not only thoroughly kneaded and elastic, but also *molded.* I used the word "State": my meaning is self-evident, namely, a herd of blonde beasts of prey, a race of conquerors and masters, which with all its warlike organization and all its organizing power pounces with its terrible claws on a population, in numbers possibly tremendously superior, but as yet formless, as yet nomad. Such is the origin of the "State." That fantastic theory that makes it begin with a contract is, I think, disposed of. He who can command, he who is a master by "nature," he who comes on the scene forceful in deed and gesture—what has he to do with contracts? Such beings defy calculation, they come like fate, without cause, reason, notice, excuse, they are there like the lightning is there, too terrible, too sudden, too convincing, too "different," to be personally even hated. Their work is an instinctive creating and impressing of forms, they are the most involuntary, unconscious artists that there are:—their appearance produces instantaneously a scheme of sovereignty which is live, in which the functions are partitioned and apportioned, in which above all no part is received or finds a place, until pregnant with a "meaning" in regard to the whole. They are ignorant of the meaning of guilt, responsibility, consideration, are these born organizers; in them predominates that terrible artist-egoism, that gleams like brass, and that knows itself justified to all eternity, in its work, even as a mother in her child. It is not in *them* that there grew the bad conscience, that is elementary—but it would not have grown *without* them, repulsive growth as it was, it would be missing, had not a tremendous quantity of freedom been expelled from the world by the stress of their hammer-strokes, their artist violence, or been at any rate made invisible and, as it were, *latent*. This *instinct of freedom* forced into being latent—it is already clear—this instinct of freedom forced back, trodden back, imprisoned within itself, and finally only able to find vent and relief in itself; this, only this, is the beginning of the "bad conscience."

18

Beware of thinking lightly of this phenomenon, by reason of its initial painful ugliness. At bottom it is the same active force which is at work on a more grandiose scale in those potent artists and organizers, and builds states, which here, internally, on a smaller and pettier scale and with a retrogressive tendency, makes itself a bad science in the "labyrinth of the breast," to use Goethe's phrase, and which builds negative ideals; it is, I repeat, that identical *instinct of freedom* (to use my own language, the will to power): only the material, on which this force with all its constructive and tyrannous nature is let loose, is here man himself, his whole old animal self—and not as in the case of that more grandiose and sensational phenomenon, the *other* man, *other* men. This secret self-tyranny, this cruelty of the artist, this delight in giving a form to one's self as a piece of difficult, refractory, and suffering material, in burning in a will, a critique, a contradiction, a contempt, a negation; this sinister and ghastly labor of love on the part of a soul, whose will is cloven in two within itself, which makes itself suffer from delight in the infliction of suffering; this wholly *active* bad conscience has finally (as one already anticipates)—true fountainhead as it is of idealism and imagination—produced an abundance of novel and amazing beauty and affirmation, and perhaps has really been the first to give birth to beauty at all. What would beauty be, forsooth, if its contradiction had not first been presented to consciousness, if the ugly had not first said to itself, "I am ugly"? At any rate, after this hint the problem of how far idealism and beauty can be traced in such opposite ideas as *"selflessness," self-denial, self-sacrifice,* becomes less problematical; and indubitably in future we shall certainly know the real and original character of the *delight* experienced by the self-less, the self-denying, the self-sacrificing: this delight is a phase of cruelty.—So much provisionally for the origin of "altruism" as a *moral* value, and the marking out the ground from which this value has grown: it is only the bad conscience, only the will for self-abuse, that provides the necessary conditions for the existence of altruism as a *value.*

19

Undoubtedly the bad conscience is an illness, but an illness like pregnancy is an illness. If we search out the conditions under which this illness reaches its most terrible and sublime zenith, we shall see what really first brought about its entry into the world. But to do this we must take a long breath, and we must first of all go back once again to an earlier point of view. The relation at civil law of the ower to his creditor (which has already been discussed in detail), has been interpreted once again (and indeed in a manner which historically is exceedingly remarkable and suspicious) into a relationship, which is perhaps more incomprehensible to us moderns than to any other era; that is, into the relationship of the *existing* generation to its *ancestors.* Within the original tribal association—we are talking of primitive times—each living generation recognizes a legal obligation towards the earlier generation, and particularly towards the earliest, which founded the family (and this is something much more than a mere sentimental obligation, the existence of which, during the longest period of man's history, is by no means indisputable). There prevails in them the conviction that it is only thanks to sacrifices and efforts of their ancestors, that the race *persists* at all—and that this has to be *paid back* to them by sacrifices and services. Thus is recognized the *owing* of a debt, which accumulates continually by reason of these ancestors never ceasing in their subsequent life as potent spirits to secure by their power new privileges and advantages to the race. Gratis, perchance? But there is no gratis for that raw and "mean-souled" age. What return can be made?—Sacrifice (at first, nourishment, in its crudest sense), festivals, temples, tributes of veneration, above all, obedience—since all customs are, *quâ* works of the ancestors, equally their precepts and commands—are the ancestors ever given enough? This suspicion remains and grows: from time to time it extorts a great wholesale ransom, something monstrous in the way of repayment of the creditor (the notorious sacrifice of the first-born, for example, blood, human blood in any case). The *fear* of ancestors and their power, the consciousness of owing debts to them, necessarily increases, according to this kind of logic, in the exact proportion that the race itself increases, that the race itself becomes more victorious, more independent, more honored, more feared. This, and not the contrary, is the fact. Each step towards race decay, all disastrous events, all symptoms of degeneration, of approaching disintegration, always *diminish* the fear of the founders' spirit, and whittle away the idea of his sagacity, providence, and potent presence. Conceive this crude kind of logic carried to its climax: it follows that the ancestors of the *most powerful* races must, through the growing fear that they exercise on the imaginations, grow themselves into monstrous dimensions, and become relegated to the gloom of a divine mystery that transcends imagination—the ancestor becomes at last necessarily transfigured into a *god*. Perhaps this is the very origin of the gods, that is, an origin from *fear*! And those who feel bound to add, "but from piety also," will have difficulty in maintaining this theory, with regard to the primeval and longest period of the human race. And of course this is even more the case as regards the *middle* period, the formative period of the aristocratic races—the aristocratic races which have given back with interest to their founders, the ancestors (heroes, gods), all those qualities which in the meanwhile have appeared in themselves, that is, the aristocratic qualities. We will later on glance again at the ennobling and promotion of the gods (which of course is totally distinct from their "sanctification"): let us now provisionally follow to its end the course of the whole of this development of the consciousness of "owing."

20

According to the teaching of history, the consciousness of owing debts to the deity by no means came to an end with the decay of the clan organization of society; just as mankind has inherited the ideas of "good" and "bad" from the race-nobility (together with its fundamental tendency towards establishing social distinctions), so with the heritage of the racial and tribal gods it has also inherited the incubus of debts as yet unpaid and the desire to discharge them. The transition is effected by those large populations of slaves and bondsmen, who, whether through compulsion or through submission and "*mimicry*," have accommodated themselves to the religion of their masters; through this channel these inherited tendencies inundate the world. The feeling of owing a debt to the deity has grown continuously for several centuries, always in the same proportion in which the idea of God and the consciousness of God have grown and become exalted among mankind. (The whole history of ethnic fights, victories, reconciliations, amalgamations, everything, in fact, which precedes the eventual classing of all the social elements in each great race-synthesis, are mirrored in the hotch-potch genealogy of their gods, in the legends of their fights, victories, and reconciliations. Progress towards universal empires invariably means progress towards universal deities; despotism, with its subjugation of the independent nobility, always paves the way for some system or other of monotheism.) The appearance of the Christian god, as the record god up to this time, has for that very reason brought equally into the world the record amount of guilt consciousness. Granted that we have gradually started on the *reverse* movement, there is no little probability in the deduction, based on the continuous decay in the belief in the Christian god, to the effect that there also already exists a considerable decay in the human consciousness of owing (ought); in fact, we cannot shut our eyes to the prospect of the complete and eventual triumph of atheism freeing mankind from all this feeling of obligation to their origin, their *causa prima*. Atheism and a kind of second innocence complement and supplement each other.

21

So much for my rough and preliminary sketch of the interrelation of the ideas "ought" (owe) and "duty" with the postulates of religion. I have intentionally shelved up to the present the actual moralization of these ideas (their being pushed back into the conscience, or more precisely the interweaving of the *bad* conscience with the idea of God), and at the end of the last paragraph used language to the effect that this moralization did not exist, and that consequently these ideas had necessarily come to an end, by reason of what had happened to their hypothesis, the credence in our "creditor," in God. The actual facts differ terribly from this theory. It is with the moralization of the ideas "ought" and "duty," and with their being pushed back into the *bad* conscience, that comes the first actual attempt to *reverse* the direction of the development we have just described, or at any rate to arrest its evolution; it is just at this juncture that the very hope of an eventual redemption *has to* put itself once for all into the prison of pessimism, it is at this juncture that the eye *has to* recoil and rebound in despair from off an adamantine impossibility, it is at this juncture that the ideas "guilt" and "duty" have to turn backwards—turn backwards against *whom?* There is no doubt about it; primarily against the "ower," in whom the bad conscience now establishes itself, eats, extends, and grows like a polypus throughout its length and breadth, all with such virulence, that at last, with the impossibility of paying the debt, there becomes conceived the idea of the impossibility of paying the penalty, the thought of its inexpiability (the idea of "eternal punishment")— finally, too, it turns against the "creditor," whether found in the *causa prima* of man, the origin of the human race, its sire, who henceforth becomes burdened with a curse ("Adam," "original sin," "determination of the will"), or in Nature from whose womb man springs, and on whom the responsibility for the principle of evil is now cast ("Diabolization of Nature"), or in existence generally, on this logic an absolute *white elephant*, with which mankind is landed (the Nihilistic flight from life, the demand for Nothingness, or for the opposite of existence, for some other existence, Buddhism and the like)—till suddenly we stand before that paradoxical and awful expedient, through which a tortured humanity has found a temporary alleviation, that stroke of genius called Christianity:— God personally immolating himself for the debt of man, God paying himself personally out of a pound of his own flesh, God as the one being who can deliver man from what man had become unable to deliver himself—the creditor playing scapegoat for his debtor, from *love* (can you believe it?), from love of his debtor!...

22

The reader will already have conjectured what took place on the stage and behind the scenes of this drama. That will for self-torture, that inverted cruelty of the animal man, who, turned subjective and scared into introspection (encaged as he was in "the State," as part of his taming process), invented the bad conscience so as to hurt himself, after the *natural* outlet for this will to hurt, became blocked—in other words, this man of the bad conscience exploited the religious hypothesis so as to carry his martyrdom to the ghastliest pitch of agonized intensity. Owing something to *God*: this thought becomes his instrument of torture. He apprehends in God the most extreme antitheses that he can find to his own characteristic and ineradicable animal instincts, he himself gives a new interpretation to these animal instincts as being against what he "owes" to God (as enmity, rebellion, and revolt against the "Lord," the "Father," the "Sire," the "Beginning of the world"), he places himself between the horns of the dilemma, "God" and "Devil." Every negation which he is inclined to utter to himself, to the nature, naturalness, and reality of his being, he whips into an ejaculation of "yes," uttering it as something existing, living, efficient, as being God, as the holiness of God, the judgment of God, as the hangmanship of God, as transcendence, as eternity, as unending torment, as hell, as infinity of punishment and guilt. This is a kind of madness of the will in the sphere of psychological cruelty which is absolutely unparalleled:—man's *will* to find himself guilty and blameworthy to the point of inexpiability, his *will* to think of himself as punished, without the punishment ever being able to balance the guilt, his *will* to infect and to poison the fundamental basis of the universe with the problem of punishment and guilt, in order to cut off once and for all any escape out of this labyrinth of "fixed ideas," his will for rearing an ideal—that of the "holy God"—face to face with which he can have tangible proof of his own un-worthiness. Alas for this mad melancholy beast man! What phantasies invade it, what paroxysms of perversity, hysterical senselessness, and *mental bestiality* break out immediately, at the very slightest check on its being the beast of action. All this is excessively interesting, but at the same time tainted with a black, gloomy, enervating melancholy, so that a forcible veto must be invoked against looking too long into these abysses. Here is *disease*, undubitably, the most ghastly disease that has as yet played havoc among men: and he who can still hear (but man turns now deaf ears to such sounds), how in this night of torment and nonsense there has rung out the cry of *love*, the cry of the most passionate ecstasy, of redemption in *love*, he turns away gripped by an invincible horror—in man there is so much that is ghastly—too long has the world been a mad-house.

23

Let this suffice once for all concerning the origin of the "holy God." The fact that *in itself* the conception of gods is not bound to lead necessarily to this degradation of the imagination (a temporary representation of whose vagaries we felt bound give), the fact that there exist nobler methods of utilizing the invention of gods than in this self-crucifixion and self-degradation of man, in which the last two thousand years of Europe have been past masters—these facts can fortunately be still perceived from every glance that we cast at the Grecian gods, these mirrors of noble and grandiose men, in which the *animal* in man felt itself deified, and did *not* devour itself in subjective frenzy. These Greeks long utilized their gods as simple buffers against the "bad conscience"—so that they could continue to enjoy their freedom of soul: this, of course, is diametrically opposed to Christianity's theory of its god. They went *very far* on this principle, did these splendid and lion-hearted children; and there is no lesser authority than that of the Homeric Zeus for making them realize occasionally that they are taking life too casually. "Wonderful," says he on one occasion—it has to do with the case of Ægistheus, a *very* bad case indeed—

> "Wonderful how they grumble, the mortals against the
>   immortals,
> *Only from us*, they presume, *comes evil*, but in their
>   folly,
> Fashion they, spite of fate, the doom of their own
>   disaster."

Yet the reader will note and observe that this Olympian spectator and judge is far from being angry with them and thinking evil of them on this score. "How *foolish* they are," so thinks he of the misdeeds of mortals—and "folly," "imprudence," "a little brain disturbance," and nothing more, are what the Greeks, even of the strongest, bravest period, have admitted to be the ground of much that is evil and fatal.—Folly, *not* sin, do you understand?... But even this brain disturbance was a problem—"Come, how is it even possible? How could it have really got in brains like ours, the brains of men of aristocratic ancestry, of men of fortune, of men of good natural endowments, of men of the best society, of men of nobility and virtue?" This was the question that for century on century the aristocratic Greek put to himself when confronted with every (to him incomprehensible) outrage and sacrilege with which one of his peers had polluted himself. "It must be that a god had infatuated him," he would say at last, nodding his head.—This solution is *typical* of the Greeks, ... accordingly the gods in those times subserved the functions of justifying man to a certain extent even in evil—in those days they took upon themselves not the punishment, but, what is more noble, the guilt.

24

I conclude with three queries, as you will see. "Is an ideal actually set up here, or is one pulled down?" I am perhaps asked.... But have ye sufficiently asked yourselves how dear a payment has the setting up of every ideal in the world exacted? To achieve that consummation how much truth must always be traduced and misunderstood, how many lies must be sanctified, how much conscience has got to be disturbed, how many pounds of "God" have got to be sacrificed every time? To enable a sanctuary to be set up *a sanctuary has got to be destroyed*: that is a law—show me an instance where it has not been fulfilled!... We modern men, we inherit the immemorial tradition of vivisecting the conscience, and practicing cruelty to our animal selves. That is the sphere of our most protracted training, perhaps of our artistic prowess, at any rate of our dilettantism and our perverted taste. Man has for too long regarded his natural proclivities with an "evil eye," so that eventually they have become in his system affiliated to a bad conscience. A converse endeavor would be intrinsically feasible —but who is strong enough to attempt it?—namely, to affiliate to the "bad conscience" all those *unnatural* proclivities, all those transcendental aspirations, contrary to sense, instinct, nature, and animalism—in short, all past and present ideals, which are all ideals opposed to life, and traducing the world. To whom is one to turn nowadays with *such* hopes and pretensions?—It is just the *good* men that we should thus bring about our ears; and in addition, as stands to reason, the indolent, the hedgers, the vain, the hysterical, the tired.... What is more offensive or more thoroughly calculated to alienate, than giving any hint of the exalted severity with which we treat ourselves? And again how conciliatory, how full of love does all the world show itself towards us so soon as we do as all the world docs, and "let ourselves go" like all the world. For such a consummation we need spirits of *different* caliber than seems really feasible in this age; spirits rendered potent through wars and victories, to whom conquest, adventure, danger, even pain, have become a need; for such a consummation we need habituation to sharp, rare air, to winter wanderings, to literal and metaphorical ice and mountains; we even need a kind of sublime malice, a supreme and most self-conscious insolence of knowledge, which is the appanage of great health; we need (to summarize the awful truth) just this *great health*!

Is this even feasible to-day?... But some day, in a stronger age than this rotting and introspective present, must he in sooth come to us, even the *redeemer* of great love and scorn, the creative spirit, rebounding by the impetus of his own force back again away from every transcendental plane and dimension, he whose solitude is misunderstanded [*sic*] of the people, as though it were a flight *from* reality;—while actually it is only his diving, burrowing, and penetrating *into* reality, so that when he comes again to the light he can at once bring about by these means the *redemption* of this reality; its redemption from the curse which the old ideal has laid upon it. This man of the future, who in this wise will redeem us from the old ideal, as he will from that ideal's necessary corollary of great nausea, will to nothingness, and Nihilism; this tocsin of noon and of the great verdict, which renders the will again free, who gives back to the world its goal and to man his hope, this Antichrist and Antinihilist, this conqueror of God and of Nothingness—*he must one day come.*

25

But what am I talking of? Enough! Enough? At this juncture I have only one proper course, silence: otherwise trespass on a domain open alone to one who is younger than I, one stronger, more "*future*" than I—open alone to *Zarathustra, Zarathustra the godless.*

Third Essay:
What is the Meaning of Ascetic Ideals?

"Careless, mocking, forceful—so does wisdom wish us:
she is a woman, and never loves any one but a warrior."

Thus Spake Zarathustra

1

What is the meaning of ascetic ideals? In artists, nothing, or too much; in philosophers and scholars, a kind of "flair" and instinct for the conditions most favorable to advanced intellectualism; in women, at best an *additional* seductive fascination, a little *morbidezza* on a fine piece of flesh, the angelhood of a fat, pretty animal; in physiological failures and whiners (in the *majority* of mortals), an attempt to pose as "too good" for this world, a holy form of debauchery, their chief weapon in the battle with lingering pain and ennui; in priests, the actual priestly faith, their best engine of power, and also the supreme authority for power; in saints, finally a pretext for hibernation, their *novissima gloriæ cupido*, their peace in nothingness ("God"), their form of madness.

But in the very fact that the ascetic ideal has meant so much to man, lies expressed the fundamental feature of man's will, his *horror vacui: he needs a goal*—and he will sooner will nothingness than not will at all.—Am I not understood?—Have I not been understood?—"Certainly not, sir?"—Well, let us begin at the beginning.

2

What is the meaning of ascetic ideals? Or, to take an individual case in regard to which I have often been consulted, what is the meaning, for example, of an artist like Richard Wagner paying homage to chastity in his old age? He had always done so, of course, in a certain sense, but it was not till quite the end, that he did so in an ascetic sense. What is the meaning of this "change of attitude,"

269

this radical revolution in his attitude—for that was what it was? Wagner veered
thereby straight round into his own opposite. What is the meaning of an artist
veering round into his own opposite? At this point (granted that we do not
mind stopping a little over this question), we immediately call to mind the best,
strongest, gayest, and boldest period, that there perhaps ever was in Wagner's
life: that was the period, when he was genuinely and deeply occupied with the
idea of "Luther's Wedding." Who knows what chance is responsible for our
now having the *Meistersingers* instead of this wedding music? And how much in
the latter is perhaps just an echo of the former? But there is no doubt but that
the theme would have dealt with the praise of chastity. And certainly it would
also have dealt with the praise of sensuality, and even so, it would seem quite
in order, and even so, it would have been equally Wagnerian. For there is no
necessary antithesis between chastity and sensuality: every good marriage, every
authentic heart-felt love transcends this antithesis. Wagner would, it seems to
me, have done well to have brought this *pleasing* reality home once again to his
Germans, by means of a bold and graceful "Luther Comedy," for there were
and are among the Germans many revilers of sensuality; and perhaps Luther's
greatest merit lies just in the fact of his having had the courage of his *sensuality*
(it used to be called, prettily enough, "evangelistic freedom "). But even in those
cases where that antithesis between chastity and sensuality does exist, there has
fortunately been for some time no necessity for it to be in any way a tragic
antithesis. This should, at any rate, be the case with all beings who are sound
in mind and body, who are far from reckoning their delicate balance between
"animal" and "angel," as being on the face of it one of the principles opposed to
existence—the most subtle and brilliant spirits, such as Goethe, such as Hafiz,
have even seen in this a *further* charm of life. Such "conflicts" actually allure one
to life. On the other hand, it is only too clear that when once these ruined swine
are reduced to worshipping chastity—and there are such swine—they only see
and worship in it the antithesis to themselves, the antithesis to ruined swine. Oh
what a tragic grunting and eagerness! You can just think of it—they worship
that painful and superfluous contrast, which Richard Wagner in his latter days
undoubtedly wished to set to music, and to place on the stage! "*For what purpose,
forsooth?*" as we may reasonably ask. What did the swine matter to him; what do
they matter to us?

3

At this point it is impossible to beg the further question of what he really had to do with that manly (ah, so unmanly) country bumpkin, that poor devil and natural, Parsifal, whom he eventually made a Catholic by such fraudulent devices. What? Was this Parsifal really meant *seriously?* One might be tempted to suppose the contrary, even to wish it—that the Wagnerian Parsifal was meant joyously, like a concluding play of a trilogy or satyric drama, in which Wagner the tragedian wished to take farewell of us, of himself, above all of tragedy, and to do so in a manner that should be quite fitting and worthy, that is, with an excess of the most extreme and flippant parody of the tragic itself, of the ghastly earthly seriousness and earthly woe of old—a parody of that *most crude phase* in the unnaturalness of the ascetic ideal, that had at length been overcome. That, as I have said, would have been quite worthy of a great tragedian; who like every artist first attains the supreme pinnacle of his greatness when he can look *down* into himself and his art, when he can *laugh* at himself. Is Wagner's Parsifal his secret laugh of superiority over himself, the triumph of that supreme artistic freedom and artistic transcendency which he has at length attained. We might, I repeat, wish it were so, for what can Parsifal, *taken seriously*, amount to? Is it really necessary to see in it (according to an expression once used against me) the product of an insane hate of knowledge, mind, and flesh? A curse on flesh and spirit in one breath of hate? An apostasy and reversion to the morbid Christian and obscurantist ideals? And finally a self-negation and self-elimination on the part of an artist, who till then had devoted all the strength of his will to the contrary, namely, the *highest* artistic expression of soul and body. And not only of his art; of his life as well. Just remember with what enthusiasm Wagner followed in the footsteps of Feuerbach. Feuerbach's motto of "healthy sensuality" rang in the ears of Wagner during the thirties and forties of the century, as it did in the ears of many Germans (they dubbed themselves "*Young* Germans"), like the word of redemption. Did he eventually *change his mind* on the subject? For it seems at any rate that he eventually wished to *change his teaching* on that subject ... and not only is that the case with the Parsifal trumpets on the stage: in the melancholy, cramped, and embarrassed lucubrations of his later years, there are a hundred places in which there are manifestations of a secret wish and will, a despondent, uncertain, unavowed will to preach actual retrogression, conversion, Christianity, mediævalism, and to say to his disciples, "All is vanity! Seek salvation elsewhere!" Even the "blood of the Redeemer" is once invoked.

4

Let me speak out my mind in a case like this, which has many painful elements—and it is a typical case: it is certainly best to separate an artist from his work so completely that he cannot be taken as seriously as his work. He is after all merely the presupposition of his work, the womb, the soil, in certain cases the dung and manure, on which and out of which it grows—and consequently, in most cases, something that must be forgotten if the work itself is to be enjoyed. The insight into the *origin* of a work is a matter for psychologists and vivisectors, but never either in the present or the future for the æsthetes, the artists. The author and creator of Parsifal was as little spared the necessity of sinking and living himself into the terrible depths and foundations of mediæval soul-contrasts, the necessity of a malignant abstraction from all intellectual elevation, severity, and discipline, the necessity of a kind of mental perversity (if the reader will pardon me such a word), as little as a pregnant woman is spared the horrors and marvels of pregnancy, which, as I have said, must be forgotten if the child is to be enjoyed. We must guard ourselves against the confusion, into which an artist himself would fall only too easily (to employ the English terminology) out of psychological "contiguity"; as though the artist himself actually were the object which he is able to represent, imagine, and express. In point of fact, the position is that even if he conceived he were such an object, he would certainly not represent, conceive, express it. Homer would not have created an Achilles, nor Goethe a Faust, if Homer had been an Achilles or if Goethe had been a Faust. A complete and perfect artist is to all eternity separated from the "real," from the actual; on the other hand, it will be appreciated that he can at times get tired to the point of despair of this eternal "unreality" and falseness of his innermost being—and that he then sometimes attempts to trespass on to the most forbidden ground, on reality, and attempts to have real *existence*. With what success? The success will be guessed—it is the *typical velleity* of the artist; the same velleity to which Wagner fell a victim in his old age, and for which he had to pay so dearly and so fatally (he lost thereby his most valuable friends).

But after all, quite apart from this velleity, who would not wish emphatically for Wagner's own sake that he had taken farewell of us and of his art in a *different* manner, not with a *Parsifal*, but in more victorious, more self-confident, more Wagnerian style—a style less misleading, a style less ambiguous with regard to his whole meaning, less Schopenhauerian, less Nihilistic?...

5

What, then, is the meaning of ascetic ideals? In the case of an artist we are getting to understand their meaning: *Nothing at all* ... or so much that it is as good as nothing at all. Indeed, what is the use of them? Our artists have for a long time past not taken up a sufficiently independent attitude, either in the world or against it, to warrant their valuations and the changes in these valuations exciting interest. At all times they have played the valet of some morality, philosophy, or religion, quite apart from the fact that unfortunately they have often enough been the inordinately supple courtiers of their clients and patrons, and the inquisitive toadies of the powers that are existing, or even of the new powers to come. To put it at the lowest, they always need a rampart, a support, an already constituted authority: artists never stand by themselves, standing alone is opposed to their deepest instincts. So, for example, did *Richard Wagner* take, "when the time had come," the philosopher Schopenhauer for his covering man in front, for his rampart. Who would consider it even thinkable, that he would have had the *courage* for an ascetic ideal, without the support afforded him by the philosophy of Schopenhauer, without the authority of Schopenhauer, which *dominated* Europe in the seventies? (This is without consideration of the question whether an artist without the milk[5] of an orthodoxy would have been possible at all.) This brings us to the more serious question: What is the meaning of a real *philosopher* paying homage to the ascetic ideal, a really self-dependent intellect like Schopenhauer, a man and knight with a glance of bronze, who has the courage to be himself, who knows how to stand alone without first waiting for men who cover him in front, and the nods of his superiors? Let us now consider at once the remarkable attitude of Schopenhauer towards *art*, an attitude which

---

5 An allusion to the celebrated monologue in William Tell.

has even a fascination for certain types. For that is obviously the reason why Richard Wagner *all at once* went over to Schopenhauer (persuaded thereto, as one knows, by a poet, Herwegh), went over so completely that there ensued the cleavage of a complete theoretic contradiction between his earlier and his later æsthetic faiths—the earlier, for example, being expressed in *Opera and Drama*, the later in the writings which he published from 1870 onwards. In particular, Wagner from that time onwards (and this is the volte-face which alienates us the most) had no scruples about changing his judgment concerning the value and position of music itself. What did he care if up to that time he had made of music a means, a medium, a "woman," that in order to thrive needed an end, a man—that is, the drama? He suddenly realized that *more* could be effected by the novelty of the Schopenhauerian theory in *majorem musicæ gloriam*—that is to say, by means of the *sovereignty* of music, as Schopenhauer understood it; music abstracted from and opposed to all the other arts, music as the independent art-in-itself, *not* like the other arts, affording reflections of the phenomenal world, but rather the language of the will itself, speaking straight out of the "abyss" as its most personal, original, and direct manifestation. This extraordinary rise in the value of music (a rise which seemed to grow out of the Schopenhauerian philosophy) was at once accompanied by an unprecedented rise in the estimation in which the musician himself was held: he became now an oracle, a priest, nay, more than a priest, a kind of mouthpiece for the "intrinsic essence of things," a telephone from the other world—from henceforward he talked not only music, did this ventriloquist of God, he talked metaphysic; what wonder that one day he eventually talked *ascetic ideals.*

6

Schopenhauer has made use of the Kantian treatment of the æsthetic problem—though he certainly did not regard it with the Kantian eyes. Kant thought that he showed honor to art when he favored and placed in the foreground those of the predicates of the beautiful, which constitute the honor of knowledge: impersonality and universality. This is not the place to discuss whether this was not a complete mistake; all that I wish to emphasize is that Kant, just like other philosophers, instead of envisaging the æsthetic problem from the standpoint of the experiences of the artist (the creator), has only considered art and beauty from the standpoint of the spectator, and has thereby imperceptibly imported the spectator himself into the idea of the "beautiful"! But if only the philosophers of the beautiful had sufficient knowledge of this "spectator"!—Knowledge of him as a great fact of personality, as a great experience, as a wealth of strong and most individual events, desires, surprises, and raptures in the sphere of beauty! But, as I feared, the contrary was always the case. And so we get from our philosophers, from the very beginning, definitions on which the lack of a subtler personal experience squats like a fat worm of crass error, as it does on Kant's famous definition of the beautiful. "That is beautiful," says Kant, "which pleases without interesting." Without interesting! Compare this definition with this other one, made by a real "spectator" and "artist"—by Stendhal, who once called the beautiful *une promesse de bonheur*. Here, at any rate, the one point which Kant makes prominent in the æsthetic position is repudiated and eliminated—*le désintéressement*. Who is right, Kant or Stendhal? When, forsooth, our æsthetes never get tired of throwing into the scales in Kant's favor the fact that under the magic of beauty men can look at even naked female statues "without interest," we can certainly laugh a little at their expense:—in regard to this ticklish point the experiences of *artists* are more "interesting," and at any rate Pygmalion was not necessarily an "unæsthetic man." Let us think all the better of the innocence of our æsthetes, reflected as it is in such arguments; let us, for instance, count to Kant's honor the country-parson naïveté of his doctrine concerning the peculiar character of the sense of touch! And here we come back to Schopenhauer, who stood in much closer neighborhood to the arts than did Kant, and yet never escaped outside the pale of the Kantian definition; how was that? The circumstance is marvelous enough: he interprets the expression, "without interest," in the most personal fashion, out of an experience which must in his case have been part and parcel of his regular routine. On few subjects does Schopenhauer speak with such certainty as on the working of æsthetic contemplation: he says of it that it simply counteracts sexual interest, like lupulin and camphor; he never gets tired of glorifying this escape from the "Life-will" as the great advantage and utility of the æsthetic state. In fact, one is tempted to ask if his fundamental conception of Will and Idea, the thought that there can only exist freedom from the "will" by means of "idea," did not originate in a generalization from this sexual experience. (In all questions concerning the Schopenhauerian philosophy, one should, by the bye, never lose sight of the consideration that it is the conception of a youth of twenty-six, so that it participates not only in what is peculiar to Schopenhauer's life, but in what is peculiar to that special period of his life.) Let us listen, for instance, to one of the most expressive among the countless passages which he has written in honor of the æsthetic state (*World as Will and Idea*, i. 231); let us listen to the tone, the suffering, the happiness, the gratitude, with which such words are uttered: "This is the painless state which Epicurus praised as the highest good and as the state of the gods; we are during that moment freed from the vile pressure of the will, we celebrate the Sabbath of the will's hard labor, the wheel of Ixion stands still." What vehemence of language! What images of anguish and protracted revulsion! How almost pathological is that temporal antithesis between "that moment" and everything else, the "wheel of Ixion," "the hard labor of the will," "the vile pressure of the will." But granted that Schopenhauer was a hundred times right for himself personally, how does that help our insight into the nature of the beautiful? Schopenhauer has described one effect of the beautiful,—the calming of the will,—but is this effect really normal? As has been mentioned, Stendhal, an equally sensual but more happily constituted nature than Schopenhauer, gives prominence to another effect of the "beautiful." "The beautiful promises happiness." To him it is just the excitement of the "will" (the "interest") by the beauty that seems the essential fact. And does not Schopenhauer ultimately lay himself open to the objection, that he is quite wrong in regarding himself as a Kantian on this point, that he has absolutely failed to understand in a Kantian sense the Kantian definition of the beautiful—that the beautiful pleased him as well by means of an interest, by means, in fact, of the strongest and most personal interest of all, that: of the victim of torture who escapes from his torture?—And to come back again to our first question, "What is the meaning of a philosopher paying homage to ascetic ideals?" We get now, at any rate, a first hint; he wishes to escape *from a torture.*

7

Let us beware of making dismal faces at the word "torture"—there is certainly in this case enough to deduct, enough to discount—there is even something to laugh at. For we must certainly not underestimate the fact that Schopenhauer, who in practice treated sexuality as a personal enemy (including its tool, woman, that *"instrumentum diaboli")*, needed enemies to keep him in a good humor; that he loved grim, bitter, blackish-green words; that he raged for the sake of raging, out of passion; that he would have grown ill, would have become a *pessimist* (for he was not a pessimist, however much he wished to be), without his enemies, without Hegel, woman, sensuality, and the whole "will for existence" "keeping on." Without them Schopenhauer would not have "kept on," that is a safe wager; he would have run away: but his enemies held him fast, his enemies always enticed him back again to existence, his wrath was just as theirs' was to the ancient Cynics, his balm, his recreation, his recompense, his *remedium* against disgust, his *happiness.* So much with regard to what is most personal in the case of Schopenhauer; on the other hand, there is still much which is typical in him—and only now we come back to our problem. It is an accepted and indisputable fact, so long as there are philosophers in the world and wherever philosophers have existed (from India to England, to take the opposite poles of philosophic ability), that there exists a real irritation and rancor on the part of philosophers towards sensuality. Schopenhauer is merely the most eloquent, and if one has the ear for it, also the most fascinating and enchanting outburst. There similarly exists a real philosophic bias and affection for the whole ascetic ideal; there should be no illusions on this score. Both these feelings, as has been said, belong to the type; if a philosopher lacks both of them, then he is—you may be certain of it—never anything but a "pseudo." What does this *mean?* For this state of affairs must first be, interpreted: in itself it stands there stupid, to all eternity, like any "Thing-in-itself." Every animal, including *la bête philosophe,* strives instinctively after an *optimum* of favorable conditions, under which he can let his whole strength have play, and achieves his maximum consciousness of power; with equal instinctiveness, and with a fine perceptive flair which is superior to any reason, every animal shudders mortally at every kind of disturbance and hindrance which obstructs or could obstruct his way to that *optimum* (it is not his way to happiness of which I am talking, but his way to power, to action, the most powerful action, and in point of fact in many cases his way to unhappiness). Similarly, the philosopher shudders mortally at *marriage*, together with all that could persuade him to it—marriage as a fatal hindrance on the way to the *optimum*. Up to the present what great philosophers have been married? Heraclitus, Plato, Descartes, Spinoza, Leibnitz, Kant, Schopenhauer— they were not married, and, further, one cannot *imagine* them as married. A married philosopher belongs to *comedy*, that is my rule; as for that exception of a Socrates—the malicious Socrates married himself, it seems, *ironice*, just to prove this *very* rule. Every philosopher would say, as Buddha said, when the birth of a son was announced to him: "Râhoula has been born to me, a fetter has been forged for me" (Râhoula means here "a little demon"); there must come an hour of reflection to every "free spirit" (granted that he has had previously an hour of thoughtlessness), just as one came once to the same Buddha: "Narrowly cramped," he reflected, "is life in the house; it is a place of uncleanness; freedom is found in leaving the house." Because he thought like this, he left the house. So many bridges to *independence* are shown in the ascetic ideal, that the philosopher cannot refrain from exultation and clapping of hands when he hears the history of all those resolute ones, who on one day uttered a nay to all servitude and went into some *desert*; even granting that they were only strong asses, and the absolute opposite of strong minds. What, then, does the ascetic ideal mean in a philosopher? This is my answer—it will have been guessed long ago: when he sees this ideal the philosopher smiles because he sees therein an *optimum* of the conditions of the highest and boldest intellectuality; he does not thereby deny "existence," he rather affirms thereby *his* existence and *only* his existence, and this perhaps to the point of not being far off the blasphemous wish, *pereat mundus, fiat philosophia, fiat philosophus, fiam!...*

8

These philosophers, you see, are by no means uncorrupted witnesses and judges of the *value* of the ascetic ideal. They think *of themselves*—what is the "saint" to them? They think of that which to them personally is most indispensable; of freedom from compulsion, disturbance, noise: freedom from business, duties, cares; of clear head; of the dance, spring, and flight of thoughts;

of good air—rare, clear, free, dry, as is the air on the heights, in which every animal creature becomes more intellectual and gains wings; they think of peace in every cellar; all the hounds neatly chained; no baying of enmity and uncouth rancor; no remorse of wounded ambition; quiet and submissive internal organs, busy as mills, but unnoticed; the heart alien, transcendent, future, posthumous—to summarize, they mean by the ascetic ideal the joyous asceticism of a deified and newly fledged animal, sweeping over life rather than resting. We know what are the three great catch-words of the ascetic ideal: poverty, humility, chastity; and now just look closely at the life of all the great fruitful inventive spirits—you will always find again and again these three qualities up to a certain extent. *Not* for a minute, as is self-evident, as though, perchance, they were part of their virtues—what has this type of man to do with virtues?—but as the most essential and natural conditions of their *best* existence, their *finest* fruitfulness. In this connection it is quite possible that their predominant intellectualism had first to curb an unruly and irritable pride, or an insolent sensualism, or that it had all its work cut out to maintain its wish for the "desert" against perhaps an inclination to luxury and dilettantism, or similarly against an extravagant liberality of heart and hand. But their intellect did effect all this, simply because it was the *dominant* instinct, which carried through its orders in the case of all the other instincts. It effects it still; if it ceased to do so, it would simply not be dominant. But there is not one iota of "virtue" in all this. Further, the *desert*, of which I just spoke, in which the strong, independent, and well-equipped spirits retreat into their hermitage—oh, how different is it from the cultured classes' dream of a desert! In certain cases, in fact, the cultured classes themselves are the desert. And it is certain that all the actors of the intellect would not endure this desert for a minute. It is nothing like romantic and Syrian enough for them, nothing like enough of a stage desert! Here as well there are plenty of asses, but at this point the resemblance ceases. But a desert nowadays is something like this—perhaps a deliberate obscurity; a getting-out-of the way of one's self; a fear of noise, admiration, papers, influence; a little office, a daily task, something that hides rather than brings to light; sometimes associating with harmless, cheerful beasts and fowls, the sight of which refreshes; a mountain for company, but not a dead one, one with *eyes* (that is, with lakes); in certain cases even a room in a crowded hotel where one can reckon on not being recognized, and on being able to talk with impunity to every one: here is the desert—oh, it is lonely enough, believe me! I grant that when Heraclitus retreated to the courts and cloisters of the colossal temple of Artemis, that "wilderness" was worthier; why do we *lack* such temples? (perchance we do not lack them: I just think of my splendid study in the *Piazza di San Marco*, in spring, of course, and in the morning, between ten and twelve). But that which Heraclitus shunned is still just what we too avoid nowadays: the noise and democratic babble of the Ephesians, their politics, their news from the "empire" (I mean, of course, Persia), their market-trade in "the things of to-day"—for there is one thing from which we philosophers especially need a rest—from the things of "to-day." We honor the silent, the cold, the noble, the far, the past, everything, in fact, at the sight of which the soul is not bound to brace itself up and defend itself—something with which one can speak without *speaking aloud.* Just listen now to the tone a spirit has when it speaks; every spirit has its own tone and loves its own tone. That thing yonder, for instance, is bound to be an agitator, that is, a hollow head, a hollow mug: whatever may go into him, everything comes back from him dull and thick, heavy with the echo of the great void. That spirit yonder nearly always speaks hoarse: has he, perchance, *thought* himself hoarse? It may be so—ask the physiologists—but he who thinks in *words,* thinks as a speaker and not as a thinker (it shows that he does not think of objects or think objectively, but only of his relations with objects—that, in point of fact, he only thinks of himself and his audience). This third one speaks aggressively, he comes too near our body, his breath blows on us—we shut our mouth involuntarily, although he speaks to us through a book: the tone of his style supplies the reason—he has no time, he has small faith in himself, he finds expression now or never. But a spirit who is sure of himself speaks softly; he seeks secrecy, he lets himself be awaited. A philosopher is recognized by the fact that he shuns three brilliant and noisy things—fame, princes, and women: which is not to say that they do not come to him. He shuns every glaring light: therefore he shuns his time and its "daylight." Therein he is as a shadow; the deeper sinks the sun, the greater grows the shadow. As for his humility, he endures, as he endures darkness, a certain dependence and obscurity: further, he is afraid of the shock of lightning, he shudders at the insecurity of a tree which is too isolated and too exposed, on which every storm vents its temper, every temper its storm. His "maternal" instinct, his secret love for that which grows in him, guides him into states where he is relieved from the necessity of taking care of *himself,* in the same way in which the "*mother*" instinct in woman has thoroughly maintained up to the present woman's dependent position. After all, they demand little enough, do these philosophers, their favorite motto is, "He who possesses is possessed." All this is *not*, as I must say again and again, to be attributed to a virtue, to a meritorious wish for moderation and simplicity; but because their supreme lord so demands of them, demands wisely and inexorably; their lord who is eager only for one thing, for which alone he musters, and for which alone he hoards everything—time, strength, love, interest. This kind of man likes not to be disturbed by enmity, he likes not to be disturbed by friendship, it is a type which forgets or despises easily. It strikes him as bad form to play the martyr, "to *suffer* for truth"—he leaves all that to the ambitious and to the stage-heroes of the intellect, and to all those, in fact, who have time enough for such luxuries (they themselves, the philosophers, have something *to do* for truth). They make a sparing use of big words; they are said to be adverse to the word "truth" itself: it has a "high falutin'" ring. Finally, as far as the chastity of philosophers is concerned, the fruitfulness of this type of mind is manifestly in another sphere than that of children; perchance in some other sphere, too, they have the survival of their name, their little immortality (philosophers in ancient India would express themselves with still greater boldness: "Of what use is posterity to him whose soul is the world?"). In this attitude there is not a trace of chastity, by reason of any ascetic scruple or hatred of the flesh, any more than it is chastity for an athlete or a jockey to abstain from women; it is rather the will of the dominant instinct, at any rate, during the period of their advanced philosophic pregnancy. Every artist knows the harm done by sexual intercourse on occasions of great mental strain and preparation; as far as the strongest artists and those with the surest instincts are concerned, this is not necessarily a case of experience—hard experience—but it is simply their "maternal" instinct which, in order to benefit the growing work, disposes recklessly (beyond all its normal stocks and supplies) of the *vigor* of its *animal* life; the greater power then *absorbs* the lesser. Let us now apply this interpretation to gauge correctly the case of Schopenhauer, which we have already mentioned: in his case, the sight of the beautiful acted manifestly like a resolving irritant on the chief power of his nature (the power of contemplation and of intense penetration); so that this strength exploded and became suddenly master of his consciousness. But this by no means excludes the possibility of that particular sweetness and fullness, which is peculiar to the æsthetic state, springing directly from the ingredient of sensuality (just as that "idealism" which is peculiar to girls at puberty originates in the same source)—it may be, consequently, that sensuality is not removed by the approach of the æsthetic state, as Schopenhauer believed, but merely becomes transfigured, and ceases to enter into the consciousness as sexual excitement. (I shall return once again to this point in connection with the more delicate problems of the *physiology of the æsthetic*, a subject which up to the present has been singularly untouched and unelucidated.)

9

A certain asceticism, a grimly gay whole-hearted renunciation, is, as we have seen, one of the most favorable conditions for the highest intellectualism, and, consequently, for the most natural corollaries of such intellectualism: we shall therefore be proof against any surprise at the philosophers in particular always treating the ascetic ideal with a certain amount of predilection. A serious historical investigation shows the bond between the ascetic ideal and philosophy to be still much tighter and still much stronger. It may be said that it was only in the *leading strings* of this ideal that philosophy really learnt to make its first steps and baby paces—alas how clumsily, alas how crossly, alas how ready to tumble down and lie on its stomach was this shy little darling of a brat with its bandy legs! The early history of philosophy is like that of all good things;—for a long time they had not the courage to be themselves, they kept always looking round to see if no one would come to their help; further, they were afraid of all who looked at them. Just enumerate in order the particular tendencies and virtues of the philosopher—his tendency to doubt, his tendency to deny, his tendency to wait (to be "ephectic"), his tendency to analyze, search, explore, dare, his tendency to compare and to equalize, his will to be neutral and objective, his will for everything which is "*sine ira et studio*":—has it yet been realized that for quite a lengthy period these tendencies went counter to the first claims of morality and conscience? (To say nothing at all of *Reason*, which even Luther chose to call *Frau Klüglin,*[6] *the sly whore.*) Has it been yet appreciated that a philosopher, in the event of his *arriving* at self-consciousness, must needs feel

---

6 Mistress Sly.—Tr.

himself an incarnate "*nitimur in vetitum*"—and consequently *guard* himself against "his own sensations," against self-consciousness? It is, I repeat, just the same with all good things, on which we now pride ourselves; even judged by the standard of the ancient Greeks, our whole modern life, in so far as it is not weakness, but power and the consciousness of power, appears pure "Hybris" and godlessness: for the things which are the very reverse of those which we honor to-day, have had for a long time conscience on their side, and God as their guardian. "Hybris" is our whole attitude to nature nowadays, our violation of nature with the help of machinery, and all the unscrupulous ingenuity of our scientists and engineers. "Hybris" is our attitude to God, that is, to some alleged teleological and ethical spider behind the meshes of the great trap of the causal web. Like Charles the Bold in his war with Louis the Eleventh, we may say, "*je combats l'universelle araignée*"; "Hybris" is our attitude to ourselves—for we experiment with ourselves in a way that we would not allow with any animal, and with pleasure and curiosity open our soul in our living body: what matters now to us the "salvation" of the soul? We heal ourselves afterwards: being ill is instructive, we doubt it not, even more instructive than being well—inoculators of disease seem to us to-day even more necessary than any medicine-men and "saviors." There is no doubt we do violence to ourselves nowadays, we crackers of the soul's kernel, we incarnate riddles, who are ever asking riddles, as though life were naught else than the cracking of a nut; and even thereby must we necessarily become day by day more and more *worthy* to be asked questions and worthy to ask them, even thereby do we perchance also become worthier to—live?

... All good things were once bad things; from every original sin has grown an original virtue. Marriage, for example, seemed for a long time a sin against the rights of the community; a man formerly paid a fine for the insolence of claiming one woman to himself (to this phase belongs, for instance, the *jus primæ noctis*, to-day still in Cambodia the privilege of the priest, that guardian of the "good old customs").

The soft, benevolent, yielding, sympathetic feelings—eventually valued so highly that they almost became "intrinsic values," were for a very long time actually despised by their possessors: gentleness was then a subject for shame, just as hardness is now (compare *Beyond Good and Evil*, Aph. 260). The submission to *law*: oh, with what qualms of conscience was it that the noble races throughout the world renounced the *vendetta* and gave the law power over themselves! Law was long a *vetitum*, a blasphemy, an innovation; it was introduced with force, like a force, to which men only submitted with a sense of personal shame. Every tiny step forward in the world was formerly made at the cost of mental and physical torture. Nowadays the whole of this point of view— "that not only stepping forward, nay, stepping at all, movement, change, all needed their countless martyrs," rings in our ears quite strangely. I have put it forward in the *Dawn of Day*, Aph. 18. "Nothing is purchased more dearly," says the same book a little later, "than the modicum of human reason and freedom which is now our pride. But that pride is the reason why it is now almost impossible for us to feel in sympathy with those immense periods of the 'Morality of Custom,' which lie at the beginning of the 'world's history,' constituting as they do the real decisive historical principle which has fixed the character of humanity; those periods, I repeat, when throughout the world suffering passed for virtue, cruelty for virtue, deceit for virtue, revenge for virtue, repudiation of the reason for virtue; and when, conversely, well-being passed current for danger, the desire for knowledge for danger, pity for danger, peace for danger, being pitied for shame, work for shame, madness for divinity, and *change* for immorality and incarnate corruption!"

10

There is in the same book, Aph. 12, an explanation of the *burden* of unpopularity under which the earliest race of contemplative men had to live— despised almost as widely as they were first feared! Contemplation first appeared on earth in a disguised shape, in an ambiguous form, with an evil heart and often with an uneasy head: there is no doubt about it. The inactive, brooding, unwarlike element in the instincts of contemplative men long invested them with a cloud of suspicion: the only way to combat this was to excite a definite *fear*. And the old Brahmans, for example, knew to a nicety how to do this! The oldest philosophers were well versed in giving to their very existence and appearance, meaning, firmness, background, by reason whereof men learnt to *fear* them; considered more precisely, they did this from an even more fundamental need, the need of inspiring in themselves fear and self-reverence. For they found even in their own souls all the valuations turned *against* themselves; they had to fight down every kind of suspicion and antagonism against "the philosophic element in themselves." Being men of a terrible age, they did this with terrible means: cruelty to themselves, ingenious self-mortification—this was the chief method of these ambitious hermits and intellectual revolutionaries, who were obliged to force down the gods and the traditions of their own soul, so as to enable themselves to *believe* in their own revolution. I remember the famous story of the King Vicvamitra, who, as the result of a thousand years of self-martyrdom, reached such a consciousness of power and such a confidence in himself that he undertook to build a *new heaven*: the sinister symbol of the oldest and newest history of philosophy in the whole world. Every one who has ever built anywhere a "*new heaven*" first found the power thereto in his *own hell.*... Let us compress the facts into a short formula. The philosophic spirit had, in order to be *possible* to any extent at all, to masquerade and disguise itself as one of the *previously fixed* types of the contemplative man, to disguise itself as priest, wizard, soothsayer, as a religious man generally: the *ascetic ideal* has for a long time served the philosopher as a superficial form, as a condition which enabled him to exist.... To be able to be a philosopher he had to exemplify the ideal; to exemplify it, he was bound to *believe* in it. The peculiarly etherealized abstraction of philosophers, with their negation of the world, their enmity to life, their disbelief in the senses, which has been maintained up to the most recent time, and has almost thereby come to be accepted as the ideal *philosophic attitude*—this abstraction is the result of those enforced conditions under which philosophy came into existence, and continued to exist; inasmuch as for quite a very long time philosophy would have been *absolutely impossible* in the world without an ascetic cloak and dress, without an ascetic self-misunderstanding. Expressed plainly and palpably, the *ascetic priest* has taken the repulsive and sinister form of the caterpillar, beneath which and behind which alone philosophy could live and slink about....

Has all that really changed? Has that flamboyant and dangerous winged creature, that "spirit" which that caterpillar concealed within itself, has it, I say, thanks to a sunnier, warmer, lighter world, really and finally flung off its hood and escaped into the light? Can we to-day point to enough pride, enough daring, enough courage, enough self-confidence, enough mental will, enough will for responsibility, enough freedom of the will, to enable the philosopher to be now in the world really—*possible*?

11

And now, after we have caught sight of the *ascetic priest*, let us tackle our problem. What is the meaning of the ascetic ideal? It now first becomes serious—vitally serious. We are now confronted with the *real representatives of the serious.* "What is the meaning of all seriousness?" This even more radical question is perchance already on the tip of our tongue: a question, fairly, for physiologists, but which we for the time being skip. In that ideal the ascetic priest finds not only his faith, but also his will, his power, his interest. His *right* to existence stands and falls with that ideal. What wonder that we here run up against a terrible opponent (on the supposition, of course, that we are the opponents of that ideal), an opponent fighting for his life against those who repudiate that ideal! … On the other hand, it is from the outset improbable that such a biased attitude towards our problem will do him any particular good; the ascetic priest himself will scarcely prove the happiest champion of his own ideal (on the same principle on which a woman usually fails when she wishes to champion "woman")—let alone proving the most objective critic and judge of the controversy now raised. We shall therefore—so much is already obvious—rather have actually to help him to defend himself properly against ourselves, than we shall have to fear being too well beaten by him. The idea, which is the subject of this dispute, is the value of our life from the standpoint of the ascetic priests: this life, then (together with the whole of which it is a part, "Nature," "the world," the whole sphere of becoming and passing away), is placed by them in relation to an existence of quite another character, which it excludes and to which it is opposed, unless it *deny* its own self: in this case, the case of an ascetic life, life is taken as a bridge to another existence. The ascetic treats life as a maze, in which one must walk backwards till one comes to the place where it starts; or he treats it as an error which one may, nay *must*, refute by action: for he demands that he should be followed; he enforces, where he can, his valuation of existence. What does this mean? Such a monstrous valuation is not an exceptional case, or a curiosity recorded in human history: it is one of the most general and persistent facts that there are. The reading from the vantage of a distant star of the capital letters of our earthly life, would perchance lead to the conclusion that the earth was the especially *ascetic planet*, a den of discontented, arrogant, and repulsive creatures, who never got rid of a deep disgust of themselves, of the world, of all life, and did themselves as much hurt as possible out of pleasure in hurting—presumably their one and only pleasure. Let us consider how regularly, how universally, how practically at every single period the ascetic priest puts in his appearance: he belongs to no particular race; he thrives everywhere; he grows out of all classes. Not that he perhaps bred this valuation by heredity and propagated it—the contrary is the case. It must be a necessity of the first order which makes this species, hostile, as it is, to *life*, always grow again and always thrive again.—*Life* itself must certainly *have an interest* in the continuance of such a type of self-contradiction. For an ascetic life is a self-contradiction: here rules resentment without parallel, the resentment of an insatiate instinct and ambition, that would be master, not over some element in life, but over life itself, over life's deepest, strongest, innermost conditions; here is an attempt made to utilize power to dam the sources of power; here does the green eye of jealousy turn even against physiological well-being, especially against the expression of such well-being, beauty, joy; while a sense of pleasure is experienced and *sought* in abortion, in decay, in pain, in misfortune, in ugliness, in voluntary punishment, in the exercising, flagellation, and sacrifice of the self. All this is in the highest degree paradoxical: we are here confronted with a rift that *wills* itself to be a rift, which *enjoys* itself in this very *suffering*, and even becomes more and more certain of itself, more and more triumphant, in proportion as its own presupposition, physiological vitality, *decreases*. "The triumph just in the supreme agony": under this extravagant emblem did the ascetic ideal fight from of old; in this mystery of seduction, in this picture of rapture and torture, it recognized its brightest light, its salvation, its final victory. *Crux, nux, lux*—it has all these three in one.

12

Granted that such an incarnate will for contradiction and unnaturalness is induced to *philosophize*; on what will it vent its pet caprice? On that which has been felt with the greatest certainty to be true, to be real; it will look for *error* in those very places where the life instinct fixes truth with the greatest positiveness. It will, for instance, after the example of the ascetics of the Vedanta Philosophy, reduce matter to an illusion, and similarly treat pain, multiplicity, the whole logical contrast of "*Subject*" and "*Object*"—errors, nothing but errors! To renounce the belief in one's own ego, to deny to one's self one's own "reality"—what a triumph! and here already we have a much higher kind of triumph, which is not merely a triumph over the senses, over the palpable, but an infliction of violence and cruelty on *reason*; and this ecstasy culminates in the ascetic self-contempt, the ascetic scorn of one's own reason making this decree: *there is* a domain of truth and of life, but reason is specially *excluded* therefrom.... By the bye, even in the Kantian idea of "the intelligible character of things" there remains a trace of that schism, so dear to the heart of the ascetic, that schism which likes to turn reason against reason; in fact, "intelligible character" means in Kant a kind of quality in things of which the intellect comprehends this much, that for it, the intellect, it is *absolutely incomprehensible*. After all, let us, in our character of knowers, not be ungrateful towards such determined reversals of the ordinary perspectives and values, with which the mind had for too long raged against itself with an apparently futile sacrilege! In the same way the very seeing of another vista, the very *wishing* to see another vista, is no little training and preparation of the intellect for its eternal "*Objectivity*"—objectivity being understood not as "contemplation without interest" (for that is inconceivable and nonsensical), but as the ability to have the pros and cons *in one's power* and to switch them on and off, so as to get to know how to utilize, for the advancement of knowledge, the *difference* in the perspective and in the emotional interpretations. But let us, forsooth, my philosophic colleagues, henceforward guard ourselves more carefully against this mythology of dangerous ancient ideas, which has set up a "pure, will-less, painless, timeless subject of knowledge"; let us guard ourselves from the tentacles of such contradictory ideas as "pure reason," "absolute spirituality," "knowledge-in-itself":—in these theories an eye that cannot be thought of is required to think, an eye which *ex hypothesi* has no direction at all, an eye in which the active and interpreting functions are cramped, are absent; those functions, I say, by means of which "abstract" seeing first became seeing something; in these theories consequently the absurd and the nonsensical is always demanded of the eye. There is only a seeing from a perspective, only a "knowing" from a perspective, and the *more* emotions we express over a thing, the *more* eyes, different eyes, we train on the same thing, the more complete will be our "idea" of that thing, our "objectivity." But the elimination of the will altogether, the switching off of the emotions all and sundry, granted that we could do so, what! would not that be called intellectual *castration*?

13

But let us turn back. Such a self-contradiction, as apparently manifests itself among the ascetics, "Life turned against Life," is—this much is absolutely obvious—from the physiological and not now from the psychological standpoint, simply nonsense. It can only be an *apparent* contradiction; it must be a kind of provisional expression, an explanation, a formula, an adjustment, a psychological misunderstanding of something, whose real nature could not be understood for a long time, and whose *real essence* could not be described; a mere word jammed into an old *gap* of human knowledge. To put briefly the facts against its being real: *the ascetic ideal springs from the prophylactic and self-preservative instincts which mark a decadent life,* which seeks by every means in its power to maintain its position and fight for its existence; it points to a partial physiological depression and exhaustion, against which the most profound and intact life-instincts fight ceaselessly with new weapons and discoveries. The ascetic ideal is such a weapon: its position is consequently exactly the reverse of that which the worshippers of the ideal imagine—life struggles in it and through it with death and *against* death; the ascetic ideal is a dodge for the *preservation* of life. An important fact is brought out in the extent to which, as history teaches, this ideal could rule and exercise power over man, especially in all those places where the civilization and taming of man was completed: that fact is, the diseased state of man up to the present, at any rate, of the man who has been tamed, the physiological struggle of man with death (more precisely, with the disgust with life, with exhaustion, with the wish for the "end"). The ascetic priest is the incarnate wish for an existence of another kind, an existence on another plane,—he is, in fact, the highest point of this wish, its official ecstasy and passion: but it is the very *power* of this wish which is the fetter that binds him here; it is just that which makes him into a tool that must labor to create more favorable conditions for earthly existence, for existence on the human plane—it is with this very power that he keeps the whole herd of failures, distortions, abortions, unfortunates, *sufferers from themselves* of every kind, fast to existence, while he as the herdsman goes instinctively on in front. You understand me already: this ascetic priest, this apparent enemy of life, this denier—he actually belongs to the really great *conservative* and *affirmative* forces of life.... What does it come from, this diseased state? For man is more diseased, more uncertain, more changeable, more unstable than any other animal, there is no doubt of it—he is *the* diseased animal: what does it spring from? Certainly he has also dared, innovated, braved more, challenged fate more than all the other animals put together; he, the great experimenter with himself, the unsatisfied, the insatiate, who struggles for the supreme mastery with beast, Nature, and gods, he, the as yet ever uncompelled, the ever future, who finds no more any rest from his own aggressive strength, goaded inexorably on by the spur of the future dug into the flesh of the present:—how should not so brave and rich an animal also be the most endangered, the animal with the longest and deepest sickness among all sick animals?... Man is sick of it, oft enough there are whole epidemics of this satiety (as about 1348, the time of the Dance of Death): but even this very nausea, this tiredness, this disgust with himself, all this is discharged from him with such force that it is immediately made into a new fetter. His "nay," which he utters to life, brings to light as though by magic an abundance of graceful "yeas"; even when he *wounds* himself, this master of destruction, of self-destruction, it is subsequently the wound itself that forces him to live.

14

The more normal is this sickliness in man—and we cannot dispute this normality—the higher honor should be paid to the rare cases of psychical and physical powerfulness, the *windfalls* of humanity, and the more strictly should the sound be guarded from that worst of air, the air of the sick-room. Is that done? The sick are the greatest danger for the healthy; it is not from the strongest that harm comes to the strong, but from the weakest. Is that known? Broadly considered, it is not for a minute the fear of man, whose diminution should be wished for; for this fear forces the strong to be strong, to be at times terrible—it preserves in its integrity the sound type of man. What is to be feared, what does work with a fatality found in no other fate, is not the great fear of, but the great *nausea* with, man; and equally so the great pity for man. Supposing that both these things were one day to espouse each other, then inevitably the maximum of monstrousness would immediately come into the world—the "last will" of man, his will for nothingness, Nihilism. And, in sooth, the way is well paved thereto. He who not only has his nose to smell with, but also has eyes and ears, he sniffs almost wherever he goes to-day an air something like that of a mad-house, the air of a hospital—I am speaking, as stands to reason, of the cultured areas of mankind, of every kind of "Europe" that there is in fact in the world. The *sick* are the great danger of man, *not* the evil, *not* the "beasts of prey." They who are from the outset botched, oppressed, broken, those are they, the weakest are they, who most undermine the life beneath the feet of man, who instill the most dangerous venom and skepticism into our trust in life, in man, in ourselves. Where shall we escape from it, from that covert look (from which we carry away a deep sadness), from that averted look of him who is misborn from the beginning, that look which betrays what such a man says to himself—that look which is a groan?" Would that I were something else," so groans this look, "but there is no hope. I am what I am: how could I get away from myself? And, verily—*I am sick of myself!*" On such a soil of self-contempt, a veritable swamp soil, grows that weed, that poisonous growth, and all so tiny, so hidden, so ignoble, so sugary. Here teem the worms of revenge and vindictiveness; here the air reeks of things secret and unmentionable; here is ever spun the net of the most malignant conspiracy—the conspiracy of the sufferers against the sound and the victorious; here is the sight of the victorious *hated.* And what lying so as not to acknowledge this hate as hate! What a show of big words and attitudes, what an art of "righteous" calumniation! These abortions! what a noble eloquence gushes from their lips! What an amount of sugary, slimy, humble submission oozes in their eyes! What do they really want? At any rate to *represent* righteousness, love, wisdom, superiority, that is the ambition of these "lowest ones," these sick ones! And how clever does such an ambition make them! You cannot, in fact, but admire the counterfeiter dexterity with which the stamp of virtue, even the ring, the golden ring of virtue, is here imitated. They have taken a lease of virtue absolutely for themselves, have these weaklings and wretched invalids, there is no doubt of it; "We alone are the good, the righteous," so do they speak, "we alone are the *homines bonæ voluntatis.*" They stalk about in our midst as living reproaches, as warnings to us—as though health, fitness, strength, pride, the sensation of power, were really vicious things in themselves, for which one would have some day to do penance, bitter penance. Oh, how they themselves are ready in their hearts to *exact* penance, how they thirst after being *hangmen!*

Among them is an abundance of revengeful ones disguised as judges, who ever mouth the word righteousness like a venomous spittle—with mouth,

I say, always pursed, always ready to spit at everything, which does not wear a discontented look, but is of good cheer as it goes on its way. Among them, again, is that most loathsome species of the vain, the lying abortions, who make a point of representing "beautiful souls," and perchance of bringing to the market as "purity of heart" their distorted sensualism swathed in verses and other bandages; the species of "self-comforters" and masturbators of their own souls. The sick man's will to represent *some* form or other of superiority, his instinct for crooked paths, which lead to a tyranny over the healthy—where can it not be found, this will to power of the very weakest? The sick woman especially: no one surpasses her in refinements for ruling, oppressing, tyrannizing. The sick woman, moreover, spares nothing living, nothing dead; she grubs up again the most buried things (the Bogos say, "Woman is a hyena"). Look into the background of every family, of every body, of every community: everywhere the fight of the sick against the healthy—a silent fight for the most part with minute poisoned powders, with pin-pricks, with spiteful grimaces of patience, but also at times with that diseased pharisaism of *pure* pantomime, which plays for choice the rôle of "righteous indignation." Right into the hallowed chambers of knowledge can it make itself heard, can this hoarse yelping of sick hounds, this rabid lying and frenzy of such "noble" Pharisees (I remind readers, who have ears, once more of that Berlin apostle of revenge, Eugen Dühring, who makes the most disreputable and revolting use in all present-day Germany of moral refuse; Dühring, the paramount moral blusterer that there is to-day, even among his own kidney, the Anti-Semites). They are all men of resentment, are these physiological distortions and worm-riddled objects, a whole quivering kingdom of burrowing revenge, indefatigable and insatiable in its outbursts against the happy, and equally so in disguises for revenge, in pretexts for revenge: when will they really reach their final, fondest, most sublime triumph of revenge? At that time, doubtless, when they succeed in pushing their own misery, in fact, all misery, *into the consciousness* of the happy; so that the latter begin one day to be ashamed of their happiness, and perchance say to themselves when they meet, "It is a shame to be happy! *there is too much misery!*" ... But there could not possibly be a greater and more fatal misunderstanding than that of the happy, the fit, the strong in body and soul, beginning in this way to doubt their right to happiness. Away with this "perverse world"! Away with this shameful soddenness of sentiment! Preventing the sick making the healthy sick—for that is what such a soddenness comes to—this ought to be our supreme object in the world—but for this it is above all essential that the healthy should remain *separated* from the sick, that they should even guard themselves from the look of the sick, that they should not even associate with the sick. Or may it, perchance, be their mission to be nurses or doctors? But they could not mistake and disown their mission more grossly—the higher must not degrade itself to be the tool of the lower, the pathos of distance must to all eternity keep their missions also separate. The right of the happy to existence, the right of bells with a full tone over the discordant cracked bells, is verily a thousand times greater: they alone are the *sureties* of the future, they alone are *bound* to man's future. What they can, what they must do, that can the sick never do, should never do! but if *they are to* be enabled to do what *only* they must do, how can they possibly be free to play the doctor, the comforter, the "Savior" of the sick?... And therefore good air! good air! and away, at any rate, from the neighborhood of all the madhouses and hospitals of civilization! And therefore good company, *our own* company, or solitude, if it must be so! but away, at any rate, from the evil fumes of internal corruption and the secret worm-eaten state of the sick! that, forsooth, my friends, we may defend ourselves, at any rate for still a time, against the two worst plagues that could have been reserved for us—against the *great nausea with man*! against the *great pity for man*!

15

If you have understood in all their depths—and I demand that you should *grasp them profoundly* and understand them profoundly—the reasons for the impossibility of its being the business of the healthy to nurse the sick, to make the sick healthy, it follows that you have grasped this further necessity—the necessity of doctors and nurses *who themselves are sick*. And now we have and hold with both our hands the essence of the ascetic priest. The ascetic priest must be accepted by us as the predestined savior, herdsman, and champion of the sick herd: thereby do we first understand his awful historic mission. The *lordship over sufferers* is his kingdom, to that points his instinct, in that he finds his own special art, his master-skill, his kind of happiness. He must himself be sick, he must be kith and kin to the sick and the abortions so as to understand them, so as to arrive at an understanding with them; but he must also be strong, even more master of himself than of others, impregnable, forsooth, in his will for power, so as to acquire the trust and the awe of the weak, so that he can be their hold, bulwark, prop, compulsion, overseer, tyrant, god. He has to protect them, protect his herds—*against* whom? Against the healthy, doubtless also against the envy towards the healthy. He must be the natural adversary and *scorner* of every rough, stormy, reinless, hard, violently-predatory health and power. The priest is the first form of the more delicate animal that scorns more easily than it hates. He will not be spared the waging of war with the beasts of prey, a war of guile (of "spirit") rather than of force, as is self-evident—he will in certain cases find it necessary to conjure up out of himself, or at any rate to represent practically a new type of the beast of prey—a new animal monstrosity in which the polar bear, the supple, cold, crouching panther, and, not least important, the fox, are joined together in a trinity as fascinating as it is fearsome. If necessity exacts it, then will he come on the scene with bearish seriousness, venerable, wise, cold, full of treacherous superiority, as the herald and mouthpiece of mysterious powers, sometimes going among even the other kind of beasts of prey, determined as he is to sow on their soil, wherever he can, suffering, discord, self-contradiction, and only too sure of his art, always to be lord of *sufferers* at all times. He brings with him, doubtless, salve and balsam; but before he can play the physician he must first wound; so, while he soothes the pain which the wound makes, *he at the same time poisons the wound.* Well versed is he in this above all things, is this wizard and wild beast tamer, in whose vicinity everything healthy must needs become ill, and everything ill must needs become tame. He protects, in sooth, his sick herd well enough, does this strange herdsman; he protects them also against themselves, against the sparks (even in the center of the herd) of wickedness, knavery, malice, and all the other ills that the plaguey and the sick are heir to; he fights with cunning, hardness, and stealth against anarchy and against the ever imminent break-up inside the herd, where *resentment,* that most dangerous blasting-stuff and explosive, ever accumulates and accumulates. Getting rid of this blasting-stuff in such a way that it does not blow up the herd and the herdsman, that is his real feat, his supreme utility; if you wish to comprise in the shortest formula the value of the priestly life, it would be correct to say the priest is the *diverter of the course of resentment.* Every sufferer, in fact, searches instinctively for a cause of his suffering; to put it more exactly, a doer,—to put it still more precisely, a sentient *responsible* doer,—in brief, something living, on which, either actually or in *effigie*, he can on any pretext vent his emotions. For the venting of emotions is the sufferer's greatest attempt at alleviation, that is to say, *stupefaction*, his mechanically desired narcotic against pain of any kind. It is in this phenomenon alone that is found, according to my judgment, the real physiological cause of resentment, revenge, and their family is to be found—that is, in a demand for the *deadening of pain through emotion*: this cause is generally, but in my view very erroneously, looked for in the defensive parry of a bare protective principle of reaction, of a "reflex movement" in the case of any sudden hurt and danger, after the manner that a decapitated frog still moves in order to get away from a corrosive acid. But the difference is fundamental. In one case the object is to prevent being hurt anymore; in the other case the object is to deaden a racking, insidious, nearly unbearable pain by a more violent emotion of any kind whatsoever, and at any rate for the time being to drive it out of the consciousness—for this purpose an emotion is needed, as wild an emotion as possible, and to excite that emotion some excuse or other is needed. "It must be somebody's fault that I feel bad"—this kind of reasoning is peculiar to all invalids, and is but the more pronounced, the more ignorant they remain of the real cause of their feeling bad, the physiological cause (the cause may lie in a disease of the *nervus sympathicus*, or in an excessive secretion of bile, or in a want of sulphate and phosphate of potash in the blood, or in pressure in the bowels which stops the circulation of the blood, or in degeneration of the ovaries, and so forth). All sufferers have an awful resourcefulness and ingenuity in finding excuses for painful emotions; they even enjoy their jealousy, their broodings over base actions and apparent injuries, they burrow through the intestines of their past and present in their search for obscure mysteries, wherein they will be at liberty to wallow in a torturing suspicion and get drunk on the venom of their own malice—they tear open the oldest wounds, they make themselves bleed from the scars which have long been healed, they make evil-doers out of friends, wife, child, and everything which is nearest to them. "I suffer: it must be somebody's fault"—so thinks every sick sheep. But his herdsman, the ascetic priest, says to him, "Quite so, my sheep, it must be the fault of someone; but thou thyself art that someone, it is all the fault of thyself alone—*it is the fault of thyself alone against thyself*: that is bold enough, false enough, but one thing is at least attained; thereby, as I have said, the course of resentment is—*diverted*.

16

You can see now what the remedial instinct of life has at least *tried* to effect, according to my conception, through the ascetic priest, and the purpose for which he had to employ a temporary tyranny of such paradoxical and anomalous ideas as "guilt," "sin," "sinfulness," "corruption," "damnation." What was done was to make the sick *harmless* up to a certain point, to destroy the incurable by means of themselves, to turn the milder cases severely on to themselves, to give their resentment a backward direction ("man needs but one thing"), and to *exploit* similarly the bad instincts of all sufferers with a view to self-discipline, self-surveillance, self-mastery. It is obvious that there can be no question at all in the case of a "medication" of this kind, a mere emotional medication, of any real *healing* of the sick in the physiological sense; it cannot even for a moment be asserted that in this connection the instinct of life has taken healing as its goal and purpose. On the one hand, a kind of congestion and organization of the sick (the word "Church" is the most popular name for it): on the other, a kind of provisional safeguarding of the comparatively healthy, the more perfect specimens, the cleavage of a *rift* between healthy and sick—for a long time that was all! and it was much! it was very much!

I am proceeding, as you see, in this essay, from an hypothesis which, as far as such readers as I want are concerned, does not require to be proved; the hypothesis that "sinfulness" in man is not an actual fact, but rather merely the interpretation of a fact, of a physiological discomfort,—a discomfort seen through a moral religious perspective which is no longer binding upon us. The fact, therefore, that any one feels "guilty," "sinful," is certainly not yet any proof that he is right in feeling so, any more than any one is healthy simply because he feels healthy. Remember the celebrated witch-ordeals: in those days the most acute and humane judges had no doubt but that in these cases they were confronted with guilt,—the "witches" *themselves had no doubt on the point,*—and yet the guilt was lacking. Let me elaborate this hypothesis: I do not for a minute accept the very "pain in the soul" as a real fact, but only as an explanation (a casual explanation) of facts that could not hitherto be precisely formulated; I regard it therefore as something as yet absolutely in the air and devoid of scientific cogency—just a nice fat word in the place of a lean note of interrogation. When any one fails to get rid of his "pain in the soul," the cause is, speaking crudely, to be found *not* in his "soul" but more probably in his stomach (speaking crudely, I repeat, but by no means wishing thereby that you should listen to me or understand me in a crude spirit). A strong and well-constituted man digests his experiences (deeds and misdeeds all included) just as he digests his meats, even when he has some tough morsels to swallow. If he fails to "relieve himself" of an experience, this kind of indigestion is quite as much physiological as the other indigestion—and indeed, in more ways than one, simply one of the results of the other. You can adopt such a theory, and yet *entre nous* be nevertheless the strongest opponent of all materialism.

17

But is he really a *physician*, this ascetic priest? We already understand why we are scarcely allowed to call him a physician, however much he likes to feel a "savior" and let himself be worshipped as a savior.[7] It is only the actual suffering, the discomfort of the sufferer, which he combats, *not* its cause, not the actual state of sickness—this needs must constitute our most radical objection to priestly medication. But just once put yourself into that point of view, of which the priests have a monopoly, you will find it hard to exhaust your amazement, at what from that standpoint he has completely seen, sought, and found. The *mitigation* of suffering, every kind of "consoling"—all this manifests itself as his very genius: with what ingenuity has he interpreted his mission of consoler, with what aplomb and audacity has he chosen weapons necessary for the part. Christianity in particular should be dubbed a great treasure-chamber of ingenious consolations,—such a store of refreshing, soothing, deadening drugs has it accumulated within itself; so many of the most dangerous and daring expedients has it hazarded; with such subtlety, refinement, Oriental refinement, has it divined what emotional stimulants can conquer, at any rate for a time, the deep depression, the leaden fatigue, the black melancholy of physiological cripples— for, speaking generally, all religions are mainly concerned with fighting a certain fatigue and heaviness that has infected everything. You can regard it as *prima facie* probable that in certain places in the world there was almost bound to prevail

---

7 In the German text "Heiland." This has the double meaning of "healer" and "savior."—H.B.S.

from time to time among large masses of the population a *sense of physiological depression*, which, however, owing to their lack of physiological knowledge, did not appear to their consciousness as such, so that consequently its "cause" and its *cure* can only be sought and essayed in the science of moral psychology (this, in fact, is my most general formula for what is generally called a "*religion*"). Such a feeling of depression can have the most diverse origins; it may be the result of the crossing of too heterogeneous races (or of classes—genealogical and racial differences are also brought out in the classes: the European "Weltschmerz," the "Pessimism" of the nineteenth century, is really the result of an absurd and sudden class-mixture); it may be brought about by a mistaken emigration—a race falling into a climate for which its power of adaptation is insufficient (the case of the Indians in India); it may be the effect of old age and fatigue (the Parisian pessimism from 1850 onwards); it may be a wrong diet (the alcoholism of the Middle Ages, the nonsense of vegetarianism—which, however, have in their favor the authority of Sir Christopher in Shakespeare); it may be blood-deterioration, malaria, syphilis, and the like (German depression after the Thirty Years' War, which infected half Germany with evil diseases, and thereby paved the way for German servility, for German pusillanimity). In such a case there is invariably recourse to a *war* on a grand scale with the feeling of depression; let us inform ourselves briefly on its most important practices and phases (I leave on one side, as stands to reason, the actual *philosophic* war against the feeling of depression which is usually simultaneous—it is interesting enough, but too absurd, too practically negligible, too full of cobwebs, too much of a hole-and-corner affair, especially when pain is proved to be a mistake, on the *naïf* hypothesis that pain must needs *vanish* when the mistake underlying it is recognized—but behold! it does anything but vanish ...). That dominant depression is *primarily fought* by weapons which reduce the consciousness of life itself to the lowest degree. Wherever possible, no more wishes, no more wants; shun everything which produces emotion, which produces "blood" (eating no salt, the fakir hygiene); no love; no hate; equanimity; no revenge; no getting rich; no work; begging; as far as possible, no woman, or as little woman as possible; as far as the intellect is concerned, Pascal's principle, "*il faut s'abêtir.*" To put the result in ethical and psychological language, "self-annihilation," "sanctification"; to put it in physiological language, "hypnotism"—the attempt to find some approximate human equivalent for what *hibernation* is for certain animals, for what æstivation is for many tropical plants, a minimum of assimilation and metabolism in which life just manages to subsist without really coming into the consciousness. An amazing amount of human energy has been devoted to this object—perhaps uselessly? There cannot be the slightest doubt but that such *sportsmen* of "saintliness," in whom at times nearly every nation has abounded, have really found a genuine relief from that which they have combated with such a rigorous *training*—in countless cases they really escaped by the help of their system of hypnotism *away* from deep physiological depression; their method is consequently counted among the most universal ethnological facts. Similarly it is improper to consider such a plan for starving the physical element and the desires, as in itself a symptom of insanity (as a clumsy species of roast-beef-eating "freethinkers" and Sir Christophers are fain to do); all the more certain is it that their method can and does pave the way to all kinds of mental disturbances, for instance, "inner lights" (as far as the case of the Hesychasts of Mount Athos), auditory and visual hallucinations, voluptuous ecstasies and effervescences of sensualism (the history of St. Theresa). The explanation of such events given by the victims is always the acme of fanatical falsehood; this is self-evident. Note well, however, the tone of implicit gratitude that rings in the very *will* for an explanation of such a character. The supreme state, salvation itself, that final goal of universal hypnosis and peace, is always regarded by them as the mystery of mysteries, which even the most supreme symbols are inadequate to express; it is regarded as an entry and homecoming to the essence of things, as a liberation from all illusions, as "knowledge," as "truth," as "being" as an escape from every end, every wish, every action, as something even beyond Good and Evil.

"Good and Evil," quoth the Buddhists, "both are fetters. The perfect man is master of them both."

"The done and the undone," quoth the disciple of the Vedanta, "do him no hurt; the good and the evil he shakes from off him, sage that he is; his kingdom suffers no more from any act; good and evil, he goes beyond them both."—An absolutely Indian conception, as much Brahmanist as Buddhist. Neither in the Indian nor in the Christian doctrine is this "Redemption" regarded as attainable by means of virtue and moral improvement, however high they may place the value of the hypnotic efficiency of virtue: keep clear on this point—indeed it simply corresponds with the facts. The fact that they remained *true* on this point is perhaps to be regarded as the best specimen of realism in the three great religions, absolutely soaked as they are with morality, with this one exception. "For those who know, there is no duty." "Redemption is not attained by the acquisition of virtues; for redemption consists in being one with Brahman, who is incapable of acquiring any perfection; and equally little does it consist in the *giving up of faults*, for the Brahman, unity with whom is what constitutes redemption, is eternally pure" (these passages are from the Commentaries of the Cankara, quoted from the first real European *expert* of the Indian philosophy, my friend Paul Deussen). We wish, therefore, to pay honor to the idea of "redemption" in the great religions, but it is somewhat hard to remain serious in view of the appreciation meted out to the *deep sleep* by these exhausted pessimists who are too tired even to dream—to the deep sleep considered, that is, as already a fusing into Brahman, as the attainment of the *unio mystica* with God. "When he has completely gone to sleep," says on this point the oldest and most venerable "script," "and come to perfect rest, so that he sees no more any vision, then, oh dear one, is he united with Being, he has entered into his own self—encircled by the Self with its absolute knowledge, he has no more any consciousness of that which is without or of that which is within. Day and night cross not these bridges, nor age, nor death, nor suffering, nor good deeds, nor evil deeds." "In deep sleep," say similarly the believers in this deepest of the three great religions, "does the soul lift itself from out this body of ours, enters the supreme light and stands out therein in its true shape: therein is it the supreme spirit itself, which travels about, while it jests and plays and enjoys itself, whether with women, or chariots, or friends; there do its thoughts turn no more back to this appanage of a body, to which the 'prana' (the vital breath) is harnessed like a beast of burden to the cart." None the less we will take care to realize (as we did when discussing "redemption") that in spite of all its pomps of Oriental extravagance this simply expresses the same criticism on life as did the clear, cold, Greekly cold, but yet suffering Epicurus. The hypnotic sensation of nothingness, the peace of deepest sleep, anæsthesia in short—that is what passes with the sufferers and the absolutely depressed for, forsooth, their supreme good, their value of values; that is what *must* be treasured by them as something positive, be felt by them as the essence of *the* Positive (according to the same logic of the feelings, nothingness is in all pessimistic religions called God).

18

Such a hypnotic deadening of sensibility and susceptibility to pain, which presupposes somewhat rare powers, especially courage, contempt of opinion, intellectual stoicism, is less frequent than another and certainly easier *training* which is tried against states of depression. I mean *mechanical activity*. It is indisputable that a suffering existence can be thereby considerably alleviated. This fact is called to-day by the somewhat ignoble title of the "Blessing of work." The alleviation consists in the attention of the sufferer being absolutely diverted from suffering, in the incessant monopoly of the consciousness by action, so that consequently there is little room left for suffering—for *narrow* is it, this chamber of human consciousness! Mechanical activity and its corollaries, such as absolute regularity, punctilious unreasoning obedience, the chronic routine of life, the complete occupation of time, a certain liberty to be impersonal, nay, a training in "impersonality," self-forgetfulness, "*incuria sui*"—with what thoroughness and expert subtlety have all these methods been exploited by the ascetic priest in his war with pain!

When he has to tackle sufferers of the lower orders, slaves, or prisoners (or women, who for the most part are a compound of labor-slave and prisoner), all he has to do is to juggle a little with the names, and to rechristen, so as to make them see henceforth a benefit, a comparative happiness, in objects which they hated—the slave's discontent with his lot was at any rate not invented by the priests. An even more popular means of fighting depression is the ordaining of a *little joy*, which is easily accessible and can be made into a rule; this medication is frequently used in conjunction with the former ones. The most frequent form in which joy is prescribed as a cure is the joy in *producing* joy (such as doing good, giving presents, alleviating, helping, exhorting, comforting, praising, treating with distinction); together with the prescription of "love your neighbour." The ascetic priest prescribes, though in the most cautious doses, what is practically a stimulation of the strongest and most life-assertive impulse—the Will for Power. The happiness involved in the "smallest superiority" which is the concomitant of all benefiting, helping, extolling, making one's self useful, is the most ample consolation, of which, if they are well-advised, physiological distortions avail themselves: in other cases they hurt each other, and naturally in obedience to the same radical instinct. An investigation of the origin of Christianity in the

Roman world shows that co-operative unions for poverty, sickness, and burial sprang up in the lowest stratum of contemporary society, amid which the chief antidote against depression, the little joy experienced in mutual benefits, was deliberately fostered. Perchance this was then a novelty, a real discovery? This conjuring up of the will for co-operation, for family organization, for communal life, for "*Cænacula*" necessarily brought the Will for Power, which had been already infinitesimally stimulated, to a new and much fuller manifestation. The herd organization is a genuine advance and triumph in the fight with depression. With the growth of the community there matures even to individuals a new interest, which often enough takes him out of the more personal element in his discontent, his aversion to himself, the "*despectus sui*" of Geulincx. All sick and diseased people strive instinctively after a herd-organization, out of a desire to shake off their sense of oppressive discomfort and weakness; the ascetic priest divines this instinct and promotes it; wherever a herd exists it is the instinct of weakness which has wished for the herd, and the cleverness of the priests which has organized it, for, mark this: by an equally natural necessity the strong strive as much for *isolation* as the weak for *union*: when the former bind themselves it is only with a view to an aggressive joint action and joint satisfaction of their Will for Power, much against the wishes of their individual consciences; the latter, on the contrary, range themselves together with positive *delight* in such a muster—their instincts are as much gratified thereby as the instincts of the "born master" (that is, the solitary beast-of-prey species of man) are disturbed and wounded to the quick by organization. There is always lurking beneath every oligarchy—such is the universal lesson of history—the desire for tyranny. Every oligarchy is continually quivering with the tension of the effort required by each individual to keep mastering this desire. (Such, *e.g.*, was the Greek; Plato shows it in a hundred places, Plato, who knew his contemporaries—and *himself.*)

19

The methods employed by the ascetic priest, which we have already learnt to know—stifling of all vitality, mechanical energy, the little joy, and especially the method of "love your neighbor" herd-organization, the awaking of the communal consciousness of power, to such a pitch that the individual's disgust with himself becomes eclipsed by his delight in the thriving of the community—these are, according to modern standards, the "innocent" methods employed in the fight with depression; let us turn now to the more interesting topic of the "guilty" methods. The guilty methods spell one thing: to produce *emotional excess*—which is used as the most efficacious anæsthetic against their depressing state of protracted pain; this is why priestly ingenuity has proved quite inexhaustible in thinking out this one question: "*By what means* can you produce an emotional excess?" This sounds harsh: it is manifest that it would sound nicer and would grate on one's ears less, if I were to say, forsooth: "The ascetic priest made use at all times of the enthusiasm contained in all strong emotions." But what is the good of still soothing the delicate ears of our modern effeminates? What is the good *on our side* of budging one single inch before their verbal Pecksniffianism. For us psychologists to do that would be at once *practical Pecksniffianism,* apart from the fact of its nauseating us. The *good taste* (others might say, the righteousness) of a psychologist nowadays consists, if at all, in combating the shamefully moralized language with which all modern judgments on men and things are smeared. For, do not deceive yourself: what constitutes the chief characteristic of modern souls and of modern books is not the lying, but the *innocence* which is part and parcel of their intellectual dishonesty. The inevitable running up against this "innocence" everywhere constitutes the most distasteful feature of the somewhat dangerous business which a modern psychologist has to undertake: it is a part of our great danger—it is a road which perhaps leads us straight to the great nausea—I know quite well the purpose which all modern books will and can serve (granted that they last, which I am not afraid of, and granted equally that there is to be at some future day a generation with a more rigid, more severe, and *healthier* taste)—the *function* which all modernity generally will serve with posterity: that of an emetic,—and this by reason of its moral sugariness and falsity, its ingrained feminism, which it is pleased to call "Idealism," and at any rate believes to be idealism. Our cultured men of to-day, our "good" men, do not lie—that is true; but it does *not* redound to their honor! The real lie, the genuine, determined, "honest" lie (on whose value you can listen to Plato) would prove too tough and strong an article for them by a long way; it would be asking them to do what people have been forbidden to ask them to do, to open their eyes to their own selves, and to learn to distinguish between "true" and "false" in their own selves. The dishonest lie alone suits them: everything which feels a good man is perfectly incapable of any other attitude to anything than that of a dishonorable liar, an absolute liar, but none the less an innocent liar, a blue-eyed liar, a virtuous liar. These "good men," they are all now tainted with morality through and through, and as far as honor is concerned they are disgraced and corrupted for all eternity. Which of them *could stand* a further truth "about man"? or, put more tangibly, which of them could put up with a true biography? One or two instances: Lord Byron composed a most personal autobiography, but Thomas Moore was "too good" for it; he burnt his friend's papers. Dr. Gwinner, Schopenhauer's executor, is said to have done the same; for Schopenhauer as well wrote much about himself, and perhaps also against himself: (εἰς ἑαντόν). The virtuous American Thayer, Beethoven's biographer, suddenly stopped his work: he had come to a certain point in that honorable and simple life, and could stand it no longer. Moral: What sensible man nowadays writes one honest word about himself? He must already belong to the Order of Holy Foolhardiness. We are promised an autobiography of Richard Wagner; who doubts but that it would be a *clever* autobiography? Think, forsooth, of the grotesque horror which the Catholic priest Janssen aroused in Germany with his inconceivably square and harmless pictures of the German Reformation; what wouldn't people do if some real psychologist were to tell us about a genuine Luther, tell us, not with the moralist simplicity of a country priest or the sweet and cautious modesty of a Protestant historian, but say with the fearlessness of a Taine, that springs from force of character and not from a prudent toleration of force. (The Germans, by the bye, have already produced the classic specimen of this toleration—they may well be allowed to reckon him as one of their own, in Leopold Ranke, that born classical advocate of every *causa fortior*, that cleverest of all the clever opportunists.)

20

But you will soon understand me.—Putting it shortly, there is reason enough, is there not, for us psychologists nowadays never getting from a certain mistrust of our *own selves*? Probably even we ourselves are still "too good" for our work, probably, whatever contempt we feel for this popular craze for morality, we ourselves are perhaps none the less its victims, prey, and slaves; probably it infects even us. Of what was that diplomat warning us, when he said to his colleagues: "Let us especially mistrust our first impulses, gentlemen! *they are almost always good*"? So should nowadays every psychologist talk to his colleagues. And thus we get back to our problem, which in point of fact does require from us a certain severity, a certain mistrust especially against "first impulses." The ascetic ideal in the service of projected emotional excess:—he who remembers the previous essay will already partially anticipate the essential meaning compressed into these above ten words. The thorough unswitching of the human soul, the plunging of it into terror, frost, ardor, rapture, so as to free it, as through some lightning shock, from all the smallness and pettiness of unhappiness, depression, and discomfort: what ways lead to *this* goal? And which of these ways does so most safely?... At bottom all great emotions have this power, provided that they find a sudden outlet—emotions such as rage, fear, lust, revenge, hope, triumph, despair, cruelty; and, in sooth, the ascetic priest has had no scruples in taking into his service the whole pack of hounds that rage in the human kennel, unleashing now these and now those, with the same constant object of waking man out of his protracted melancholy, of chasing away, at any rate for a time, his dull pain, his shrinking misery, but always under the sanction of a religious interpretation and justification. This emotional excess has subsequently to be *paid for*, this is self-evident—it makes the ill more ill—and therefore this kind of remedy for pain is according to modern standards a "guilty" kind.

The dictates of fairness, however, require that we should all the more emphasize the fact that this remedy is applied with *a good conscience*, that the ascetic priest has prescribed it in the most implicit belief in its utility and indispensability;—often enough almost collapsing in the presence of the pain which he created;—that we should similarly emphasize the fact that the violent physiological revenges of such excesses, even perhaps the mental disturbances, are not absolutely inconsistent with the general tenor of this kind of remedy; this remedy, which, as we have shown previously, is *not* for the purpose of healing diseases, but of fighting the unhappiness of that depression, the alleviation and deadening of which was its object. The object was consequently achieved. The keynote by which the ascetic priest was enabled to get every kind of agonizing and ecstatic music to play on the fibers of the human soul—was, as everyone knows, the exploitation of the feeling of "*guilt*." I have already indicated in the previous essay the origin of this feeling—as a piece of animal psychology and nothing else: we were thus confronted with the feeling of "guilt," in its crude state, as it were. It was first in the hands of the priest, real artist that he was in the feeling of guilt, that it took shape—oh, what a shape!

"Sin"—for that is the name of the new priestly version of the animal "bad-conscience" (the inverted cruelty)—has up to the present been the greatest event in the history of the diseased soul: in "sin" we find the most perilous and fatal masterpiece of religious interpretation. Imagine man, suffering from himself, some way or other but at any rate physiologically, perhaps like an animal shut up in a cage, not clear as to the why and the wherefore! imagine him in his desire for reasons—reasons bring relief—in his desire again for remedies, narcotics at last, consulting one, who knows even the occult—and see, lo and behold, he gets a hint from his wizard, the ascetic priest, his *first* hint on the "cause" of his trouble: he must search for it in *himself*, in his guiltiness, in a piece of the past, he must understand his very suffering as a *state of punishment*. He has heard, he has understood, has the unfortunate: he is now in the plight of a hen round which a line has been drawn. He never gets out of the circle of lines. The sick man has been turned into "the sinner"—and now for a few thousand years we never get away from the sight of this new invalid, of "a sinner"—shall we ever get away from it?—wherever we just look, everywhere the hypnotic gaze of the sinner always moving in one direction (in the direction of guilt, the *only* cause of suffering); everywhere the evil conscience, this "*greuliche Thier*,"[8] to use Luther's language; everywhere rumination over the past, a distorted view of action, the gaze of the "green-eyed monster" turned on all action; everywhere the willful misunderstanding of suffering, its transvaluation into feelings of guilt, fear of retribution; everywhere the scourge, the hairy shirt, the starving body, contrition; everywhere the sinner breaking himself on the ghastly wheel of a restless and morbidly eager conscience; everywhere mute pain, extreme fear, the agony of a tortured heart, the spasms of an unknown happiness, the shriek for "redemption." In point of fact, thanks to this system of procedure, the old depression, dullness, and fatigue were absolutely conquered, life itself became *very* interesting again, awake, eternally awake, sleepless, glowing, burnt away, exhausted and yet not tired—such was the figure cut by man, "the sinner," who was initiated into these mysteries. This grand old wizard of an ascetic priest

---

8 "Horrible beast."

fighting with depression—he had clearly triumphed, *his* kingdom had come: men no longer grumbled at pain, men *panted* after pain: "*More pain!* More pain!" So for centuries on end shrieked the demand of his acolytes and initiates. Every emotional excess which hurt; everything which broke, overthrew, crushed, transported, ravished; the mystery of torture-chambers, the ingenuity of hell itself—all this was now discovered, divined, exploited, all this was at the service of the wizard, all this served to promote the triumph of his ideal, the ascetic ideal. "*My kingdom is not of this world*," quoth he, both at the beginning and at the end: had he still the right to talk like that?—Goethe has maintained that there are only thirty-six tragic situations: we would infer from that, did we not know otherwise, that Goethe was no ascetic priest. He—knows more.

21

So far as all *this* kind of priestly medicine-mongering, the "guilty" kind, is concerned, every word of criticism is superfluous. As for the suggestion that emotional excess of the type, which in these cases the ascetic priest is fain to order to his sick patients (under the most sacred euphemism, as is obvious, and equally impregnated with the sanctity of his purpose), has ever really been of use to any sick man, who, forsooth, would feel inclined to maintain a proposition of that character? At any rate, some understanding should be come to as to the expression "be of use." If you only wish to express that such a system of treatment has *reformed* man, I do not gainsay it: I merely add that "reformed" conveys to my mind as much as "tamed," "weakened," "discouraged," "refined," "daintified," "emasculated" (and thus it means almost as much as injured). But when you have to deal principally with sick, depressed, and oppressed creatures, such a system, even granted that it makes the ill "better," under any circumstances also makes them more *ill*: ask the mad-doctors the invariable result of a methodical application of penance-torture, contrition, and salvation ecstasies. Similarly ask history. In every body politic where the ascetic priest has established this treatment of the sick, disease has on every occasion spread with sinister speed throughout its length and breadth. What was always the "result"? A shattered nervous system, in addition to the existing malady, and this in the greatest as in the smallest, in the individuals as in masses. We find, in consequence of the penance and redemption-training, awful epileptic epidemics, the greatest known to history, such as the St. Vitus and St. John dances of the Middle Ages; we find, as another phase of its after-effect, frightful mutilations and chronic depressions, by means of which the temperament of a nation or a city (Geneva, Bale) is turned once for all into its opposite;—this *training*, again, is responsible for the witch-hysteria, a phenomenon analogous to somnambulism (eight great epidemic outbursts of this only between 1564 and 1605);—we find similarly in its train those delirious death-cravings of large masses, whose awful "shriek," "*evviva la morte!*" was heard over the whole of Europe, now interrupted by voluptuous variations and anon by a rage for destruction, just as the same emotional sequence with the same intermittencies and sudden changes is now universally observed in every case where the ascetic doctrine of sin scores once more a great success (religious neurosis *appears* as a manifestation of the devil, there is no doubt of it. What is it? *Quæritur*). Speaking generally, the ascetic ideal and its sublime-moral cult, this most ingenious, reckless, and perilous systematization of all methods of emotional excess, is writ large in a dreadful and unforgettable fashion on the whole history of man, and unfortunately not only on history. I was scarcely able to put forward any other element which attacked the health and race efficiency of Europeans with more destructive power than did this ideal; it can be dubbed, without exaggeration, *the real fatality* in the history of the health of the European man. At the most you can merely draw a comparison with the specifically German influence: I mean the alcohol poisoning of Europe, which up to the present has kept pace exactly with the political and racial pre–dominance of the Germans (where they inoculated their blood, there too did they inoculate their vice). Third in the series comes syphilis—*magno sed proximo intervallo*.

22

The ascetic priest has, wherever he has obtained the mastery, corrupted the health of the soul, he has consequently also corrupted *taste in artibus et litteris*—he corrupts it still. "Consequently?" I hope I shall be granted this "consequently"; at any rate, I am not going to prove it first. One solitary indication, it concerns the arch-book of Christian literature, their real model, their "book-in-itself." In the very midst of the Græco-Roman splendor, which was also a splendor of books, face to face with an ancient world of writings which had not yet fallen into decay and ruin, at a time when certain books were still to be read, to possess which we would give nowadays half our literature in exchange, at that time the simplicity and vanity of Christian agitators (they are generally called Fathers of the Church) dared to declare: "We too have our classical literature, we *do not need that of the Greeks*"—and meanwhile they proudly pointed to their books of legends, their letters of apostles, and their apologetic tractlets, just in the same way that to-day the English "Salvation Army" wages its fight against Shakespeare and other "heathens" with an analogous literature. You already guess it, I do not like the "New Testament"; it almost upsets me that I stand so isolated in my taste so far as concerns this valued, this over-valued Scripture; the taste of two thousand years is *against* me; but what boots it! "Here I stand! I cannot help myself"[9]—I have the courage of my bad taste. The Old Testament—yes, that is something quite different, all honor to the Old Testament! I find therein great men, an heroic landscape, and one of the rarest phenomena in the world, the incomparable naïveté *of the strong heart*; further still, I find a people. In the New, on the contrary, just a hostel of petty sects, pure rococo of the soul, twisting angles and fancy touches, nothing but conventicle air, not to forget an occasional whiff of bucolic sweetness which appertains to the epoch (*and* the Roman province) and is less Jewish than Hellenistic. Meekness and braggadocio cheek by jowl; an emotional garrulousness that almost deafens; passionate hysteria, but no passion; painful pantomime; here manifestly every one lacked good breeding. How dare any one make so much fuss about their little failings as do these pious little fellows! No one cares a straw about it—let alone God. Finally they actually wish to have "the crown of eternal life," do all these little provincials! In return for what, in sooth? For what end? It is impossible to carry insolence any further. An immortal Peter! who could stand *him*! They have an ambition which makes one laugh: the *thing* dishes up cut and dried his most personal life, his melancholies, and common-or-garden troubles, as though the Universe itself were under an obligation to bother itself about them, for it never gets tired of wrapping up God Himself in the petty misery in which its troubles are involved. And how about the atrocious form of this chronic hobnobbing with

---

9 "Here I stand! I cannot help myself. God help me! Amen"—were Luther's words before the Reichstag at Worms.—H.B.S.

God? This Jewish, and not merely Jewish, slobbering and clawing importunacy towards God!—There exist little despised "heathen nations" in East Asia, from whom these first Christians could have learnt something worth learning, a little tact in worshiping; these nations do not allow themselves to say aloud the name of their God. This seems to me delicate enough, it is certain that it is *too* delicate, and not only for primitive Christians; to take a contrast, just recollect Luther, the most "eloquent" and insolent peasant whom Germany has had, think of the Lutherian tone, in which he felt quite the most in his element during his *tête-à-têtes* with God. Luther's opposition to the mediæval saints of the Church (in particular, against "that devil's hog, the Pope"), was, there is no doubt, at bottom the opposition of a boor, who was offended at the *good etiquette* of the Church, that worship-etiquette of the sacerdotal code, which only admits to the holy of holies the initiated and the silent, and shuts the door against the boors. These definitely were not to be allowed a hearing in this planet—but Luther the peasant simply wished it otherwise; as it was, it was not German enough for him. He personally wished himself to talk direct, to talk personally, to talk "straight from the shoulder" with his God. Well, he's done it. The ascetic ideal, you will guess, was at no time and in no place, a school of good taste, still less of good manners—at the best it was a school for sacerdotal manners: that is, it contains in itself something which was a deadly enemy to all good manners. Lack of measure, opposition to measure, it is itself a "*non plus ultra.*"

23

The ascetic ideal has corrupted not only health and taste, there are also third, fourth, fifth, and sixth things which it has corrupted—I shall take care not to go through the catalogue (when should I get to the end?). I have here to expose not what this ideal effected; but rather only what it *means*, on what it is based, what lies lurking behind it and under it, that of which it is the provisional expression, an obscure expression bristling with queries and misunderstandings. And with *this* object only in view I presumed "not to spare" my readers a glance at the awfulness of its results, a glance at its fatal results; I did this to prepare them for the final and most awful aspect presented to me by the question of the significance of that ideal. What is the significance of the *power* of that ideal, the monstrousness of its power? Why is it given such an amount of scope? Why is not a better resistance offered against it? The ascetic ideal expresses one will: where is the opposition will, in which an opposition ideal expresses itself? The ascetic ideal has an aim—this goal is, putting it generally, that all the other interests of human life should, measured by its standard, appear petty and narrow; it explains epochs, nations, men, in reference to this one end; it forbids any other interpretation, any other end; it repudiates, denies, affirms, confirms, only in the sense of its own interpretation (and was there ever a more thoroughly elaborated system of interpretation?); it subjects itself to no power, rather does it believe in its own precedence over every power—it believes that nothing powerful exists in the world that has not first got to receive from "it" a meaning, a right to exist, a value, as being an instrument in its work, a way and means to its end, to one end. Where is the *counterpart* of this complete system of will, end, and interpretation? Why is the counterpart lacking? Where is the other "one aim"? But I am told it is not lacking, that not only has it fought a long and fortunate fight with that ideal, but that further it has already won the mastery over that ideal in all essentials: let our whole modern *science* attest this—that modern science, which, like the genuine reality-philosophy which it is, manifestly believes in itself alone, manifestly has the courage to be itself, the will to be itself, and has got on well enough without God, another world, and negative virtues.

With all their noisy agitator-babble, however, they effect nothing with me; these trumpeters of reality are bad musicians, their voices do not come from the deeps with sufficient audibility, they are not the mouthpiece for the abyss of scientific knowledge—for to-day scientific knowledge is an abyss—the word "science," in such trumpeter-mouths, is a prostitution, an abuse, an impertinence. The truth is just the opposite from what is maintained in the ascetic theory. Science has to-day absolutely no belief in itself, let alone in an ideal superior to itself, and wherever science still consists of passion, love, ardor, suffering, it is not the opposition to that ascetic ideal, but rather the *incarnation of its latest and noblest form*. Does that ring strange? There are enough brave and decent working people, even among the learned men of to-day, who like their little corner, and who, just because they are pleased so to do, become at times indecently loud with their demand, that people to-day should be quite content, especially in science—for in science there is so much useful work to do. I do not deny it—there is nothing I should like less than to spoil the delight of these honest workers in their handiwork; for I rejoice in their work. But the fact of science requiring hard work, the fact of its having contented workers, is absolutely no proof of science as a whole having to-day one end, one will, one ideal, one passion for a great faith; the contrary, as I have said, is the case. When science is not the latest manifestation of the ascetic ideal—but these are cases of such rarity, selectness, and exquisiteness, as to preclude the general judgment being affected thereby—science is a *hiding-place* for every kind of cowardice, disbelief, remorse, *despectio sui*, bad conscience—it is the very *anxiety* that springs from having no ideal, the suffering from the *lack* of a great love, the discontent with an enforced moderation. Oh, what does all science not cover to-day? How much, at any rate, does it not try to cover? The diligence of our best scholars, their senseless industry, their burning the candle of their brain at both ends— their very mastery in their handiwork—how often is the real meaning of all that to prevent themselves continuing to see a certain thing? Science as a self-anæsthetic: *do you know that?* You wound them—every one who consorts with scholars experiences this—you wound them sometimes to the quick through just a harmless word; when you think you are paying them a compliment you embitter them beyond all bounds, simply because you didn't have the *finesse* to infer the real kind of customers you had to tackle, the *sufferer* kind (who won't own up even to themselves what they really are), the dazed and unconscious kind who have only one fear—*coming to consciousness.*

24

And now look at the other side, at those rare cases, of which I spoke, the most supreme idealists to be found nowadays among philosophers and scholars. Have we, perchance, found in them the sought-for *opponents* of the ascetic ideal, its *anti-idealists?* In fact, they *believe* themselves to be such, these "unbelievers" (for they are all of them that): it seems that this idea is their last remnant of faith, the idea of being opponents of this ideal, so earnest are they on this subject, so passionate in word and gesture;—but does it follow that what they believe must necessarily be *true?* We "knowers" have grown by degrees suspicious of all kinds of believers, our suspicion has step by step habituated us to draw just the opposite conclusions to what people have drawn before; that is to say, wherever the strength of a belief is particularly prominent to draw the conclusion of the difficulty of proving what is believed, the conclusion of its actual *improbability*. We do not again deny that "faith produces salvation": *for that very reason* we do deny that faith *proves* anything,—a strong faith, which produces happiness, causes suspicion of the object of that faith, it does not establish its "truth," it does establish a certain probability of—*illusion*. What is now the position in these cases? These solitaries and deniers of to-day; these fanatics in one thing, in their claim to intellectual cleanness; these hard, stern, continent, heroic spirits, who constitute the glory of our time; all these pale atheists, anti-Christians, immoralists, Nihilists; these sceptics, "ephectics," and "hectics" of the intellect (in a certain sense they are the latter, both collectively and individually); these supreme idealists of knowledge, in whom alone nowadays the intellectual conscience dwells and is alive—in point of fact they believe themselves as far away as possible from the ascetic ideal, do these "free, very free spirits": and yet, if I may reveal what they themselves cannot see—for they stand too near themselves: this ideal is simply *their* ideal, they represent it nowadays and perhaps no one else, they themselves are its most spiritualized product, its most advanced picket of skirmishers and scouts, its most insidious delicate and elusive form of seduction.—If I am in any way a reader of riddles, then I will be one with this sentence: for some time past there have been no free spirits; *for they still believe in truth*. When the Christian Crusaders in the East came into collision with that invincible order of assassins, that order of free spirits *par excellence,* whose lowest grade lives in a state of discipline such as no order of monks has ever attained, then in some way or other they managed to get an inkling of that symbol and tally-word, that was reserved for the highest grade alone as their *secretum*, "Nothing is true, everything is allowed,"—in sooth, that was *freedom* of thought, thereby was *taking leave* of the very belief in truth. Has indeed any European, any Christian freethinker, ever yet wandered into this proposition and its labyrinthine consequences? Does he know *from experience* the Minotauros of this den.—I doubt it—nay, I know otherwise. Nothing is more really alien to these "mono-fanatics," these *so-called* "free spirits," than freedom and unfettering in that sense; in no respect are they more closely tied, the absolute fanaticism of their belief in truth is unparalleled. I know all this perhaps too much from experience at close quarters—that dignified philosophic abstinence to which a belief like that binds its adherents, that stoicism of the intellect, which eventually vetoes negation as rigidly as it does affirmation, that wish for standing still in front of the actual, the *factum brutum*, that fatalism in "*petits faits*" (*ce petit faitalism*, as I call it), in which French Science now attempts a kind of moral superiority over German, this renunciation of interpretation generally (that is, of forcing, doctoring, abridging, omitting, suppressing, inventing, falsifying, and all the other *essential* attributes of interpretation)—all this, considered broadly, expresses the asceticism of virtue, quite as efficiently as does any repudiation of the senses (it is at bottom only a *modus* of that repudiation.) But what forces it into that unqualified will for truth is the faith *in the ascetic ideal itself*, even though it take the form of its unconscious imperatives,—make no mistake about it, it is the faith, I repeat, in a *metaphysical* value, an *intrinsic* value of truth, of a character which is only warranted and guaranteed in this ideal (it stands and falls with that ideal). Judged strictly, there does not exist a science without its "hypotheses," the thought of such a science is inconceivable, illogical: a philosophy, a faith, must always exist first to enable science to gain thereby a direction, a meaning, a limit and method, a *right* to existence. (He who holds a contrary opinion on the subject—he, for example, who takes it upon himself to establish philosophy "upon a strictly scientific basis"—has first got to "turn up-side-down" not only philosophy but also truth itself—the gravest insult which could possibly be offered to two such respectable females!) Yes, there is no doubt about it—and here I quote my *Joyful Wisdom*, cp. Book V. Aph. 344: "The man who is truthful in that daring and extreme fashion, which is the presupposition of the faith in science, *asserts thereby a different world* from that of life, nature, and history; and in so far as he asserts the existence of that different world, come, must he not similarly repudiate its counterpart, this world, *our* world? The belief on which our faith in science is based has remained to this day a metaphysical belief—even we knowers of to-day, we godless foes of metaphysics, we too take our fire from that conflagration which was kindled by a thousand-year-old faith, from that Christian belief, which was also Plato's belief, the belief that God is truth, that truth is *divine*.... But what if this belief becomes more and more incredible, what if nothing proves itself to be divine, unless it be error, blindness, lies—what if God, Himself proved Himself to be our *oldest lie*?"—It is necessary to stop at this point and to consider the situation carefully. Science itself now *needs* a justification (which is not for a minute to say that there is such a justification). Turn in this context to the most ancient and the most modern philosophers: they all fail to realize the extent of the need of a justification on the part of the Will for

Truth—here is a gap in every philosophy—what is it caused by? Because up to the present the ascetic ideal dominated all philosophy, because Truth was fixed as Being, as God, as the Supreme Court of Appeal, because Truth was not allowed to be a problem. Do you understand this "allowed"? From the minute that the belief in the God of the ascetic ideal is repudiated, there exists *a new problem*: the problem of the value of truth. The Will for Truth needed a critique—let us define by these words our own task—-the value of truth is tentatively *to be called in question*.... (If this seems too laconically expressed, I recommend the reader to peruse again that passage from the *Joyful Wisdom* which bears the title, "How far we also are still pious," Aph. 344, and best of all the whole fifth book of that work, as well as the Preface to *The Dawn of Day*.)

25

No! You can't get round me with science, when I search for the natural antagonists of the ascetic ideal, when I put the question: "*Where* is the opposed will in which the *opponent ideal* expresses itself?" Science is not, by a long way, independent enough to fulfil this function; in every department science needs an ideal value, a power which creates values, and in whose *service* it *can believe* in itself —science itself never creates values. Its relation to the ascetic ideal is not in itself antagonistic; speaking roughly, it rather represents the progressive force in the inner evolution of that ideal. Tested more exactly, its opposition and antagonism are concerned not with the ideal itself, but only with that ideal's outworks, its outer garb, its masquerade, with its temporary hardening, stiffening, and dogmatizing—it makes the life in the ideal free once more, while it repudiates its superficial elements. These two phenomena, science and the ascetic ideal, both rest on the same basis—I have already made this clear—the basis, I say, oft the same over-appreciation of truth (more accurately the same belief in the *impossibility* of valuing and of criticizing truth), and consequently they are *necessarily* allies, so that, in the event of their being attacked, they must always be attacked and called into question together. A valuation of the ascetic ideal inevitably entails a valuation of science as well; lose no time in seeing this clearly, and be sharp to catch it! (*Art*, I am speaking provisionally, for I will treat it on some other occasion in greater detail,—art, I repeat, in which lying is sanctified and the *will for deception* has good conscience on its side, is much more fundamentally opposed to the ascetic ideal than is science: Plato's instinct felt this—Plato, the greatest enemy of art which Europe has produced up to the present. Plato *versus* Homer, that is the complete, the true antagonism—on the one side, the whole–hearted "transcendental," the great defamer of life; on the other, its involuntary panegyrist, the *golden* nature. An artistic subservience to the service of the ascetic ideal is consequently the most absolute artistic *corruption* that there can be, though unfortunately it is one of the most frequent phases, for nothing is more corruptible than an artist.) Considered physiologically, moreover, science rests on the same, basis as does the ascetic ideal: a certain *impoverishment of life* is the presupposition of the latter as of the former—add, frigidity of the emotions, slackening of the *tempo*, the substitution of dialectic for instinct, *seriousness* impressed on mien and gesture (seriousness, that most unmistakable sign of strenuous metabolism, of struggling, toiling life). Consider the periods in a nation in which the learned man comes into prominence; they are the periods of exhaustion, often of sunset, of decay—the effervescing strength, the confidence in life, the confidence in the future are no more. The preponderance of the mandarins never signifies any good, any more than does the advent of democracy, or arbitration instead of war, equal rights for women, the religion of pity, and all the other symptoms of declining life. (Science handled as a problem! what is the meaning of science?—upon this point the Preface to the *Birth of Tragedy*.) No! this "modern science"—mark you this well—is at times the *best* ally for the ascetic ideal, and for the very reason that it is the ally which is most unconscious, most automatic, most secret, and most subterranean! They have been playing into each other's hands up to the present, have these "poor in spirit" and the scientific opponents of that ideal (take care, by the bye, not to think that these opponents are the antithesis of this ideal, that they are the *rich* in spirit—that they are *not*; I have called them the *hectic* in spirit). As for these celebrated victories of science; there is no doubt that they are *victories*—but victories over what? There was not for a single minute any victory among their list over the ascetic ideal, rather was it made stronger, that is to say, more elusive, more abstract, more insidious, from the fact that a wall, an outwork, that had got built on to the main fortress and disfigured its appearance, should from time to time be ruthlessly destroyed and broken down by science. Does anyone seriously suggest that the downfall of the theological astronomy signified the downfall of that ideal?—Has, perchance, man grown *less in need* of a transcendental solution of his riddle of existence, because since that time this existence has become more random, casual, and superfluous in the *visible* order of the universe? Has there not been since the time of Copernicus an unbroken progress in the self-belittling of man and his *will* for belittling himself? Alas, his belief in his dignity, his uniqueness, his irreplaceableness in the scheme of existence, is gone—he has become animal, literal, unqualified, and unmitigated animal, he who in his earlier belief was almost God ("child of God," "demi-God"). Since Copernicus man seems to have fallen on to a steep plane—he rolls faster and faster away from the center—whither? into nothingness? into the "thrilling sensation of his own nothingness"—Well! this would be the straight way—to the old ideal?— All science (and by no means only astronomy, with regard to the humiliating and deteriorating effect of which Kant has made a remarkable confession, "it annihilates my own importance"), all science, natural as much as *unnatural*—by unnatural I mean the self-critique of reason—nowadays sets out to talk man out of his present opinion of himself, as though that opinion had been nothing but a bizarre piece of conceit; you might go so far as to say that science finds its peculiar pride, its peculiar bitter form of stoical ataraxia, in preserving man's *contempt of himself,* that state which it took so much trouble to bring about, as man's final and most serious claim to self-appreciation (rightly so, in point of fact, for he who despises is always "one who has not forgotten how to appreciate"). But does all this involve any real effort to *counteract* the ascetic ideal? Is it really seriously suggested that Kant's *victory* over the theological dogmatism about "God," "Soul," "Freedom," "Immortality," has damaged that ideal in any way (as the theologians have imagined to be the case for a long time past)?— And in this connection it does not concern us for a single minute, if Kant himself intended any such consummation. It is certain that from the time of Kant every type of transcendentalist is playing a winning game—they are emancipated from the theologians; what luck!—he has revealed to them that secret art, by which they can now pursue their "heart's desire" on their own responsibility, and with all the respectability of science. Similarly, who can grumble at the agnostics, reverers, as they are, of the unknown and the absolute mystery, if they now worship *their very query* as God? (Xaver Doudan talks somewhere of the *ravages* which *l'habitude d'admirer l'inintelligible au lieu de rester tout simplement dans l'inconnu* has produced—the ancients, he thinks, must have been exempt from those ravages.) Supposing that everything, "known" to man, fails to satisfy his desires, and on the contrary contradicts and horrifies them, what a divine way out of all this to be able to look for the responsibility, not in the "desiring" but in "knowing"!—"There is no knowledge. *Consequently*—there is a God"; what a novel *elegantia syllogismi!* what a triumph for the ascetic ideal!

26

Or, perchance, does the whole of modern history show in its demeanor greater confidence in life, greater confidence in its ideals? Its loftiest pretension is now to be a *mirror*; it repudiates all teleology; it will have no more "proving"; it disdains to play the judge, and thereby shows its good taste—it asserts as little as it denies, it fixes, it "describes." All this is to a high degree ascetic, but at the same time it is to a much greater degree *nihilistic*; make no mistake about this! You see in the historian a gloomy, hard, but determined gaze,—an eye that *looks out* as an isolated North Pole explorer looks out (perhaps so as not to look within, so as not to look back?)—there is snow—here is life silenced, the last crows which caw here are called "whither?" "Vanity," "Nada"—here nothing more flourishes and grows, at the most the metapolitics of St. Petersburg and the "pity" of Tolstoy. But as for that other school of historians, a perhaps still more "modern" school, a voluptuous and lascivious school which ogles life and the ascetic ideal with equal fervor, which uses the word "artist" as a glove, and has nowadays established a "corner" for itself, in all the praise given to contemplation; oh, what a thirst do these sweet intellectuals excite even for ascetics and winter landscapes! Nay! The devil take these "contemplative" folk! How much liefer would I wander with those historical Nihilists through the gloomiest, grey, cold mist!—nay, I shall not mind listening (supposing I have to choose) to one who is completely unhistorical and anti-historical (a man, like Dühring for instance, over whose periods a hitherto shy and unavowed species of "beautiful souls" has grown intoxicated in contemporary Germany, *the species anarchistica* within the educated proletariate). The "contemplative" are a hundred times worse—I never knew anything which produced such intense nausea as one of those "objective" *chairs*,[10] one of those scented mannikins-about-town of history, a thing half-priest, half-satyr (Renan *parfum*), which betrays by the high, shrill falsetto of his applause what he lacks and where he lacks it, who betrays where in this case the Fates have plied their ghastly shears, alas! in too surgeon-like a fashion! This is distasteful to me, and irritates my patience; let him keep patient at such sights who has nothing to lose thereby,—such a sight enrages me, such spectators embitter me against the "play," even more than does the play itself (history itself, you understand); Anacreontic moods imperceptibly come over me. This Nature, who gave to the steer its horn, to the lion its χάσμ ὀδόντων, for what purpose did Nature give me my foot?—To kick, by St. Anacreon, and not merely to run away! To trample on all the worm-eaten "chairs," the cowardly contemplators, the lascivious eunuchs of history, the flirters with ascetic ideals, the righteous hypocrites of impotence! All reverence on my part to the ascetic ideal, *in so far as it is honorable*! So long as it believes in itself and plays no pranks on us! But I like not all these coquettish bugs who have an insatiate ambition to smell of the infinite, until eventually the infinite smells of bugs; I like not the whited sepulchers with their stagey reproduction of life; I like not the tired and the used up who wrap themselves in wisdom and look "objective"; I like not the agitators dressed up as heroes, who hide their dummy-heads behind the stalking-horse of an ideal; I like not the ambitious artists who would fain play the ascetic and the priest, and are at bottom nothing but tragic clowns; I like not, again, these newest speculators in idealism, the Anti-Semites, who nowadays roll their eyes in the patent Christian-Aryan-man-of-honor fashion, and by an abuse of moralist attitudes and agitation dodges, so cheap as to exhaust any patience, strive to excite all the blockhead elements in the populace (the invariable success of *every* kind of intellectual charlatanism in present-day Germany hangs together with the almost indisputable and already quite palpable desolation of the German mind, whose cause I look for in a too exclusive diet, of papers, politics, beer, and Wagnerian music, not forgetting the condition precedent of this diet, the national exclusiveness and vanity, the strong but narrow principle, "Germany, Germany above everything,"[11] and finally the *paralysis agitans* of "modern ideas"). Europe nowadays is, above all, wealthy and ingenious in means of excitement; it

---

10   E.g. Lectureships.
11   An allusion to the well-known patriotic song.—H.B.S.

apparently has no more crying necessity than *stimulantia* and alcohol. Hence the enormous counterfeiting of ideals, those most fiery spirits of the mind; hence too the repulsive, evil-smelling, perjured, pseudo–alcoholic air everywhere. I should like to know how many cargoes of imitation idealism, of hero-costumes and high falutin' clap-trap, how many casks of sweetened pity liqueur (Firm: *la religion de la souffrance*), how many crutches of righteous indignation for the help of these flat-footed intellects, how many *comedians* of the Christian moral ideal would need to-day to be exported from Europe, to enable its air to smell pure again. It is obvious that, in regard to this over-production, a new *trade* possibility lies open; it is obvious that there is a new business to be done in little ideal idols and obedient "idealists"—don't pass over this tip! Who has sufficient courage? We have in *our hands* the possibility of idealizing the whole earth. But what am I talking about courage? we only need one thing here—a hand, a free, a very free hand.

27

Enough! enough! let us leave these curiosities and complexities of the modern spirit, which excite as much laughter as disgust. Our problem can certainly do without them, the problem of *meaning* of the ascetic ideal—what has it got to do with yesterday or to-day? those things shall be handled by me more thoroughly and severely in another connection (under the title "A Contribution to the History of European Nihilism," I refer for this to a work which I am preparing: *The Will to Power, an Attempt at a Transvaluation of All Values*). The only reason why I come to allude to it here is this: the ascetic ideal has at times, even in the most intellectual sphere, only one real kind of enemies and *damagers*: these are the comedians of this ideal—for they awake mistrust. Everywhere otherwise, where the mind is at work seriously, powerfully, and without counterfeiting, it dispenses altogether now with an ideal (the popular expression for this abstinence is "Atheism")—*with the exception of the will for truth.* But this will, this *remnant* of an ideal, is, if you will believe me, that ideal itself in its severest and cleverest formulation, esoteric through and through, stripped of all outworks, and consequently not so much its remnant as its *kernel.* Unqualified honest atheism (and its air only do we breathe, we, the most intellectual men of this age) is *not* opposed to that ideal, to the extent that it appears to be; it is rather one of the final phases of its evolution, one of its syllogisms and pieces of inherent logic—it is the awe-inspiring catastrophe of a two-thousand-year training in truth, which finally forbids itself *the lie of the belief in God*. (The same course of development in India—quite independently, and consequently of some demonstrative value—the same ideal driving to the same conclusion the decisive point reached five hundred years before the European era, or more precisely at the time of Buddha—it started in the Sankhyam philosophy, and then this was popularized through Buddha, and made into a religion.)

What, I put the question with all strictness, has really *triumphed* over the Christian God? The answer stands in my *Joyful Wisdom*, Aph. 357: "the Christian morality itself, the idea of truth, taken as it was with increasing seriousness, the confessor-subtlety of the Christian conscience translated and sublimated into the scientific conscience into intellectual cleanness at any price. Regarding Nature as though it were a proof of the goodness and guardianship of God; interpreting history in honor of a divine reason, as a constant proof of a moral order of the world and a moral teleology; explaining our own personal experiences, as pious men have for long enough explained them, as though every arrangement, every nod, every single thing were invented and sent out of love for the salvation of the soul; all this is now done away with, all this has the conscience *against* it, and is regarded by every subtler conscience as disreputable, dishonorable, as lying, feminism, weakness, cowardice—by means of this severity, if by means of anything at all, are we, in sooth, *good Europeans* and heirs of Europe's longest and bravest self-mastery.". .. All great things go to ruin by reason of themselves, by reason of an act of self-dissolution: so wills the law of life, the law of necessary "self-mastery" even in the essence of life—ever is the law-giver finally exposed to the cry, "*patere legem quam ipse tulisti*"; in thus wise did Christianity *go to ruin as a dogma*, through its own morality; in thus wise must Christianity go again to ruin to-day as a morality—we are standing on the threshold of this event. After Christian truthfulness has drawn one conclusion after the other, it finally draws its *strongest conclusion*, its conclusion against itself; this, however, happens, when it puts the question, "*what is the meaning of every will for truth?*" And here again do I touch on my problem, on our problem, my unknown friends (for as yet *I know* of no friends): what sense has our whole being, if it does not mean that in our own selves that will for truth has come to its own consciousness *as a problem*?—By reason of this attainment of self-consciousness on the part of the will for truth, morality from henceforward—there is no doubt about it—goes *to pieces*: this is that great hundred-act play that is reserved for the next two centuries of Europe, the most terrible, the most mysterious, and perhaps also the most hopeful of all plays.

28

If you except the ascetic ideal, man, the animal man had no meaning. His existence on earth contained no end; "What is the purpose of man at all?" was a question without an answer; the *will* for man and the world was lacking; behind every great human destiny rang as a refrain a still greater "Vanity!" The ascetic ideal simply means this: that something *was lacking*, that a tremendous *void* encircled man—he did not know how to justify himself, to explain himself, to affirm himself, he *suffered* from the problem of his own meaning. He suffered also in other ways, he was in the main a *diseased* animal; but his problem was not suffering itself, but the lack of an answer to that crying question, "*To what purpose* do we suffer?" Man, the bravest animal and the one most inured to suffering, does *not* repudiate suffering in itself: he *wills* it, he even seeks it out, provided that he is shown a meaning for it, a *purpose* of suffering. *Not* suffering, but the senselessness of suffering was the curse which till then lay spread over humanity—*and the ascetic ideal gave it a meaning*! It was up till then the only meaning; but any meaning is better than no meaning; the ascetic ideal was in that connection the *"faute de mieux" par excellence* that existed at that time. In that ideal suffering *found an explanation*; the tremendous gap seemed filled; the door to all suicidal Nihilism was closed. The explanation—there is no doubt about it—brought in its train new suffering, deeper, more penetrating, more venomous, gnawing more brutally into life: it brought all suffering under the perspective of *guilt*; but in spite of all that—man was *saved* thereby, he had a *meaning*, and from henceforth was no more like a leaf in the wind, a shuttle-cock of chance, of nonsense, he could now "will" something—absolutely immaterial to what end, to what purpose, with what means he wished: *the will itself was saved*. It is absolutely impossible to disguise *what* in point of fact is made clear by every complete will that has taken its direction from the ascetic ideal: this hate of the human, and even more of the animal, and more still of the material, this horror of the senses, of reason itself, this fear of happiness and beauty, this desire to get right away from all illusion, change, growth, death, wishing and even desiring—all this means—let us have the courage to grasp it—a will for Nothingness, a will opposed to life, a repudiation of the most fundamental conditions of life, but it is and remains *a will*—and to say at the end that which I said at the beginning—man will wish *Nothingness* rather than not wish *at all.*

Peoples and Countries

Translated by J.M. Kennedy

[The following twenty-seven fragments were intended by Nietzsche to form a supplement to Chapter Eight of *Beyond Good and Evil.*]

1

The Europeans now imagine themselves as representing, in the main, the highest types of men on earth.

2

A characteristic of Europeans: inconsistency between word and deed; the Oriental is true to himself in daily life. How the European has established colonies is explained by his nature, which resembles that of a beast of prey.

This inconsistency is explained by the fact that Christianity has abandoned the class from which it sprang.

This is the difference between us and the Hellenes: their morals grew up among the governing castes. Thucydides' morals are the same as those that exploded everywhere with Plato.

Attempts towards honesty at the Renaissance, for example: always for the benefit of the arts. Michael Angelo's conception of God as the "Tyrant of the World" was an honest one.

3

I rate Michael Angelo higher than Raphael, because, through all the Christian clouds and prejudices of his time, he saw the ideal of a culture *nobler* than the Christo-Raphaelian: whilst Raphael truly and modestly glorified only the values handed down to him, and did not carry within himself any inquiring, yearning instincts. Michael Angelo, on the other hand, saw and felt the problem of the law-giver of new values: the problem of the conqueror made perfect, who first had to subdue the "hero within himself," the man exalted to his highest pedestal, master even of his pity, who mercilessly shatters and annihilates everything that does not bear his own stamp, shining in Olympian divinity. Michael Angelo was naturally only at certain moments so high and so far beyond his age and Christian Europe: for the most part he adopted a condescending attitude towards the eternal feminine in Christianity; it would seem, indeed, that in the end he broke down before her, and gave up the ideal of his most inspired hours. It was an ideal which only a man in the strongest and highest vigor of life could bear; but not a man advanced in years! Indeed, he would have had to demolish Christianity with his ideal! But he was not thinker and philosopher enough for that Perhaps Leonardo da Vinci alone of those artists had a really super-Christian outlook. He knows the East, the "land of dawn," within himself as well as without himself. There is something super-European and silent in him: a characteristic of every one who has seen too wide a circle of things good and bad.

4

How much we have learnt and learnt anew in fifty years! The whole Romantic School with its belief in "the people" is refuted! No Homeric poetry as "popular" poetry! No deification of the great powers of Nature! No deduction from language-relationship to race-relationship! No "intellectual contemplations" of the supernatural! No truth enshrouded in religion!

The problem of truthfulness is quite a new one. I am astonished. From this standpoint we regard such natures as Bismarck as culpable out of carelessness, such as Richard Wagner out of want of modesty; we would condemn Plato for his *pia fraus*, Kant for the derivation of his Categorical Imperative, his own belief certainly not having come to him from this source.

Finally, even doubt turns against itself: doubt in doubt. And the question as to the *value* of truthfulness and its extent lies *there*.

5

What I observe with pleasure in the German is his Mephistophelian nature; but, to tell the truth, one must have a higher conception of Mephistopheles than Goethe had, who found it necessary to *diminish* his Mephistopheles in order to magnify his "inner Faust." The true German Mephistopheles is much more dangerous, bold, wicked, and cunning, and *consequently* more open-hearted: remember the nature of Frederick the Great, or of that much greater Frederick, the Hohenstaufen, Frederick II.

The real German Mephistopheles crosses the Alps, and believes that everything there belongs to him. Then he recovers himself, like Winckelmann, like Mozart. He looks upon Faust and Hamlet as caricatures, invented to be laughed at, and upon Luther also. Goethe had his good *German* moments, when he laughed inwardly at all these things. But then he fell back again into his cloudy moods.

6

Perhaps the Germans have only grown up in a wrong climate! There is something in them that might be Hellenic!—something that is awakened when they are brought into touch with the South—Winckelmann, Goethe, Mozart. We should not forget, however, that we are still young. Luther is still our last event; our last book is still the Bible. The Germans have never yet "moralized." Also, the very food of the Germans was their doom: its consequence, Philistinism.

7

The Germans are a dangerous people: they are experts at inventing intoxicants. Gothic, rococo (according to Semper), the historical sense and exoticism, Hegel, Richard Wagner—Leibniz, too (dangerous at the present day)—(they even idealized the serving soul as the virtue of scholars and soldiers, also as the simple mind). The Germans may well be the most composite people on earth.

"The people of the Middle," the inventors of porcelain, and of a kind of Chinese breed of Privy Councillor.

8

The smallness and baseness of the German soul were not and are not consequences of the system of small states; for it is well known that the inhabitants of much smaller states were proud and independent: and it is not a large state *per se* that makes souls freer and more manly. The man whose soul obeys the slavish command: "Thou shalt and must kneel!" in whose body there is an involuntary bowing and scraping to titles, orders, gracious glances from above—well, such a man in an "Empire" will only bow all the more deeply and lick the dust more fervently in the presence of the greater sovereign than in the presence of the lesser: this cannot be doubted. We can still see in the lower classes of Italians that aristocratic self-sufficiency; manly discipline and self-confidence still form a part of the long history of their country: these are virtues which once manifested themselves before their eyes. A poor Venetian gondolier makes a far better figure than a Privy Councillor from Berlin, and is even a better man in the end—anyone can see this. Just ask the women.

9

Most artists, even some of the greatest (including the historians) have up to the present belonged to the serving classes (whether they serve people of high position or princes or women or "the masses"), not to speak of their dependence upon the Church and upon moral law. Thus Rubens portrayed the nobility of his age; but only according to *their* vague conception of taste, not according to his own measure of beauty on the whole, therefore, against his own taste. Van Dyck was nobler in this respect: who in all those whom he painted added a certain amount of what he himself most highly valued: he did not descend from himself, but rather lifted up others to himself when he "rendered."

The slavish humility of the artist to his public (as Sebastian Bach has testified in undying and outrageous words in the dedication of his High Mass) is perhaps more difficult to perceive in music; but it is all the more deeply engrained. A hearing would be refused me if I endeavored to impart my views on this subject. Chopin possesses distinction, like Van Dyck. The disposition of Beethoven is that of a proud peasant; of Haydn, that of a proud servant. Mendelssohn, too, possesses distinction—like Goethe, in the most natural way in the world.

10

We could at any time have counted on the fingers of one hand those German learned men who possessed wit: the remainder have understanding, and a few of them, happily, that famous "childlike character" which divines.... It is our privilege: with this "divination" German science has discovered some things which we can hardly conceive of, and which, after all, do not exist, perhaps. It is only the Jews among the Germans who do not "divine" like them.

11

As Frenchmen reflect the politeness and *esprit* of French society, so do Germans reflect something of the deep, pensive earnestness of their mystics and musicians, and also of their silly childishness. The Italian exhibits a great deal of republican distinction and art, and can show himself to be noble and proud without vanity.

12

A larger number of the higher and better-endowed men will, I hope, have in the end so much self-restraint as to be able to get rid of their bad taste for affectation and sentimental darkness, and to turn against Richard Wagner as much as against Schopenhauer. These two Germans are leading us to ruin; they flatter our dangerous qualities. A stronger future is prepared for us in Goethe, Beethoven, and Bismarck than in these racial aberrations. We have had no philosophers yet.

13

The peasant is the commonest type of noblesse, for he is dependent upon himself most of all. Peasant blood is still the best blood in Germany—for example, Luther, Niebuhr, Bismarck.

Bismarck a Slav. Let any one look upon the face of Germans. Everything that had manly, exuberant blood in it went abroad. Over the smug populace remaining, the slave-souled people, there came an improvement from abroad, especially by a mixture of Slavonic blood.

The Brandenburg nobility and the Prussian nobility in general (and the peasant of certain North German districts), comprise at present the most manly natures in Germany. That the manliest men shall rule: this is only the natural order of things.

14

The future of German culture rests with the sons of the Prussian officers.

15

There has always been a want of wit in Germany, and mediocre heads attain there to the highest honors, because even they are rare. What is most highly prized is diligence and perseverance and a certain cold-blooded, critical outlook, and, for the sake of such qualities, German scholarship and the German military system have become paramount in Europe.

16

Parliaments may be very useful to a strong and versatile statesman: he has something there to rely upon (every such thing must, however, be able to resist!)—upon which he can throw a great deal of responsibility. On the whole, however, I could wish that the counting mania and the superstitious belief in majorities were not established in Germany, as with the Latin races, and that one could finally invent something new even in politics! It is senseless and dangerous to let the custom of universal suffrage—which is still but a short time under cultivation, and could easily be uprooted—take a deeper root: whilst, of course, its introduction was merely an expedient to steer clear of temporary difficulties.

17

Can anyone interest himself in this German Empire? Where is the new thought? Is it only a new combination of power? All the worse, if it does not know its own mind. Peace and *laisser aller* are not types of politics for which I have any respect. Ruling, and helping the highest thoughts to victory—the only things that can make me interested in Germany. England's small-mindedness is the great danger now on earth. I observe more inclination towards greatness in the feelings of the Russian Nihilists than in those of the English Utilitarians. We require an intergrowth of the German and Slav races, and we require, too, the cleverest financiers, the Jews, for us to become masters of the world.

(a) The sense of reality.
(b) A giving-up of the English principle of the people's right of representation We require the representation of the great interests.
(c) We require an unconditional union with Russia, together with a mutual plan of action which shall not permit any English schemata to obtain the mastery in Russia. No American future!
(d) A national system of politics is untenable, and embarrassment by Christian views is a very great evil. In Europe all sensible people are sceptics, whether they say so or not.

18

I see over and beyond all these national wars, new "empires," and whatever else lies in the foreground. What I am concerned with—for I see it preparing itself slowly and hesitatingly—is the United Europe. It was the only real work, the one impulse in the souls, of all the broad-minded and deep-thinking men of this century—this preparation of a new synthesis, and the tentative effort to anticipate the future of "the European." Only in their weaker moments, or when they grew old, did they fall back again into the national narrowness of the "Fatherlanders"—then they were once more "patriots." I am thinking of men like Napoleon, Heinrich Heine, Goethe, Beethoven, Stendhal, Schopenhauer. Perhaps Richard Wagner likewise belongs to their number, concerning whom, as a successful type of German obscurity, nothing can be said without some such "perhaps."

But to the help of such minds as feel the need of a new unity there comes a great explanatory economic fact: the small States of Europe—I refer to all our present kingdoms and "empires"—will in a short time become economically untenable, owing to the mad, uncontrolled struggle for the possession of local and international trade. Money is even now compelling European nations to amalgamate into one Power. In order, however, that Europe may enter into the battle for the mastery of the world with good prospects of victory (it is easy to perceive against whom this battle will be waged), she must probably "come to an understanding" with England. The English colonies are needed for this struggle, just as much as modern Germany, to play her new rôle of broker and middleman, requires the colonial possessions of Holland. For no one any longer believes that England alone is strong enough to continue to act her old part for fifty years more; the impossibility of shutting out *homines novi* from the government will ruin her, and her continual change of political parties is a fatal obstacle to the carrying out of any tasks which require to be spread out over a long period of time. A man must to-day be a soldier first and foremost that he may not afterwards lose his credit as a merchant. Enough; here, as in other matters, the coming century will be found following in the footsteps of Napoleon—the first man, and the man of greatest initiative and advanced views, of modern times. For the tasks of the next century, the methods of popular representation and parliaments are the most inappropriate imaginable.

19

The condition of Europe in the next century will once again lead to the breeding of manly virtues, because men will live in continual danger. Universal military service is already the curious antidote which we possess for the effeminacy of democratic ideas, and it has grown up out of the struggle of the nations. (Nation—men who speak one language and read the same newspapers. These men now call themselves "nations," and would far too readily trace their descent from the same source and through the same history; which, however, even with the assistance of the most malignant lying in the past, they have not succeeded in doing.)

20

What quagmires and mendacity must there be about if it is possible, in the modern European hotch-potch, to raise questions of "race"! (It being premised that the origin of such writers is not in Horneo and Borneo.)

21

Maxim: To associate with no man who takes any part in the mendacious race swindle.

22

With the freedom of travel now existing, groups of men of the same kindred can join together and establish communal habits and customs. The overcoming of "nations."

23

To make Europe a center of culture, national stupidities should not make us blind to the fact that in the higher regions there is already a continuous reciprocal dependence. France and German philosophy. Richard Wagner and Paris (1830-50). Goethe and Greece. All things are impelled towards, a synthesis of the European past in the highest types of mind.

24

Mankind has still much before it—how, generally speaking, could the ideal be taken from the past? Perhaps merely in relation to the present, which latter is possibly a lower region.

25

This is our distrust, which recurs again and again; our care, which never lets us sleep; our question, which no one listens to or wishes to listen to; our Sphinx, near which there is more than one precipice: we believe that the men of present-day Europe are deceived in regard to the things which we love best, and a pitiless demon (no, not pitiless, only indifferent and puerile)—plays with our hearts and their enthusiasm, as it may perhaps have already played with everything that lived and loved; I believe that everything which we Europeans of to-day are in the habit of admiring as the values of all these respected things called "humanity," "mankind," "sympathy," "pity," may be of some value as the debilitation and moderating of certain powerful and dangerous primitive impulses. Nevertheless, in the long run all these things are nothing else than the belittlement of the entire type "man," his mediocrization, if in such a desperate situation I may make use of such a desperate expression. I think that the *commedia umana* for an epicurean spectator-god must consist in this: that the Europeans, by virtue of their growing morality, believe in all their innocence and vanity that they are rising higher and higher, whereas the truth is that they are sinking lower and lower—*i.e.,* through the cultivation of all the virtues which are useful to a herd, and through the repression of the other and contrary virtues which give rise to a new, higher, stronger, masterful race of men—the first-named virtues merely develop the herd-animal in man and stabilitate the animal "man," for until now man has been "the animal as yet unstabilitated."

26

Genius and Epoch.—Heroism is no form of selfishness, for one is shipwrecked by it.... The direction of power is often conditioned by the state of the period in which the great man happens to be born; and this fact brings about the superstition that he is the expression of his time. But this same power could be applied in several different ways; and between him and his time there is always this difference: that public opinion always worships the herd instinct,—*i.e.,* the instinct of the weak,—while he, the strong man, rights for strong ideals.

27

The fate now overhanging Europe is simply this: that it is exactly her strongest sons that come rarely and late to the spring-time of their existence; that, as a rule, when they are already in their early youth they perish, saddened, disgusted, darkened in mind, just because they have already, with the entire passion of their strength, drained to the dregs the cup of disillusionment, which in our days means the cup of knowledge, and they would not have been the strongest had they not also been the most disillusioned. For that is the test of their power—they must first of all rise out of the illness of their epoch to reach their own health. A late spring-time is their mark of distinction; also, let us add, late merriment, late folly, the late exuberance of joy! For this is the danger of to-day: everything that we loved when we were young has betrayed us. Our last love—the love which makes us acknowledge her, our love for Truth—let us take care that she, too, does not betray us!